The Psychology of Emotion in Restorative Practice

of related interest

Implementing Restorative Practices in Schools
A Practical Guide to Transforming School Communities
Margaret Thorsborne and Peta Blood
ISBN 978 1 84905 377 8
eISBN 978 0 85700 737 7

Just Schools
A Whole School Approach to Restorative Justice
Belinda Hopkins
ISBN 978 1 84310 132 1
eISBN 978 1 84642 432 8

Just Care
Restorative Justice Approaches to Working
with Children in Public Care
Belinda Hopkins
Foreword by Jonathan Stanley
ISBN 978 1 84310 981 5
eISBN 978 0 85700 087 3

The Pocket Guide to Restorative Justice
Pete Wallis and Barbara Tudor
ISBN 978 1 84310 629 6
eISBN 978 1 84642 748 0

Restorative Justice
How it Works
Marian Liebmann
ISBN 978 1 84310 074 4
eISBN 978 1 84642 631 5

A Community-Based Approach to the
Reduction of Sexual Reoffending
Circles of Support and Accountability
Stephen Hanvey, Terry Philpot and Chris Wilson
ISBN 978 1 84905 198 9
eISBN 978 0 85700 423 9

The Psychology of Emotion in Restorative Practice

HOW AFFECT SCRIPT PSYCHOLOGY EXPLAINS HOW AND WHY RESTORATIVE PRACTICE WORKS

Edited by Vernon C. Kelly, Jr. and Margaret Thorsborne

Foreword by Andrew Becroft

Jessica Kingsley *Publishers*
London and Philadelphia

The illustrations in Figure 6.3 on p.147 are reproduced by
permission of St Luke's Innovative Resources

First published in 2014
by Jessica Kingsley Publishers
73 Collier Street
London N1 9BE, UK
and
400 Market Street, Suite 400
Philadelphia, PA 19106, USA

www.jkp.com

Library of Congress Cataloging in Publication Data
A CIP catalog record for this book is available from the Library of Congress

British Library Cataloguing in Publication Data
A CIP catalogue record for this book is available from the British Library

ISBN 978 1 84905 974 9
eISBN 978 0 85700 866 4

Printed and bound in Great Britain

To
Donald L. Nathanson,
our colleague and friend, in honour of his extraordinary
contributions to our understanding of shame

Contents

Foreword

Andrew Becroft

It's not every day that one faces a 'charge' of being the (partial) reason for a book being written. The authors of this text have 'laid' exactly such an allegation against me. In this case, the dubious distinction is entirely an honour. I willingly plead guilty. My plea in mitigation is that, in November 2011, I was asked, as after dinner speaker, to address the combined Restorative Practices International's (RPI)/Restorative Justice Aotearoa (RJA) Conference in Wellington, New Zealand. The brief was to be provocative and challenging. Somewhat enthusiastically, and perhaps a little bluntly, I provided some reflections on restorative justice from the perspective of what we know in New Zealand as youth justice Family Group Conferences (FGCs). The first reflection was to suggest that, at least in New Zealand, we are strong on practice but short on theory, that we are practice-orientated and analysis/theory weak.

We New Zealanders like to think we know a thing or two about restorative justice. In 1989 the seminal Children, Young Persons and their Families Act 1989 (the CYPF Act) provided for FGCs, both as a diversionary mechanism for serious offences (where the police wish to charge a young person but cannot arrest him/her), and as a decision-making tool for virtually all important decisions in the Youth Court. They are triggered, and are mandatory, in the Youth Court, when a young person indicates that he/she 'does not deny' the charge. This difficult-to-explain (especially to young offenders) 'double negative' opens the door to a FGC. The aim of the FGC is to discuss how a young person can be encouraged to accept responsibility for the offending and be held accountable, and second, to recognize and address a young person's needs and the causes of the offending, so that the young person is given (in the powerful words of our legislation) the opportunity 'to develop in responsible, beneficial, and socially acceptable ways' (Section (4)(f)(ii) of the CYPF Act).

Now it is worth noting that the words 'restorative justice' were not even mentioned in the CYPF Act. It was 1989 after all. The concept was in its infancy and certainly not in vogue, at least for policy-makers and legislators. However, very quickly, the FGC, with its entitlement for victims and their supporters to attend, came to be practised along restorative justice lines. In one sense, in the very early 1990s, I am sure that many involved in facilitating FGCs did not even know that what they were doing was pioneering a restorative justice model. It took the rest of the world to tell us, and then researchers such as Drs Gabrielle Maxwell and Alison Morris, and judges such as Judge Fred McElrea, started to carefully describe and analyse our 'restorative' practice and procedure.

It is also important to recognize that the FGC is *not* (as is sometimes unrealistically touted, and indeed hinted at – wrongly – in this book) the wholesale adoption of an indigenous Māori method of dispute resolution and a rejection of the western legal system. The model certainly originated, in significant part, from the strong dissatisfaction by Māori with the previous paternalistic/welfare-based child welfare and youth justice systems. And aspects of Māori custom are incorporated into the FGC. For instance, in Māori custom and law, *tikanga o ngā hara* (or the law of wrongdoing) is based on notions of collective rather than individual responsibility. Understanding why an individual has offended and addressing the causes collectively is seen as a benefit to society as a whole.

The *whānau* (or family) meeting model, used by extended families in some areas to resolve disputes, was seen as a prototype for a new method of resolving disputes in a way that was culturally appropriate for Māori and also an empowering process for all New Zealand families. The adoption of this model accords with a shift in modern western legal systems towards alternative methods of dispute resolution, such as mediation. Two specific factors promoted participation by the young Māori offender in the FGC process:

- the inclusion of *whānau* (family), *hapā* (subtribe) and *iwi* (tribe) in repairing the harm; and

- the opportunity to have the conference in chosen familiar surroundings, including on *marae* (traditional meeting area).

However, the FGC is better understood as a modern mechanism of justice that is culturally appropriate. It contains some elements of the traditional Māori system of *whānau* decision-making, but also elements that are foreign to it (such as the presence of representatives of the State). It also modifies elements of the traditional system, such as the roles played by the family and victims. Nevertheless, these are important features of the system because Māori children and young people comprise around half of all youth apprehended by the police in New Zealand, and over half of those prosecuted in the Youth Court.

Twenty-three years on, New Zealand has a proud record of practising restorative justice – primarily in the youth justice arena (where we have now conducted at least 160,000 FGCs!), but it has also spread to the adult courts, and more recently to schools, workplaces and even cities, such as Whanganui in the North Island of New Zealand. When well prepared and conducted, FGCs have in them the 'seeds of genius', and they are certainly the jewels in the crown of the New Zealand youth justice system. As Judge McElrea observed, the 1989 Act truly ushered in 'a new paradigm' for conducting youth justice.

But all that said, and as I raised in 2011, in New Zealand I think we are remarkably short on reflective analysis and writing on the values that underpin the practice and the theories that explain restorative justice processes. That is why I am so encouraged by this book. It addresses this deficit head on. In particular, beginning with Chapter 1, Vernon Kelly powerfully argues that in order to have any theoretical basis for the methods of restorative practice, we must first understand the 'biology' of how and why we care. He describes 'affect script psychology', which, he suggests, is 'the most comprehensive, biologically-based theory of motivation yet proposed' and which can shine '...a bright light on how and why restorative practice reduces harm'. If Kelly's theories are accepted, then all those involved in restorative practice work must get to grips with the biology and the motivations for human behaviour. Much will be demanded of our practitioners. Only with this understanding can restorative justice truly help to unpack the emotions behind the offending and harboured by the victim to provide a platform for restoration. Dr Lauren Abramson builds on Kelly's thinking and then demonstrates how it applies in practice. Kelly's work in Chapter 2 on the 'four relationship windows' (*neglectful:* low expectations/ low support; *punitive:* high expectations/low support; *permissive:* low expectations/high support; and *restorative:* high expectations/high support) from the perspective of affect script psychology also pays careful reading.

The remaining chapters of the book continue to build on this basis and demonstrate how these theoretical ideas are being applied. Part 2, dealing with the theory in action in communities and the criminal justice settings, is of particular interest for me, as a judge sitting in the youth and adult jurisdictions. Part 3, focusing on organizational settings, and Part 4, exploring restorative practice in education, demonstrate just how pervasive and 'revolutionary' the influence of restorative theory can be. Indeed few, if any, areas of community life are not susceptible to the benefits of restorative practice. Incidentally, all these parts of the book address the remaining challenges I issued at the 2011 conference. For the record, those challenges were:

- Who is the FGC for? The victim and/or the young offender/ or the community, or all three?

- Too much focus on the 'deed', and not enough on the 'need'? In other words, in the emotion of the moment and in the power of the 'victim–offender transaction' and restoration, are we prone to gloss over or overlook the underlying causes of offending, which, if left unaddressed, will make reoffending almost inevitable? Hardly a good advertisement for restorative practice.

- Restorative justice misunderstood by the public! Are the true believers providing good education and information, or are they selling restorative justice short?

- Exciting opportunities to be grasped! These include the growing and successful use of restorative justice practice in schools (surely a better way, if possible, than the exclusion route for school students); workplace restorative justice;

community justice centres; and the use of restorative justice practice more widely in whole communities.

All these issues are addressed in this very helpful text. Little did I realize when I issued these challenges that such a comprehensive and thoughtful book would be produced, in part, to answer some of these questions – which in truth were the questions that the whole restorative justice community had been quietly asking for some years. There was hardly anything new in what I was saying – an after dinner speaker just has greater license to speak freely.

The book comes at a good time. There is a wide-ranging community debate as to the proper approach to dealing with criminals in a way that properly meets victims' needs, much discussion as to how we can keep some of our toughest young people within the education system, and how effective communities can be developed that do not marginalize, but include, those at greatest risk of offending and being blighted by poor life outcomes. Restorative practice provides answers to these issues. But rhetoric and emotion are not enough. Sound theory must back up and underpin good practice. Restorative practice is at risk without it.

The writer of the *Book of Proverbs* in the Bible observed thousands of years ago that 'where there is no vision the people perish' (Chapter 29, v.18). We desperately need a vision for restorative justice that can galvanize community-wide practice to resolve some of the toughest issues (described in this book) that we face as humans. Without a sound and clearly articulated vision, systems risk atrophying and may whither on the vine. The same is true for restorative justice thinking and practice itself. This book is a valuable contribution to generating an ongoing vision for restorative practice that will challenge us all.

I conclude with words of a song produced by a young offender as part of his FGC plan, many years ago now. He had been involved, but at the margins, in an aggravated robbery of a corner store. The FGC involved over 30 people and lasted over six hours. I am told it was extraordinarily powerful. Heemi (not his real name) had dropped out of school, was involved with alcohol and binge-drinking of alcohol, and was facing significant other issues. Nobody knew that he had talents as a writer and a singer. As a result of the FGC, he composed and recorded this song for the owners of the store that he had helped to rob. It demonstrates the power of a properly conducted restorative justice conference, and its words reinforce the message of this book.

I'm sorry for all the pain that I caused
Putting your family through something I could have stopped
And now I'm staring at the stars thinking of what I have done
Something stupid of course what was I thinking of
Looking for my mentality but that was lost
Back in the days BC I'd be pinned to a cross
But instead I'm writing this rhyme because you gave me a chance
So in the words that I write
You should know that they came from my heart
You opened my eyes despising what I had done
Look above and find the strength to carry on…

The stupid things I've done in my life
Creating enemies that want to bring a lot of strife
We'd fight
On the streets
Is probably where you would see me
Drugged out struggling to breathe
But now I'm down on my knees
With a million apologies
Please time freeze wish I could turn back the time
Rewind but its all over and done
A new era begun
The sun has risen
And it's shining through
This song I compose is dedicated to you.

Andrew Becroft
Principal Youth Court Judge for New Zealand, Wellington

Acknowledgements

There are many to whom we are grateful for their involvement in this project. The authors, all, for their patience and commitment outside regular work, for their passionate writing, editing and re-editing after we had read and suggested, usually only minor, changes. Their understanding of affect script psychology (ASP) and restorative justice (RJ) and its practice gives us hope that the marriage of both will result in better practice that can be sustained in the long term and bring both to mainstream thinking.

Our own families have lived the project with us and provided the nurturing encouragement of their emotional connectedness and the many cups of tea during the numerous moments that required both. To Sharon and Mick, our love, always.

We would like to thank Jessica Kingsley Publishers for their interest in this project and for taking the risk of doing something quite new.

Finally, we would like to thank Judge Andrew Becroft for issuing the challenge to the still emerging field of RJ and its many related practices. He was decidedly accurate that there needs be a cogent, general theory to guide the research necessary for this promising, emotionally humanitarian field to gain more widespread validation. His message rang out loud and clear to us! The result is this volume you have before you. Its ultimate dedication is to restorative practitioners everywhere who work tirelessly to bring healing in an emotionally disconnected world.

Introduction

Vernon C. Kelly Jr. and Margaret Thorsborne

New Zealand Principal Youth Court Judge, Andrew Becroft, is partly responsible for the writing of this book. He was one of the inspirational keynote speakers at the Third International Conference of Restorative Practices International (RPI)[1] in Wellington, New Zealand, in 2011. In his address, he urged delegates to find a theory that would support and explain the emergence of a range of innovative, successful practices in restorative justice (RJ). As fate would have it, co-editor Vernon Kelly, the last morning's keynote speaker at the same conference, answered the call for a substantive theory with a compelling presentation of affect script psychology (ASP). His insights into human motivation, learned from the work of Silvan Tomkins, provided a very clear explanation for how and why restorative practice, when done properly, provides healing for all involved – whether at work, in families, in criminal justice settings, in schools or in communities of one sort or another.

It might be important at this point, in case you have picked up this book because it looked a bit interesting, to *not* assume that everyone knows what we mean by the terms 'restorative justice' and 'restorative practice' (RP). The word 'justice' should give some clue. For some, the word evokes thoughts about responses to crime and wrongdoing that involve fair process; for others, punishment. Still others think 'social' justice. Whatever the word association for the reader, our meaning in this book is about the response to wrongdoing (or offensive acts) that cause harm to others – whether it is in the context of society and the criminal justice system, or in families, schools, communities or workplaces. Restorative *practice* is the 'doing' of RJ. In this approach

---

1   This conference was the result of collaboration between RPI and Restorative Justice Aotearoa (RJA).

to problem-solving, skilled facilitators bring together the community of people directly affected by an incident or crime. In a process of dialogue, stories are told, motivations explained, harm explored and a plan developed to address the harm to individuals, families and the wider community, and to address the causes of the offending and put in place measures to reduce the likelihood of reoffending. It is a kind of face-to-face accountability that is highly confronting, emotional and yet healing for all participants when they come willingly to the process. It is this process of bringing people together – a focus on relationships – that distinguishes it from more retributive responses to crime that tend to keep the people involved apart. How is healing possible when we remain disconnected?

Perhaps the most widely read and quoted theoretician in the field of RJ is Australian criminologist and Distinguished Professor at the Australian National University, John Braithwaite. In his study of how various cultures deal with wrongdoing, especially the use of whole–community meetings by the indigenous people of New Zealand, the Māori, he recognized that the success or failure of what later became known as *restorative conferences* depended upon the pivotal role played by the emotion shame. In his seminal work, *Crime, Shame and Reintegration* (1989), he set the tone for all future restorative interventions by making clear that those wrongdoers most likely to reoffend are those who feel stigmatized – *shamed* into feeling they are inherently flawed, bad people – by traditional punishments for their behaviour, in part, because they feel ostracized from their community. Those least likely to reoffend are those who are involved in interventions that cause them to feel shame about their behaviour but also to feel that the community they've offended wants them back – reintegrated – because they are seen by all as worthwhile people whose lives are important and meaningful.

The recognition of the significance of shame and the need for further research prompted Braithwaite and his colleagues (Ahmed *et al.* 2001) to engage in explorations into various theories of shame – including the psychological, the sociological, the anthropological, the ethical and more. Their work leaves one with a much greater appreciation of the many faces of shame, but also with a feeling that there is no foundational theory to explain what is inherent in human beings that makes it possible for all of us to experience shame. After all, it cannot simply pop up out of thin air! Nor does their research or theorizing explain the motivating forces behind the interpersonal dynamics of restorative conferences that engender reintegration through shaming. We believe that what they were missing is hinted at when they wrote, 'In this book we sidestep all the biological questions about shame: Is it a human universal?' (p.3).

Human beings are neurobiological entities before they become psychological, social and ethical beings. While Ahmed *et al.* (2001) touch superficially on the work of Silvan Tomkins, their research and subsequent theories could well have led to a more all-inclusive theory of how and why restorative processes and reintegration through shaming work, had they fully grasped the depth and consequences of the biological and evolutionary insights provided by ASP. Nor had any other theoreticians in the decade between the 2001 publishing of the aforementioned volume and the 2011 Wellington conference developed any significant unifying theory. Judge Becroft was right: the RJ/RP movement needed a cogent theory.

The co-editors had the good fortune of attending the workshops of a number of the Wellington conference faculty who were already well versed in ASP. They gave presentations elegantly interweaving the theory into stories about their daily work using RP in a variety of settings. Their material was so invigorating that it was a small leap to the idea of putting together an edited volume of case studies in RJ/RP to answer Judge Becroft's challenge.

Case studies are nothing new as an approach to writing a volume, but what we have done this time around is different. We invited both practitioners from the conference and several others with whose work we were familiar to each write a case study or tell their own story. Within their chapters, each author has provided an explanation about what happened from an ASP perspective, linked back to Vernon Kelly's first two chapters that outline the theory. We have drawn from a variety of fields – school, workplace, criminal justice and policing, family violence, arts and neighbourhoods. We selected the authors whose stories are generously shared in this volume for two reasons: their deep familiarity with the everyday doing of RJ/RP and their understanding of ASP.

The Chapters

We have arranged this volume into four parts with chapters written to reflect the case study setting:

Part 1: The Theory Underpinning Restorative Justice – Affect Script Psychology (Chapters 1 and 2)

Part 2: The Theory in Action in Communities and the Criminal Justice Setting (Chapters 3–6)

Part 3: The Theory in Action in Organizational Settings (Chapters 7 and 8)

Part 4: The Theory in Action in Education (Chapters 9 and 10)

Part 1: The Theory Underpinning Restorative Justice – Affect Script Psychology

Chapter 1: *Caring, Restorative Practice and the Biology of Emotion* is by Dr Vernon Kelly Jr., MD, whose immersion in the work of Silvan S. Tomkins eventually led to his co-founding The Silvan S. Tomkins Institute with Donald Nathanson, MD, in the early 1990s in Philadelphia, Pennsylvania, USA. In this chapter, Kelly presents a consolidated version of Tomkins's theories about the biological and evolutionary roots of human motivation – what Tomkins called human being theory – the how and why we 'care'. He relates the theory to principles central to restorative practices including what constitutes harm and the biology of shame.

Chapter 2: *Interpersonal Caring, Social Disciple and a Blueprint for Restorative Healing,* also written by Dr Kelly, interweaves insights from ASP into the scripts motivating interpersonal relationships and how those scripts impact the dynamics of interactions between those in authority and their subordinates based on insights from the Social Discipline Window. He then describes the emotional transformation that occurs in a well-prepared, well-facilitated restorative process. He clarifies how every culture is governed by the same biology, with each developing its own scripts (rules) to keep the balance determined by the Central Blueprint. He also tackles the somewhat controversial topic of forgiveness and helps us understand why sometimes we can forgive and other times not.

Part 2: The Theory in Action in Communities and the Criminal Justice Setting

Chapter 3: *Being Emotional, Being Human: Creating Healthy Communities and Institutions by Honoring Our Biology* is by Lauren Abramson, PhD, the founder and CEO of the Community Conferencing Center (CCC) in Baltimore, Maryland, USA. Lauren, of all our other authors, has had very close encounters with ASP, as she was for a time a student of Silvan Tomkins himself. She brings this depth of understanding to her writing. It is clear from her stories that the CCC has wrought some stunning results in terms of justice outcomes in her community. This chapter adds another layer of understanding about ASP on top of Kelly's first two chapters. If you are a chapter 'jumper', then do try to read this one next after his first two chapters, before tackling the others.

Chapter 4: *Restorative Practice in a Policing Environment: Understanding Affect Will Help* is by an experienced, seasoned police officer, John Lennox, who is now a restorative consultant in Tasmania, Australia. John describes first several aspects of the 'daily grind' of policing and then how his understanding of ASP changed his approach to policing both with groups and with individuals. This change of approach allowed him to better understand the crime itself, and then manage its fallout and its tragedies. He includes details of a restorative conference he facilitated for a case of arson in a school. Some of his stories are uplifting, others deeply sad.

Chapter 5: *Forgiveness* is by Katy Hutchison, a Canadian from Vancouver Island, BC, Canada, who is a strong advocate of restorative justice. Katy is not a restorative practitioner – she is a participant in her own story of the journey through the murder of her husband Bob and her experiences with the criminal justice system and eventually RJ. This story, written in hindsight with the advantage of a deep understanding of ASP, is a deeply moving account of tragedy, face-to-face encounters with the young man who killed her husband in a fit of drug-fuelled rage, recovery and eventually, forgiveness.

Chapter 6: *A Necessary Discovery: Why the Theory is Important* is by a group of practitioners, Matthew Casey, William Curry, Anne Burton and Katherine Gribben, in a not-for-profit organization in Goulburn, New South Wales, Australia. Primarily tasked to work with families in crisis, this group was introduced to RJ in 2000. They ultimately discovered that restorative conferencing is not always possible or practical when dealing with chaotic family situations, nor is it necessarily effective. Further enquiry has culminated in their unique 'Explicit Affective Practice' framework, described in an independently funded evaluation as a fusion between RJ and ASP (Broderick and Bazeley 2012). In a practice divergent from more traditional forms of family therapy, they concisely share Tomkins's theory with client families along with identifiable restorative tools towards an understanding and management of behaviours. The practice is a uniform agency response with particular emphasis on wholesome relationships. Their case work, especially with spouse abusers, is remarkable.

Part 3: The Theory in Action in Organizational Settings

Chapter 7: *Keep Calm and Carry On: From Fear to Fun over Two Years in a British Youth Arts Organization* is written with typical British humour by Siân Williams, a restorative consultant who spends her time between her base in London and Malawi, Africa. This case is a perfect example of how a keen knowledge of both RJ and ASP helped her transform a deeply negative, competitive culture in a youth arts organization into one of healthy, positive relationships and genuine collaboration between all the key groups in this venture, including staff, young people and the public. It required her to hold steady when it looked terrifying in the early days of her work – to keep calm and carry on!

Chapter 8: *Drama Queens* is by Margaret Thorsborne, restorative consultant and co-editor of this volume, based on the Sunshine Coast, Queensland, Australia, with offices in Australia and London. She relates the story of a transformation in a high school faculty beset with a highly toxic relationship between two teachers – a relationship that had infected the rest of the group. The faculty had been suffering from the fallout from a number of issues that, as is too often the case in organizations, escalated over time because they were never resolved when small. An understanding of ASP and RJ allowed the design of a process that followed the rules of the Central Blueprint, and allowed Marg and her colleague Sharon Borrows to help the group reach some positive outcomes. Like Siân in the previous chapter, they were able to stay centred in the face of very toxic affect and trust the process and the natural biology of emotion to get some very positive outcomes that were a great relief for all involved.

Part 4: The Theory in Action in Education

Chapter 9: *Affect and Emotion in a Restorative School* is by Graeme George, a restorative practitioner and teacher in a boys' school in Brisbane, Queensland, Australia. Graeme's long involvement in restorative practice and a comprehensive restructure of his school has resulted in his immersion in ASP and RJ. This chapter reflects his deep interest in boys' education, and his research into the emotions of shame and guilt help us to distinguish between the two. He has developed a framework for understanding the shame involved in learning, and how the teacher might work alongside learners to help them develop resilience and stay engaged, even when the subject matter is quite daunting. His insights into the complex emotions involved in education provides a template for educators at all levels to get the best out of their students and themselves.

Chapter 10: *They Suck, School Sucks, I Suck: The Secret Emotional Life of a Child with a Brain That Learns Differently* is by Bill Hansberry, educator, restorative consultant and therapist, based in Adelaide, Australia. Bill writes graphically about the learning difficulties of a young boy with attention deficit hyperactivity disorder (ADHD), the shame he experiences and the behaviours he defaults to in order to deal with such negative feelings. This chapter has important and very practical lessons for educators of young children with such learning difficulties, and shows how a punitive approach has no chance of improving their educational outcomes. An approach based on restorative principles informed by ASP, on the other hand, will help them develop self-regulation and create a greater sense of connectedness in the school community.

References

Ahmed, E., Harris, N., Braithwaite, J. and Braithwaite, V. (2001) *Shame Management Through Reintegration.* Cambridge: Cambridge University Press.

Braithwaite, J. (1989) *Crime, Shame and Reintegration.* Cambridge: Cambridge University Press.

Broderick, S. and Bazeley P. (2012) *Outcomes of the Explicit Affective Practice. A report of the Evaluation of the Family Support and Counselling Activities Provided by the Goulburn Family Support Service.* Available at http://gfss.ned.org.au/images/Outcomes_of_Explicit_Affective_Practice_Evaluation_Report.pdf, accessed on 24 September 2013.

Part 1

The Theory Underpinning Restorative Justice

Affect Script Psychology

CHAPTER 1

Caring, Restorative Practice and the Biology of Emotion

Vernon C. Kelly, Jr.

Introduction

Restorative interventions work because human beings *care*. Amongst other things: people care about what others feel and think about them; they care that others have been harmed and are in need of repair; they care that they may have harmed others and don't know how to fix it; they care that others care for them; they care if others act as if they don't care for them; and they sometimes care to act as if they don't care because they have been harmed. Furthermore, all human behavior is motivated by what we care about.

In order to provide a theoretical basis for the methods of restorative practice and the motivations of victims and offenders, it is necessary to delve into how and why we care. Such an exploration must acknowledge that we are biological beings, living in social settings from birth on, and that the unique psychology of each of us evolves from a complex interplay of these factors. Ultimately, this will lead to a discussion of how human emotion and the dynamic interplay of emotions between people creates the atmosphere essential for successful restorative interventions.

Our commonly inherited biology is the critical factor in social bonding behaviors, be it between two individuals or larger groups of people. In part, this is because everyone *knows* what it feels like to experience joy, fear, excitement, anger and shame, even though the ratio of positive to negative feelings varies widely in each individual. Furthermore, everyone is affected by the emotions of others in quite similar ways.

In these next two chapters, I present a brief overview[1] of the biological basis of human emotional dynamics. My main goals are:

- To provide a theoretical basis for understanding the techniques used by those involved in all forms of restorative practice (RP), including restorative justice (RJ).

- To clarify what is meant by restorative practitioners when they say someone has experienced *harm* because of the actions of another person(s).

- To explain how and why restorative conferences and circles affect the behavior and emotions of both victims and offenders in dramatic, predictable ways.

Affect Script Psychology
The Motivational System
THE AFFECTS

In the early 1960s, Silvan Tomkins (1962, 1963) posited a biologically based theory of emotion, cognition and personality in the first two books of a four-volume series entitled *Affect Imagery Consciousness (AIC)*. In what has grown into the system known as affect script psychology (ASP), the term *affect* has a very specific meaning. An affect is a biological program, wired into the central nervous system of all newborn infants. The *affect system* in human brains is comprised of nine affects:

Positive affects	*Neutral affect*	*Negative affects*
interest-excitement	surprise-startle	distress-anguish
enjoyment-joy		fear-terror
		anger-rage
		shame-humiliation
		disgust
		dissmell

---

1   This overview only skims the surface of ASP. See the Suggested Reading section at the end of the chapter to gain a fuller appreciation of how all human behavior, emotion and personality development emerge from the same nine innate affects found in all infants.

Each one of these affect *programs* is set off or triggered when our sensory system (sight, smell, taste, touch, hearing and/or pain) perceives a certain signal in the environment around us or inside of us – the *stimulus conditions* of the environment. It is the evolved function of these affect programs to provide us with information about what is going on so that we pay attention to the most important events taking place in our world at that moment. Each affect is triggered by a very specific set of stimulus conditions. Fear-terror, for instance, is the response to our senses picking up on something too big, too loud or too fast going on. On the other hand, when our senses encounter some novel stimulus that is *just right*, interest-excitement is triggered. Distress-anguish is the response when too much has been happening for too long, and enjoyment-joy the affect triggered when that too much finally stops happening.

The triggering of each of the nine affects is an automatic process – it does not require thought. As such, the triggering of an affect can be compared to the knee jerk response. If the stimulus conditions are exactly right, a particular affect is triggered, just as the lower leg jerks upward when the knee is tapped in exactly the right spot. Both of these responses occur because that is the way human biology works. It is how we are wired by all the nerves and nerve endings found throughout the body. We have no conscious ability to control either set of responses. In Tomkins's opinion, the automatic responses of the affect system serve a function critical for the survival of our species. They focus our attention immediately on one thing at a time, making us consciously aware of whatever is the most important thing happening at that moment. Each moment of consciousness, he suggests, is preceded by an affect. In other words, we only become consciously aware of something if it first triggers an affect.

The significance of Tomkins's insight conveyed in that last sentence cannot be overstated. It is often a difficult concept to accept because it implies a massive shift from the theories of almost all current and past 'experts' in human emotion and behavior – theories that most of us learned and believed from early childhood on. Simply stated, it means that affect motivates everything humans do and think.

You would be right to ask, 'How can this be? Aren't humans often logical and rational?' Yes, we certainly can be. But consider this lengthy question: given that we are biological beings with a carbon-based chemistry made up of molecules and atoms from which all of our organs including our brains are constructed, what in our biological makeup *motivates* logic and rationality? With all of the advances in the field of neuroscience, we have moved away from the archaic notion that there is a black box of *logic* in our brains. Logic does not develop out of thin air. It's not present at birth. Something causes us – motivates us – to want to become logical. The foundation of that something must be present at birth as part of our inherited biological attributes. It is beyond the scope of this chapter to detail Tomkins's findings from his study of the faces of infants, but he uncovered the fact that each of the nine affect programs includes a specific facial pattern which is visible in infants either immediately upon birth or very soon after. Affect, therefore, is with us from the very start. It influences the way we think, from our earliest musings as children to the more complex thinking of the mature brain. The biological foundation of logic is the affect system.

As I have already mentioned, each of the nine inborn affects is an automatic reaction to and gives us immediate information about our environment without us first having to think about it. The information from the positive affects of *interest* and *enjoyment* is that something pleasant is happening. The information from the negative affects of *distress, fear, anger, disgust, dissmell* (foul-smelling things) and *shame* is that something unpleasant is happening. The neutral affect *surprise-startle* simply resets attention to prepare us for what comes next.

The idea that the affects are either pleasant/rewarding or unpleasant/unrewarding is essential for the next part of this discussion. But first, it is important to stress the fact that affects are simple biologic events that take place out of conscious awareness. In ASP, we use the term *feelings* to describe what takes place once we become consciously aware that an affect has been triggered. For instance, if someone says, 'I'm afraid', the sequence of events that took place is: first, a stimulus was perceived by the person's senses (e.g. they saw, heard or felt something too loud or too big or too fast); then, second, their affect system responded with fear, producing a number of bodily reactions; and then, and only then, did they became aware of the fear. The biological (and survival) advantage of such a sequence of events is that one does not have to stop and think about a saber tooth tiger charging at them; instead, they simply experience fear and then, based on prior learning, can choose the fight or flight response most suitable for the situation.

THE CENTRAL BLUEPRINT

The affect system with its nine affects is but one feature of how and why we care. It is vitally important because it directs attention to what is going on around us. It also provides us with a *flavor* to what our senses detect. Anything that triggers positive affect is inherently rewarding and we want more of it, whereas negative affect experiences are inherently punishing and we want less of them.

The affect system works in conjunction with many other brain systems. Memory allows us to store information about what we like and don't like. The ability to analyze experiences allows us to pinpoint the positive and negative aspects of an event and compare it with other events. All of these things combined act as a continual feedback system and create in each person a general plan of action – sometimes conscious and often unconscious – known in ASP as the Central Blueprint. The how and why of caring and the primary motivation of all human behavior is directed by the four rules of the Blueprint. We are continually motivated by our inborn biologic systems to:

1. maximize positive affect

2. minimize negative affect

3. minimize the inhibition of affect, and

4. maximize the power to maximize positive affect, minimize negative affect, and minimize the inhibition of affect.

Wellbeing results from a life lived with numbers 1–3 as balanced as circumstances permit. When that is the case, number 4 progressively generates more and more advanced skills to carry out 1–3. However, some physical illnesses or negative life events such as abuse can create distortions in Central Blueprint balance, leading to unhealthy behaviors. For instance, a chronically abused person might resort to a life dedicated solely to maximizing positive affect through addictive behaviors without regard for the consequences that lead to negative affect. Or someone who has had an experience that harmed them deeply might turn solely to behaviors dedicated to minimizing negative affect – perhaps by withdrawing from all social contact – thereby limiting what they used to maximize positive affect and have fun. As will be seen throughout this book, effective restorative practices *restore* the ability of individuals and communities to live and function in emotionally balanced ways consistent with the biological directives of the Central Blueprint.

The Cognitive System

To this point, the discussion of motivation, and the most primitive aspects of how and why we care, has centered entirely on the evolved biological workings of the human brain. Simply stated, we are all wired from birth to experience positive and negative affect based on stimulus conditions around us and to have our reactions to those feelings managed by a Central Blueprint. We care – are motivated – to automatically seek more positive feelings and to stop negative feelings.

As the infant brain matures, we become more and more aware of what we are feeling and able to think about it. We develop the motor skills and control of our bodies, including the ability to speak, that permit us to more actively pursue positive feelings and avoid the negative ones. Furthermore, the cognitive or thinking components of our brains begin to be able to anticipate what might feel good or bad based on what felt good or bad in the past.

Our brain is without question the most powerful survival tool at our disposal. Perhaps its most valuable asset is its capacity for simplification. For instance, by amplifying a stimulus, the affect system simplifies things by making us focus on just one thing at a time, even when there are a myriad of other things bombarding our senses simultaneously. In other words, if something triggers interest, we immediately focus on just that; if it triggers fear, we immediately focus on just that. If this simplification did not occur, our limited channel for conscious awareness would be overwhelmed. Overwhelmed creatures are much less likely to survive.

If, however, we only possessed an affect system that caused our awareness to jump from one thing to the next to the next to the next and so on, the human race would not have advanced very far. We would have remained disorganized and infant-like, moving randomly from one toy to the next, to the next, and so on. Luckily, our *cognitive system* begins early on to organize experience into patterns that can be remembered and used to anticipate the future. This is yet another way that things are simplified and survival made easier. The cognitive system receives information, somewhat like data input into a computer, and then duplicates and transforms that information into conscious reports or thoughts. (The details of this complex process can be found in Volume IV of *AIC* (Tomkins 1992).) The information received by the cognitive system comes from both memory of past reports and reports about what is happening at the moment. This simplifies things by making it unnecessary to learn everything anew each time it happens. In conjunction with a child's growing control over his or her muscular system, the organizing functions of the cognitive system permit us to develop motor and language skills that can be repeated and used to communicate with those around us.

The motivational system and cognitive system are both independent and interdependent systems. This means each works on its own but constantly also interacts with the other. If we had only a motivational system, then we would feel things but have no idea what to do with or about those feelings. If we had only a cognitive system, then we would have information but lack motivation to do anything about it. The motivational system provides urgency to our thoughts, and our thoughts give direction and meaning to our feelings. Together, the motivational system and cognitive system create what Tomkins called *minding*. He used the term *mind* to indicate that things mind to us – in other words, that we care.

Script Formation: Foundations of Personality

To more fully understand the how and why of caring, it is necessary to consider one special ability of the brain that is a product of our mind. In ASP, this is called *script formation*. (One might be tempted to label this *emotional learning*, but since one of the nine affects precedes all experience of which humans become conscious, all learning is ultimately motivated by emotion, making the term redundant.)

I begin the study of scripts by considering the simplest unit of conscious experience. It is comprised of the following sequence: our sensory system receives a message (a **stimulus**) and an **affect** program is triggered with several facial and bodily responses. Tomkins named this stimulus-affect-response (SAR) unit a *scene*. Waking life consists of many, many scenes occurring each day. By itself, each scene is essentially meaningless. But through memory and the ability to recognize patterns, the mind organizes scenes that are similar into groups of scenes.

There are several advantages for survival when scenes are organized into groups. The most important is that once groups of scenes are stored in memory, we do not have to relearn everything each time it happens. Instead, we can compare each new scene to things we already know. This permits us to rapidly make sense out of almost anything that we see or hear or feel without having to rethink it. This frees up our brain, which has limits on how much we can hold in conscious awareness at any given moment in time, so that new learning can take place more easily. For instance, when you see a chair, you do not have to re-examine it in order to know that it – and everything similar to it – is something to sit on. You know its purpose and what to do with it immediately. Likewise, you do not have to rethink how to cross a busy street or wear a shirt or relate to people you know.

The technical term used to describe how script formation aids in survival is *information advantage*. By storing in memory groups of related scenes, such as all the things we have sat upon, we have now learned about sitting and the things we can sit on. Our cognitive system transforms this information into a simple theory that, once learned, does not have to be learned again. The theory will then be applied to all forms of sitting and objects to sit upon. Therefore, whenever we receive through our eyes the small amount of information that there is a chair in front of us, we can apply this theory about a large amount of information without having to think about it. This is analogous to using a lever so that with a small amount of force we can move a large object.

Here is another relatively simple example of the creation of a script: a hungry baby cries. (The stimulus is hunger, the affect is distress, and the response is crying.) Her caregiver picks her up, feeds her, and she experiences relief of hunger. (Stimulus – relief of hunger and distress; affect – enjoyment-joy/contentment; response – smile/

body relaxes.) Each time this happens, her cognitive system begins to collect the scenes that are similar and organize them into groups and remember them. As time passes, she learns that almost every time she experiences distress and cries, a *person* will appear to help her reduce the negative affect of distress – whether it's created by hunger or something else. She will then begin have a great deal of interest in the appearance of that person and associate her or him with both the general group known as *people* and the very specific person or people who attend to her regularly, often known as mother and father. The affects of distress, enjoyment and interest are the powerful motivators behind this learning.

This is how the cognitive system, working hand in hand with the motivational system, forms *attachment scripts*. The most basic message of these scripts is that people help relieve my distress, give me enjoyment and are interested in me, and therefore I am interested in them. In other words, the infant now cares about people, and cares that people care about her.

Attachment scripts go through many modifications over time based on each person's interactions with parents, extended family and their cultural milieu. A child's mind is constantly updating attachment scripts to balance what is happening in her or his relationships based on the Central Blueprint requirement to maximize positive affect and minimize negative affect. The result of this ongoing process of attachment or relational script formation is the development in the child's personality of specific ways of relating to people. Tomkins's insights into personality formation led him to write (1981, p.31): 'From the outset, I have supposed the person to be a bio-psycho-social entity at the intersect of both more complex higher social systems and lower biologic systems.'

At this point, it is useful to define *emotions* to distinguish them from affects and feelings. *Affects* are simply short-lived biological responses to stimulus conditions. They do not last very long. We have all inherited nine affects over which we have no real control. They happen because of our neurological wiring. The term *feelings* describes the situation when someone becomes consciously aware that an affect has been triggered. *Emotions* are scripted responses, arising from the complex interaction between the social relationships of a child's birth culture, that child's inborn temperament and the brain's motivational and cognitive systems effects on these interactions. Emotion is clearly a bio-psycho-social phenomenon.

While there are only nine inborn affects, there are an infinite variety of emotional reactions or scripts that arise from the nine. At birth, we all look and act very much alike – even with the differences in features of our multiracial species – because we all have the same nine affects and the facial expressions that accompany them. As adults, we all seem very different *emotionally* because of the dissimilarity of our backgrounds. Each person is unique because no two people share exactly the same history. As a result, once we know someone, we can distinguish that person from everyone who has ever lived – even identical twins – if we know them well enough.

The vast differences in scripted emotional and behavioral responses are one of the reasons people from different cultures often have difficulty coexisting peacefully. If someone looks and acts differently, and we cannot interpret what their emotions or behaviors mean, and if we cannot communicate with them, it creates an uncomfortable, even fearful state of affairs. Human beings create walls – both emotional and physical – to defend against those whose appearance creates fear in them. This raises the question: How can we *ever* understand each other? The answer is found in the universality of our biologic inheritance. We all know what it is to feel fear, joy, anger, shame, interest, distress, disgust and dissmell. It is our shared biology that makes RP possible and effective, as you shall learn in the pages of this book that follow.

Attachment scripts are just one example of the multitude of scripts we form over a lifetime. We have scripts for eating, for dressing, for playing sports, for driving vehicles, for working machinery, for dealing with stressful situations, for language, for writing, for having fun, for reading, for learning, for interpreting what others say, for beliefs about politics, religion and art, for dealing with each of the nine affects and so forth. Scripts are the way we create order out of the ever-changing world in which we live. They give us stability because, once formed, they are resistant to change. This stability provides our species with a survival advantage. Because we do not have to relearn everything each time it happens, we can more quickly assess situations and base the most favorable response on both past learning and the ever-present Central Blueprint direction to maximize positive affect and minimize negative affect.

Personality can be thought of as the combined effect of a person's many accumulated scripts. Every personality is unique because the scripts arise from singular life experiences and biologic differences in temperament (including genetic inheritance). Likewise, each person's scripted emotions, and the expression of those emotions, are unique. One person may yell and scream when angry, while another, equally as angry, might simply raise an eyebrow. This substantial difference in emotional expression is a direct reflection of the familial and cultural background of each person. Behavioral responses are also scripted differently in everyone. This will be discussed in more detail below, but when considering why people act the way they do in any situation, it is important to keep in mind that affect motivates everything.

Several other features of our biology and how we care need mentioning before turning to a more detailed discussion of the mechanisms behind restorative practice. The first is that of *affective resonance*. Each of our nine affects is triggered as a specific response to the stimulus conditions around us. The face and rest of the body exhibit our responses whenever an affect is triggered. Others looking at and hearing us notice our response. What they see and hear is a stimulus for their responses. This then triggers in them the same affect we are exhibiting. Hence, one begins to feel angry if talking with someone who is angry about something. Or one feels sad (distress) if the other person is sad. Or happy if that person is happy, and so forth with all nine of the affects. This is the biologically based phenomenon known as affective resonance. It is the reason feelings are contagious. It is a major component of script formation as the affects that motivate us often reflect the affect(s) of those around us. Affective resonance is, therefore, a very powerful influence in how we care during restorative interventions and why such interventions can effect significant change in emotions and behaviors. (More about this later in the chapter.)

SOCIAL SCRIPTS
One can never completely disassociate personality scripts and the behaviors accompanying them from the influence (affects) of others.

The brief mention earlier of attachment script formation outlined the first affects shared by infant and caregiver. Simply stated, the inborn affects of interest and enjoyment (contentment) experienced by infants motivate the child to notice and to learn that other people are a source of positive experience. Every living person must have experienced some degree of this because, at the very least, to survive one must have been fed by another and felt the contentment when hunger was relieved. The earliest, most primitive social (interpersonal) scripts, the ones that create the need, desire and wish to have relationships, can be stated in the following way.

One is motivated toward social interaction because:

- When I feel bad, another person can make me feel good.

- People are interested in and enjoy me and that makes me feel good and want to be interested in and enjoy them.

These early social scripts become more powerful due to a number of biological forces. Studies show that physical contact increases the production of the bonding hormone oxytocin, which, in turn, triggers parasympathetic activity and general body relaxation with reduction of negative affect (Gamer and Büchel 2012). (Interestingly, Guastella, Mitchell and Dadds (2008) noted that as part of this response, oxytocin promotes increased focus on the eye region of the face. Since the face is the primary site of the expression of affect, increased focus fosters increased interaffective responses between caregiver and child mediated by affective resonance.) These and other forces work together to create social scripts of such great power that human beings are essentially compelled – by a high degree of interest – to care very deeply throughout their entire lifetime about being with others of our species, be it in pairs, families or communities.

Just as the Central Blueprint always directs the way individuals care, it does the same when two, three or more interact with one another. In the mid-1990s, I used ASP to redefine *emotional intimacy* (Kelly 1996). More recently, I updated this work in a book (Kelly 2012) intended for people in all walks of life. What I discovered in my research was that couples in emotionally intimate relationships have the deepest, most satisfying emotional connection when they successfully:

1. mutualize and maximize positive affect

2. mutualize and minimize negative affect

3. mutualize and minimize the inhibition of affect, and

4. mutualize and maximize the power to mutualize and maximize positive affect, mutualize and minimize negative affect, and mutualize and minimize the inhibition of affect.

It makes sense that as each individual feels the impact of the emotions and behaviors of another, their Central Blueprint directs them toward interpersonal behaviors aimed at feeling good and not feeling bad. The healthiest interpersonal scripts arise in those relationships where the two people mutually agree to help one another maximize positive affect and minimize negative affect by paying attention to what each other feels. (The most effective interpersonal communications – a critical factor used in all analyses of relationship success or failure – are those that include clear information about what each partner feels.) We are able to mutualize feelings with another because we care about ourselves and about them, and because we care that they care about us.

With some variations, a similar phenomenon occurs in the relationships in all communities, be they large or small. The social scripts of an individual directed by the Central Blueprint promote that person's caring about others and that others care for him/her. The flow of emotion in a group – powerfully influenced by affective resonance since amplification of affect occurs when shared and reflected back and forth between people – also follows the rules of the Central Blueprint. This holds implications for restorative conferences and circles that are addressed in Chapter 2.

The Biology and Influence of Shame

We feel shame and hurt if an individual or the community at large rejects us, causing us to want to withdraw from the situation. While this is something we have all experienced, it is but one aspect of how the innate affect shame influences emotion and behavior. The first association most people have to the word 'shame' is that it means someone has done something to be ashamed of. The word 'shame' evokes bad feelings because it reminds us of unpleasantness from our past. Upon closer examination of the biological origins of shame in our species, however, it turns out that shame has an important general function that goes well beyond simply feeling ashamed of oneself.

Like all the other innate affects, shame evolved solely to give us information about something going on in our immediate environment. According to Tomkins (1962, 1991), the evolution of a built-in signal to notify us of the presence of impediment to positive affect was inevitable. The positive affects of interest-excitement and enjoyment-joy are highly rewarding emotionally. Wellbeing depends upon our ability to maximize these affects and experience them as frequently as we can. Caring for others and ourselves requires that we be able to monitor (be aware of) their presence or absence. It would be impossible to monitor these positive affects without having readily available the *information* that, while in the midst of having interest or enjoyment, something came along to interfere with the experience. Obviously, this could not be a signal of a positive affect nature. That would only confuse matters. It had to be an affect that felt bad enough to make us notice that there was interference with something that previously felt good. Shame affect emerged from this need. Its ultimate purpose is to inform us, by making us feel bad, that our happiness is at risk.

Tomkins was conflicted about his use of the word 'shame' for this innate affect. However, he felt it was the best choice because his research indicated that the facial response of anyone, including very young infants, to impediments to their positive affects is the same. This is true whether the shame is in its mildest form as embarrassment or at its most intense as humiliation. There is a diverting down of the eyes, a slumping of the head to one side as the muscles of the neck go limp, and sometimes the appearance of a blush. His ultimate choice of the word 'shame' for this innate affect had to do with the many ways in which scripting converts it into a myriad of shame emotions. He reasoned that using 'shame' as the name for the entire family of shame emotions would be analogous to the way the word 'salt' is commonly used. While we usually mean table salt or sodium chloride when we say salt, we know that there are thousands of different kinds of salts (many salts come from a chemical reaction between acids and bases to form neutral compounds). Some salts are necessary for life, while others are dangerous when ingested and can cause death. Similarly, shame is necessary for wellbeing because it is a signal that something is in the way of our interest or enjoyment, while shame that leads to deep humiliation can set in motion thoughts and behaviors that end in homicide and/or suicide.[2]

As noted by Braithwaite in 1989, shame is a critical element in RJ. I would add that successful RP in all settings hinges on the ability of those involved to understand and use shame as a positive force based on its inherited biologic function as a signal that positive emotions are within our reach if we can remove that which blocks them.

Shame continually influences the way we care in our relationships. This is as true in our family, school, workplace and community relationships as it is in our most intimate relationship with a significant other (Kelly 2012). Because social scripts create the motivation in everyone to seek positive interactions with others, shame is vitally important as an indicator that something is amiss. Children are highly interested in feeling the interest of their parents toward them and experience shame when that interest is blocked. It often requires trained observers to notice the initial shame reaction because, even in young children, it is short-lived — as are all the innate affects when first triggered. Beginning in very young children, however, the process of script formation rapidly converts the affect shame into *emotional* responses based on each child's temperament and relationship with her/his caregivers.

For instance, the protest of the child in whom shame has been triggered may take the form of distressed or angry crying or even withdrawal. A successful protest alerts the caregiver that something is wrong and she needs to refocus on the child. She may pick him up or speak softly to him, and soon the protest stops because the impediment to her child's interest in her (caregiver's) interest is gone and so is the shame. Both in spite of and because of how bad shame feels, it is nonetheless the affect that signals the need for and then motives the behaviors of reconnection and reconciliation. It is critical for the balanced functioning of the Central Blueprint in

---

2   For more detailed information about the understanding of shame based on ASP, see Nathanson (1992) and the DVD *Managing Shame, Preventing Violence* available from The Tomkins Institute (www.tomkins.org).

relationships because its presence always means there is desire for positive emotional connections with others.

Shame and Guilt

Earlier, I described how emotion is the scripted outcome of the interaction between social and biological forces in a person's life. Many prior theories of emotion and motivation have been incomplete because they did not account for human biology – difficult to understand since we are biologic beings first and only become complex psychological beings over time. This has led to some confusion in the restorative practices literature, especially when it comes to defining and understanding the impact of shame and guilt in restorative processes. The basis of the discussion that follows is the idea that human emotion does not materialize out of thin air. There is a very real, observable biological foundation from which all of it emerges. In Chapter 2, this same concept is applied to a discussion of the bio-psycho-social forces directing the processes that take place during restorative conferences. But for now the focus is on the *emotions* of shame and guilt and how they have the same biologic starting point – the *affect* shame-humiliation. (Note that the emotions embarrassment, mortification and shyness also have a basis in the affect shame-humiliation and are not considered here due to space limitations.)

The bottom line is that while it is true that *shame* and *guilt* are commonly used to describe experiences that feel very different emotionally, they nevertheless both involve situations *where good feelings have turned bad*. Since this is one of the discoveries of ASP that is not immediately obvious, it is useful for those who practice restoratively and for those who do research in that arena to understand this conceptually. Shame and guilt are *emotions* that arise when our interest in being seen by self and others as competent, morally sound or intelligent is blocked by something we do or say. But their scripting takes very different paths.

Generally speaking, the experience of the emotion shame (note again the reference here to the *emotion* shame, not the innate *affect* shame from which its scripting originates) involves a more intense turning inward to focus on defects within the self, while the emotion guilt involves a focus on the harm we have caused others combined with fear of punishment for our deeds. Although more biologically based research needs to done in this area, the findings of ASP suggest that those with more shame-prone personalities have been turned inward by parenting styles, experiences and socialization methods that repeatedly create great emotional distance between children and their caregivers. This promotes a scripted system of beliefs within the child that she/he is by nature bad, defective, stupid and unlovable and there is nothing much she/he can do about it. Examples of adult–child interactions promoting shame-proneness might include physical abuse ('Because you deserve it!'), abandonment threats ('I'll send you away forever!') or actual abandonment and lectures about defectiveness ('You're useless and will never amount to any good!').

On the other hand, parenting styles, experiences and socialization methods where the adults more regularly keep the child focused on the interpersonal interaction between the two, the effect of the child's behavior on others and the fear of what might happen if negative behaviors keep repeating are more likely to create a proneness to guilty emotions. Examples might include 'Look what you did to me,' 'See how you made me feel' and 'That's not the way grown-ups behave'. In scenarios such as these, the affect shame-humiliation is triggered initially because the child's interest in the parent's approval is blocked by the parent's negative response to the behavior being addressed. (Keep in mind that the evolved biologic function of shame is to signal that there is some impediment to positive feelings.) But a caregiver keeping a child focused on the feelings of others and/or the moral standards of the family and community transforms shame about negative behavior into the world of interpersonal relationships and the fear of punishment by others. As bad as this may feel, it gives the child hope that there is something she can do to correct her misdeeds because *she has the experience that others are interested in her if she will only mend her ways.* The child cut off from others, on the other hand, is likely to remain deeply mired in shameful feelings about a defective self and experience no such hope.

Although there are extreme cases, most personalities contain a mixture of shame- and guilt-proneness. In Chapter 9, George details research that has provided important information about the negative outcomes for children who by the age of eight are more shame-prone than guilt-prone.

The Compass of Shame

The next part of this chapter is concerned with the influence of shame *affect* on the formation of scripts and the behaviors related to those scripts. As detailed by Nathanson (1992), even though shame affect and the scripted emotions of shame, guilt, embarrassment, mortification and shyness are simply information about impediment to positive affect, there are many situations in which that information cannot be used in constructive ways. Depending on the degree of intensity of an unmanageable shame response – mild in embarrassment to severe in mortification – one must erect defenses that correspond in intensity. Nathanson outlined four script libraries into which he grouped these defenses. Because he believed pairs of these scripts to be opposites and because they point the way conceptually to shame that otherwise might remain hidden, he named this construct the *Compass of Shame*, depicted in Figure 1.1.

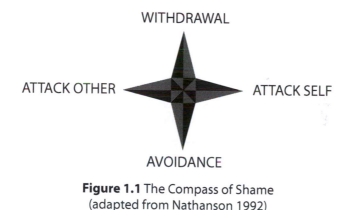

Figure 1.1 The Compass of Shame
(adapted from Nathanson 1992)

The usefulness of what follows is that it outlines *behaviors* where the underlying motivation is based on the fact that those who exhibit them are experiencing shame that they do not know how to manage any other way. Shame, guilt, embarrassment, shyness and all the other emotions that arise when some impediment blocks positive affect are painful states. We want them to go away and will do almost anything to have them stop. You will note in the discussion that follows ways in which you have behaved because everyone has had difficult-to-manage shame experiences. Whether any particular behavior becomes permanently scripted into one's personality depends upon how painful and enduring the shame is that one is defending against.

ATTACK OTHER

This group of behaviors works by shifting attention away from the self and on to another person or thing. Anger is often involved because angry feelings and the accompanying bursts of adrenalin make more vulnerable feelings like shame disappear. However, for many individuals anger is also taboo, and they hide it behind such things as passive-aggressive behaviors like sarcasm.

Here is a partial list of behaviors, exhibited when shame is covered up by the use of *attack other* methods of defense:

- Angry put-downs: 'You're an idiot!'

- Abusive recrimination: 'You did it wrong, just like you always do.'

- Physical attacks: spousal abuse, bar fights, road-rage fights.

- Sarcasm: derived from the Greek word *sarkasmos*, meaning 'to tear flesh'.

- Hatred and vengeance: expressed either verbally or by nasty treatment of the other.

- Sexual sadism: taking the role of dominator/dominatrix in BDSM activity.

- Murder: the most extreme form of *attack other* behavior.

ATTACK SELF

These shame defenses appear, at first, to increase shame, not reduce it. However, these are behaviors that represent a compromise that if I shame myself first, then I control the amount of shame I feel. These are often people whose caregivers used shame and *attack other* as their primary methods of socializing their children. The children therefore learn to put themselves down to help blunt their caregiver's attacks.

Here is a partial list of behaviors, exhibited when shame is dealt with by the use of *attack self* methods of defense:

- Self-recrimination: 'I can't do anything right.'

- Sexual masochism: taking the submissive role in BDSM activity.

- Self-mutilation: cutting, burning and other reckless behaviors.

- Suicide: the most extreme form of *attack self* behavior.

WITHDRAWAL

This group of behaviors works by removing people from situations that cause shame. They are aware that shame is present or might be present and withdraw into their house or room or into their own head. They keep their real feelings to themselves for fear that anything they expose will be stupid or silly, or will in some way open them up to ridicule by others. They have great fear that others see them – literally and figuratively – as defective; as a result, they prefer to hide.

Here is a partial list of behaviors, exhibited when someone deals with shame by the use of *withdrawal*:

- Solo activity: often becomes a lifestyle choice in *shy* people.

- Silence: refusal to speak.

- Sexual withdrawal: can be through impotence, frigidity.

- Agoraphobia: the most serious form can be crippling for reaching life's goals.

AVOIDANCE

These behaviors use denial in various forms in an attempt to remove feelings of shame from conscious awareness. People who use avoidance defenses frequently have patterns that also promote the use of *attack other*, especially if their denial is confronted. When avoidance behaviors become part of their character, it gives rise to people with *big egos*, with rigidly judgmental opinions of others. These are people who cannot admit to being wrong and who often receive the label *narcissist*.

Here is a partial list of behaviors, exhibited when someone deals with shame by the use of *avoidance* methods of defense:

- Macho: 'I am strong, you are weak, and I'll prove it by beating you up.' (When combined with *attack other*, this leads to bullying behaviors.)

- Alcoholism and drug abuse: shame reduced with chemicals.

- Over-intellectualization: 'I'm smarter than you.'

- Over-competitiveness: must always win or be involved in the attempt.

- Obsessive wealth gathering: covering up any signs of being lesser with money.

- Verbal gibberish: just going on and on to cover up what's underneath all the talk.

- Sexual infidelity: 'I just can't help it – these other women want me.'

The importance of using the Compass of Shame to aid in the recognition of behaviors motivated by the Central Blueprint directive to minimize the negative affect shame will be seen throughout this book. This is equally true for restorative efforts on behalf of offenders, as well as their victims, whether it be in the criminal justice system, the workplace or in schools. In order to care for others effectively, one must have an approach based upon a solid understanding of how others care and how that motivates their behavior.

For instance, a bully is always someone engaged in *attack other* behaviors to reduce his own shame. It should be a clear message to anyone dealing with the situation that such behaviors signal vulnerability within that person. Punitive methods of managing a bully generally create more shame because there is little concern shown for what he cares about that motivates his behavior. His behavior is punished and his person ignored. When ignored, people experience an impediment to that most basic of all human interpersonal needs – that others be interested in them. It is this cyclical pattern of re-shaming offenders that makes reoffending – often the repetition of shame-based behaviors – more probable.

Shame–Jealousy–Competitiveness

One commonplace, but often misunderstood, group of behaviors based on shame is represented by the triangle in Figure 1.2. As you read the ensuing chapters, you will encounter a number of examples where jealousy and competitiveness play a role. I submit the image of the triangle as a cue that where one finds any one of these, the other two are likely to be present. In fact, jealousy and competitiveness 'feed' on one another. The more jealous one feels, the more one may compete to be better, smarter, more athletic, richer, sexier or more beautiful than others are. The more one competes, the more one notices those who are 'better' in some way, and hence the more jealous one becomes. In general, the greater the shame being defended against, the more intense the jealous and competitive behaviors will be.

Figure 1.2 Shame–Jealousy–Competitiveness

COMPETITIVE SCRIPTS

Jealous actions/thoughts and competitiveness are examples of behaviors that represent combinations of Compass of Shame scripts. Competitiveness is a frequent factor in the development of the self – sometimes healthy and, at other times, unhealthy, creating an imbalance in Central Blueprint functions. Nathanson (1992, p.371) wrote:

> Since so much of our self-concept is derived from comparison with others, and since it is through the medium of competition that we set up purposeful systems of comparison, it stands to reason that shame stemming from some perceived but irremediable deficiency of the self can be mitigated by shifting attention toward the pride and status achieved when one wins at something. Directly proportional to the amount of energy devoted to competition is always the degree of chronic shame linked to a persistently lowered self-image.

Competitiveness is mostly an *avoidance* script wherein one attempts to deny and overcome weak, helpless feelings by defeating others. But when the feelings of shame and low self-esteem are intense, the defensive script of competitiveness becomes more intense and combines with *attack other*. In these situations, the need to win carries with it the need to dominate and crush the opponent – be they real or imagined – in order to humiliate them. Of course, when one doesn't 'win', the result can lead to *attack self* behaviors.

Like many other scripts, there are positive and negative aspects to competitiveness. Who hasn't felt little, helpless or weak at times? We are all wired to experience shame at those moments. It helps motivate us to develop scripts so we do not have to feel little, helpless or weak. To compete as a means to reduce feelings of vulnerability arising from shame is something everyone does, and there are many forms of competition that are creative, healthy and useful. This is in contrast to the behaviors of a person locked in a lifelong struggle to overcome shame from 'a persistently lowered self-image'. The *attack other* of their competitive scripts is intended to make others feel terrible in the process of being 'beaten'.

JEALOUSY SCRIPTS

Jealousy also involves the use of *avoidance* and *attack other* mechanisms to focus attention away from deficiencies – real or imagined – within the self. It becomes others who are 'filthy' rich or 'disgustingly' beautiful who are making one's life miserable. In love triangles, the problem is not 'me', but that devious other who is plotting to win over my lover and steal them away from me. It is often the case with attempts to reduce shame through Compass of Shame scripts that the resulting behaviors increase one's shame. Jealousy, for example, can feed on itself by creating more shame because of feelings of not being rich enough or attractive enough. The resulting shame will intensify the need for more intense jealous vigilance, even to the point of creating paranoia about everything one's lover does or says.

REVENGE

When shame is of unbearable intensity – the humiliation to mortification side of the shame-humiliation scale of emotions – jealousy and competitiveness can amplify each other to create the need for the *attack other* behavior of revenge. Many disastrous love triangles, for example, have ended in murder. If *attack self* becomes involved, that is when murder/suicides take place.

It is not uncommon to find situations involving intense shame–jealousy–competitiveness that leave people mired in thoughts of revenge. (This is especially true in places where a punitive approach to wrongdoing dominates the cultural ethos. For a refreshingly rare exception, see Chapter 5 to read the story of how Katy Hutchison's capacity for forgiveness saved her, her family and an offender.) When these thoughts dominate a person's thinking, it gives them the false notion that getting some kind of revenge is the only way they will feel better. They are wrong in this belief. They can only feel better if they become involved in restorative approaches to help them deal with their shame. If revenge permanently disguises their feelings of shame, preventing them from doing work on the self to reduce shame, they will never feel better.

The Emotional Dynamics of Harm

It is a given that restorative interventions endeavor to reduce harm. But what constitutes harm? Can we always recognize its presence? And how do restorative processes reduce harm in individuals or communities? In order to answer these questions, one must have a clear understanding of the foundations of human emotional functioning – the *how* and *why* of caring.

One of the fundamental principles of ASP is that the negative affects, wired into human biology from birth, are inherently punishing. As already discussed, wellbeing depends upon a person's ability to balance the guidelines of the Central Blueprint to maximize positive affect, minimize negative affect and minimize the inhibition of affect. When people are free from restrictions – by either external or internal forces – to respond to their negative affect, the information from those affects motivates behaviors that change the factors creating the bad feelings. With each occurrence where a SAR scene of some stimulus-creating negative affect is responded to by change that ends the negative affect, scripts of efficacy, personal worth and wellbeing blossom and grow. The presence of efficacy scripts increases the probability that one will be able to live balancing Central Blueprint directives.

Emotional harm happens when circumstances inhibit one's freedom to respond to and eliminate negative affect. Children are, of course, most vulnerable to harm because their physical and mental resources are limited. But there are many situations in which adults too face such limitations. Offenders may have superior strength or wield weapons that render helpless the victim of rape, robbery or an assault. More subtle, but just as restricting, are the offenders who have control because they hold power over one's person or job or future career or school grades. If one is not present during an offense against a loved one, there can be a feeling of shame and guilt that one was not there to protect him or her. If the damage to one's person, property or loved ones was brought about by the forces of nature – earthquakes, tsunamis, storms, fires – or the unmitigated forces of humankind – wars – one also feels powerless to effect change that would reduce or control the negative affect.

Whether they occur once or repeatedly, negative affect-triggering situations over which one has little or no control – especially when fear, distress and/or shame occur – are sources of emotional harm. The gravity of the harm caused will be in direct proportion to the intensity of the negative affect experienced by the person and its duration. The longer one goes on experiencing the negative emotion, the greater the effect of the harm on that person's wellbeing. (Note: in this same vein, abuse is defined as intentional behavior toward another that creates intense affect that the other is powerless to control. Usually the affect is negative. However, in the case of sexual abuse of children, for instance, the child may experience excitement and overstimulation that he does not want and cannot control. This often leads to confusion and great shame on part of the abused person because he may misinterpret the fact that he experienced some positive feelings to mean he was an accomplice in the sexual behavior. Such shame is one of the factors that causes so many either to never report the abuse or to wait until they are much older.)

Because the wired-in demand to minimize negative affect never ceases to operate, persistent negative affect from harm or abuse leads to the development of behaviors and scripts that throw the Central Blueprint out of balance. For instance, one's entire existence might become dominated by the need to maximize positive affect that overwhelms the negative. Examples of this are constant thrill seeking – often with dangerous behaviors – or 'partying' to the detriment of normal daily functioning. Many sexually abused women end up as prostitutes or as actors in pornography. On the other hand, one might become overly invested in behaviors that minimize negative affect. Examples of this strategy are withdrawal from any association with others, obsessional avoidance of anything that seems dangerous or the excessive use of drugs and/or alcohol to dull the pain.

Shame is the most common outcome of events that cause harm because those events are impediments to one's interest in being competent to control one's life and wellbeing. We all *care* to be masters of our own fate. Nathanson's (1992, p.317) research into the effects of shame uncovered a 'cognitive phase' that occurs soon after shame has been triggered, during which one develops reasons – regardless of whether or not they are true – for the dreadful feeling of shame. These thoughts include such notions as being weak, incompetent, stupid, ugly, helpless, defective and a loser. The greater the shame, the more the feeling and its accompanying thoughts will force one to resort to one or more of the Compass of Shame scripts (defenses) of *attack other, attack self, withdrawal* or *avoidance*. That one has experienced or is experiencing harm can easily be missed when feelings are hidden behind shame-reducing behaviors. In the chapters that follow, the reader will encounter a number of real-life situations in which restorative practitioners have been able to recognize either the presence of hidden shame by the behavior(s) exhibited or the potential for it. The ability to recognize and/or prevent shame greatly enhances the efficacy of restorative interventions.

Conclusion

All human behavior stems from how and why we care, whether that behavior is helpful or detrimental to the individual or the community. To minimize people by treating them as if *all* they are is their *behavior* is to misunderstand the essence of what makes us human. Punitive methods of dealing with detrimental behaviors are destined to fail because they dehumanize the person, creating more shame and harm in people whose behaviors most likely stem from the fact that they've already been harmed.

ASP – the most comprehensive, biologically based theory of motivation yet proposed – shines a bright light on how and why RP reduces harm.

References

Braithwaite, J. (1989) *Crime, Shame and Reintegration*. Cambridge: Cambridge University Press.

Gamer, M. and Büchel, C. (2012) 'Oxytocin specifically enhances valence-dependent parasympathetic responses.' *Psychoneuroendocrinology 37*, 1, 87–93.

Guastella, A.J., Mitchell, P.B. and Dadds, M.R. (2008) 'Oxytocin increases gaze to the eye region of human faces.' *Biological Psychiatry 63*, 1, 3–5.

Kelly, V.C. (1996) 'Affect and the Redefinition of Intimacy.' In D.L. Nathanson (ed.) *Knowing Feeling: Affect, Script, and Psychotherapy*. New York, NY: Norton.

Kelly, V.C. (2012) *The Art of Intimacy and the Hidden Challenge of Shame*. Rockland, ME: Maine Authors Publishing.

Nathanson, D.L. (1992) *Shame and Pride: Affect, Sex, and the Birth of the Self*. New York, NY: W.W. Norton.

Tomkins, S. (1962) *Affect Imagery Consciousness. Volume I: The Positive Affects*. New York, NY: Springer.

Tomkins, S. (1963) *Affect Imagery Consciousness. Volume II: The Negative Affects*. New York, NY: Springer.

Tomkins, S. (1981) 'The quest for primary motives: Biography and autobiography of an idea.' *Journal of Personality and Social Psychology 41*, 2, 306–329. Reprinted in V.E. Demos (ed.) (1995) *Exploring Affect*. Cambridge: Cambridge University Press.

Tomkins, S. (1991) *Affect Imagery Consciousness. Volume III: The Negative Affects:* Anger and Fear. New York, NY: Springer.

Tomkins, S. (1992) *Affect Imagery Consciousness. Volume IV: Cognition: Duplication and Transformation of Information*. New York, NY: Springer.

Suggested Reading

Demos, E.V. (ed.) (1995) *Exploring Affect: The Selected Writings of Silvan S. Tomkins.* Cambridge: Cambridge University Press.

Hutchison, K. (2006) *Walking After Midnight.* Oakland, CA: New Harbinger.

Holinger, P.C. and Doner, K. (2003) *What Babies Say Before They Can Talk.* New York, NY: Fireside.

Kelly, V. (2009) *A Primer of Affect Psychology.* Available at www.tomkins.org/uploads/Primer_of_Affect_Psychology.pdf, accessed on 26 October 2010.

Kelly, V.C. (2012) *The Art of Intimacy and the Hidden Challenge of Shame.* Rockland, ME: Maine Authors Publishing.

Nathanson, D.L. (1992) *Shame and Pride: Affect, Sex, and the Birth of the Self.* New York, NY: W.W. Norton.

Tomkins, S. (2008) *Affect Imagery Consciousness: The Complete Edition.* New York, NY: Springer.

CHAPTER 2

Interpersonal Caring, Social Disciple and a Blueprint for Restorative Healing

Vernon C. Kelly, Jr.

Introduction

In Chapter 1, I outlined the biological roots of attachment and how people learn to be cared for and to care for others. The best descriptor of interpersonal transactions between people is *emotional connections* (Kelly 2012) because they are motivated by and continually monitored by our commonly inherited affect systems – the source of all emotion. Activation of each of the nine pre-wired affect programs of the affect system depends upon the stimulus conditions around us and happens before we even have a chance to 'think'. Importantly, each affect is also an activator of itself by affective resonance. Hence, an infant in distress will activate distress in her caregiver by stimuli such as her cry of distress (activation by auditory stimulus) or the look of distress on her face (activation by visual stimulus). Similarly, her interest or joy will set off similar affects in those around her.

Emotional connection to others rapidly becomes more complex as infants grow and begin to experience others in their world in interaction with the maturing of their central nervous systems. Innate affect combined with experience and memory leads to the formation of intricate emotional scripts. As discussed previously in relationship to the affect shame-humiliation, such scripts often involve the need to hide feelings and emotions from others and/or the self. Sometimes this culminates in personality styles and behaviors that make it difficult for others to know what one (self or other) is really feeling – in spite of the adult capacity for intellectually directed empathy.

However, even around those with whom it is difficult to *know* what they are feeling, emotional connections are still subject to our wired-in capacity to care through affective resonance. It is because of this that we generally know if we care – feel positive affect – for someone or do not care – feel negative affect – for someone. In fact, human beings are exquisitely sensitive through affective resonance to the ebb and flow, the positives and negatives in emotional connections with others, whether we are familiar with them or do not know them at all.

We care deeply about how the behaviors and emotions of others affect us because of that most primitive of attachment (social) scripts that creates in essentially all people *the interest in others being interested in us and our interest in being interested in them*. It is the power of this basic social script, combined with intellectual naïveté, that motivates children to accept without question the beliefs, social values and other standards of the family culture in which they are raised.

The motivation for this is both positive and negative. Children want to bathe in the positive interest of others as it washes over them, and they feel the negative sting of shame if anything – especially disapproval by parents or other individuals in their social group – interrupts that interest. The emotions experienced by such interpersonally triggered shame are rejection, hurt, isolation, distance and loneliness. These shame-based feelings turn people inward during shame's cognitive phase and generate many negative thoughts about the self. No one cares to be perceived – by self or others – as stupid, ugly, defective, incompetent or any of the other nasty things shame can cause us to think and feel about ourselves.

The Central Blueprint constantly monitors each moment of our interactions with others, motivating us to maximize positive affect and minimize negative affect. Following Central Blueprint rules, our motivational and cognitive systems cooperate to regularly form and update social scripts based on the outcome of our interpersonal experiences. Because we all develop a lifelong, powerful interest and enjoyment in the interest and enjoyment of others in us and because of shame's inborn biological function – to signal when positive affect is blocked – shame and its emotional offspring guilt (see Chapter 1) feature prominently in social script formation.

Shame's effects on people can be either useful or seriously damaging. It is useful when one can accurately read shame's signals that another's or our own interest in connecting emotionally is being interfered with and then do something to change the situation. In other words, if we feel bad about a relationship and have the power to discuss those feelings with the other person and work things out, then shame helps us restore good feelings. But experiencing shame is damaging when we are unable to make such changes. It leads to a sense of helplessness and more shame – shame powerful enough to motivate us to hide from our feelings using destructive Compass of Shame strategies and behaviors. This happens often when someone is not in control of the conditions blocking the flow of positive emotion in their important relationships. Children and adolescents, for instance, frequently have little control over their emotional connections with parents, teachers and the other adults in their lives. These same conditions can exist for those whose life or career situations place others in power over them – for example, the power to hire or fire them.

In this chapter, I first utilize the concepts of affect script psychology (ASP) and briefly discuss some of the possible emotional consequences of differing approaches to relationships with reference to the Social Discipline Window. Then I present a blueprint for the emotional dynamics of healing and restoration made possible by the proper use of circles and restorative conferencing.

Figure 2.1 depicts a version of the Social Discipline Window adapted from Wachtel (1999), Coloroso (2003) and Thorsborne and Blood (2013). It represents four different approaches by which authority figures, including parents, might deal with misbehavior or wrongdoing in those for (and over) whom they have responsibility. It has found worldwide application in helping people understand the most basic premise of the restorative practice paradigm – traditional methods of punishment for socially unacceptable behaviors and outright wrongdoing done TO offenders make them feel more like stigmatized outcasts, whereas restorative interventions done WITH offenders invite them into the community to share in the process of repairing the harm created by their offense, making it more likely that the community will be repaired and the offender will be reintegrated into that community and be less likely to reoffend in the future.

Emotional Connection and the Social Discipline Window

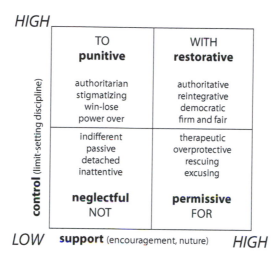

Figure 2.1 The Social Discipline Window
(adapted from Watchel 1999; Coloroso 2003; Thorsborne and Blood 2013)

After examining the application of the Social Discipline Window in school settings, Vaandering (2010, p.7) added the following:

> Given that the root of rj [restorative justice] lies in an integrated, relational world and life views promoted since ancient times through indigenous and spiritual traditions (Zehr, 2005; Bianchi, 1994; Pranis, Stuart & Wedge, 2003), the Social Discipline Window in its emphasis on controlling wrongdoing and supporting 'rightdoing' steps away from rj principles by promoting a response to behaviour, rather than relationship. When rj is limited to issues of management and discipline it inadvertently gets redirected to answering questions about rules, blame and punishment. In order to redirect thinking so that questions of harm done, the need of those hurt, and repair are addressed, concepts of relationship must be highlighted.

In order to address this apparent paradox, Vaandeering proposes '[i]n its stead, a Relationship Window that describes people's engagement with each other as objects or humans' (p.12). This window (adapted from Vaandering 2010) is depicted in Figure 2.2.

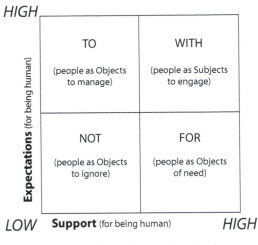

Figure 2.2 The Relationship Window
(adapted from Vaandering 2010)

Vaandering (2010, p.12) concludes:

> This window, which is grounded in the foundational understanding
> of justice as honouring the worth and well-being of humanity,
> builds a matrix that has the potential for serving as a simple
> framework that moves beyond a response to people's behaviour
> to a means to guide how people engage with each other and their
> environments at all times.

Let us examine each of the four windows from an ASP perspective to
explore further the emotional implications of each of these relational
styles. It is useful to keep in mind that at the heart of all human
caring for emotional connection with others is the basic social script
– motivated by affect – of a great *interest* in seeking and wanting the
interest of others toward the self. In other words, we are programmed
from early in life to always seek positive emotional connections with
others.

NOT (Neglectful): Low Expectations and Low Support

Whether it is a parent relating to a child or an authority figure relating
to someone over whom they have control, this relational style carries
the same message to the younger or 'lesser' person: *the other does*

not care for or about me. Given the innate wiring of the human affect system, the only possible emotional response of the lesser person to this state of affairs is to feel bad. The specific negative affect triggered is shame because its inherited function is to signal to us when what we are interested in caring for is interfered with (see Chapter 1).

In the case of a disinterested primary caregiver, who is either too wrapped up in her own problems or perhaps depressed and unable to show interest in anything or anybody, the child regularly experiences shame and must deal with its consequences every day. This is particularly damaging if there are no other significant caregivers available. The personalities of young children raised in such distant emotional atmospheres are formed under a Central Blueprint that must, of necessity, become overly focused on the strategy of minimizing negative affect. One need only look at the Compass of Shame (see Chapter 1) to imagine where this can lead. Such children frequently invest heavily in the strategy of *withdrawal,* and can develop into quiet, shy people who hide their feelings and are hard to reach emotionally. There is a serious disturbance in their emotional connections to others because of a need to withdraw for fear of experiencing further hurt and shame.

To make matters worse, since the immature brains of the young view everything as caused by or about them, they usually blame themselves for the lack of interest shown them by their caregivers. This leads to *attack self* feelings and behaviors, a deep sense of worthlessness and more shame. Such people do not care for themselves and find it challenging to care about others. It is fortunate, and lessens the negative impact, when at least one or two other adults who care about them and show interest in them populate their world. However, as these shamed children mature, their Compass of Shame scripts, which may also include damaging *attack other* and *avoidance* behaviors, make it difficult for them to establish secure emotional connections with others and for others to connect with them.

Somewhat similar conditions apply in schools or the workplace when those in authority convey to students or workers that they don't have any expectations of them and are not willing to be supportive. In other words, they are treated as *objects* whose individuality does not matter. Such authority figures may or may not be aware of their impact. They may even believe there is little or no emotional connection with their students or workers and that this 'emotional stuff' is not part of their job – but this is never true. All people are emotionally attuned to everyone with whom they are in contact because of affective resonance. (Note that one must be careful when using either Wachtel's terms 'indifferent and passive' or Vaandering's term 'people as objects to ignore' to describe those in authority who use this style. It can dehumanize them and cause one to miss the fact that they too have interpersonal scripts that are likely based on shame. For instance, they may be caught in interpersonal withdrawal scripts due to shame issues from their past or current relationships. To apply universally, the caring in restorative practice needs to address them also, even if such an approach is not always successful.)

The effect of such authority figures on those under them is to trigger shame during almost all exchanges. The most adaptive response of those affected – the 'lesser' people – is to realize that the source of the negative affect they feel during interactions is the authority figure's lack of interest, and then to minimize interactions with them and cease being interested in what that person thinks or feels about them. This adaptation is not possible when the authority figure or boss holds power over them. Nor is it possible when the subordinate person is a child or adolescent facing teachers or administrators with whom they are in daily contact and in whom they have a high level of interest in seeking knowledge and guidance.

The damage caused by these NOT emotional connections depends upon a number of factors. The greater the self-esteem of the child or worker and the less often they are in contact with the authority figure, the easier it is for them to shrug off the negative to minimize the impact on their wellbeing. On the other hand, the poorer the self-esteem, especially in the case of children or adolescents with pre-existing emotional and/or behavioral problems, and the more frequent the shame-inducing contact with the authority figure, the more powerful will be the shame experienced. The level of intensity of this negative, punishing emotion pushes people into equally powerful, compensatory Compass of Shame defensive responses.

Paradoxically, many Compass of Shame responses produce behaviors that make it more likely that the child or worker will be confronted by those in authority. For instance, they might engage in *attack other* behaviors such as bullying or rage attacks, or *avoidance* behaviors using drugs/alcohol, or *withdrawal* behaviors of truancy and absenteeism, or tragically, *attack self* behaviors culminating in suicide. Whichever strategy is used, it usually begins a downwardly spiraling set of problems with more shame, more defense, more shame, more defense and so forth.

TO (Punitive): High Expectations and Low Support

This window represents the classical situation found in criminal justice systems worldwide. It was observations of its ineffectiveness by police officers, judges and ancillary personnel working with offenders entering the system that prompted the re-emergence of the system now known as *restorative justice*. A large percentage of offenders thrown into this punitive system did not seem to be learning from their mistakes. In fact, it appeared they were further alienated to cultural standards and norms, and rates of reoffending were very high. It was also clear that these processes, with wrongdoers accountable only to the state or institution, were failing those most harmed by the behavior. Victims of wrongdoing were excluded almost totally from decisions about what needed to happen to make things right for them. It was – and remains – clear that something is wrong with this system, as prisons around the world, filled to capacity, require the building of more and more of these institutions. There is no question that serious responses for offenses against people and grave violations of cultural standards of behavior are necessary, but we also need an understanding of the emotional consequences of dealing with offenders without providing proper support. It will be helpful to consider first the effects of TO situations outside the criminal justice system.

The emotional connections created in circumstances – families, schools and workplaces – with high expectations and low support are marginally preferable to those where there are low expectations and low support. There can, at least, be a sense that those in authority have some interest in the child or worker doing better and, by implication, that there is an interest in the actual person him or herself. However, Wachtel's implication is that the expectations here are less than personal, more a general part of the demands of the individual's institution or workplace or state. Vaandering suggests that, in this case, the people are being managed en masse and not as individuals.

Generally, this window represents those situations wherein the interactions are primarily of a punitive nature meant to enforce high, primarily impersonal expectations. This would include such standards in school settings as grades, dress/uniform codes, physical appearance, socially acceptable behavior under the rubric of being 'good' little girls and boys and being 'seen but not heard'. In the workplace, it might include meeting certain quotas and goals or fitting into a company's cultural norms for dress and appearance.

These expectations are not harmful in and of themselves. Those in authority often insist that they are good for the person, that they build character and make one better suited to be good citizens. The problem is the *low* support with obedience demanded without explanations required and no ability to question authority. Reward/punishment systems are established with no regard for the individuals involved, and, therefore, individuals in the system experience an atmosphere wherein their feelings or ideas do not matter. They sense constant pressure that, if they do wrong or poorly, they will be punished in impersonal ways that carry the message that who they are – their very existence – is irrelevant to those in charge. (This is also the case for children raised by caregivers more interested in how others 'see' their children than the individual needs of each child.) The young person or adult treated this way has no voice, no opportunity for feeling understood or for telling their story.

Low support, high expectation settings create an emotional bind for people. Because of early social scripting, everyone starts out wanting those in authority – be they teachers, parents, employers, the police or judges – to be interested in them. Therefore, most people initially attempt to meet all expectations, no matter how high, in order to maintain the interest of others so they can feel that a positive emotional connection with those others is present. But if those in authority show little support when rules are broken or standards are not met, this is experienced as a lack of interest consistent with Vaandering's concept of people as 'objects to ignore', and shame will inevitably be triggered. The lack of positive interpersonal connection in this case makes people feel emotionally isolated and alone. The shame creates feelings of rejection by those in authority. Lying to avoid punishment and shame can be a common response, and become so ingrained that the behavior becomes an avoidance script.

The Central Blueprint motivates shamed individuals stuck in these authoritarian settings to minimize negative affect by reducing interest in the expectations of the community that is demanding their expectations be met without providing a sense of caring. Often they will adopt defensive postures and behaviors indicative of Compass of Shame scripts. They may increase their negative interactions with those in authority by acting chronically discontented, withdrawn, mistrustful and defiant (Grille 2005). And they are likely to 'reoffend' because they care less and less about the community that seems to not care about them.

FOR (Permissive): Low Expectations and High Support

This category refers to situations where those in authority, be they parents, teachers or bosses, provide too much support, either because they do not believe the child or worker can do things for themselves or because they believe it is the best way to show love and help a child succeed. Such parents have recently received the label of 'snow-plough' parents, implying that what they do is plough all obstacles out of their child's path to prevent them from ever losing or not succeeding. It is beyond the scope of this volume to delve into all the possible motivations of such parents – one would no doubt find a mixture of love, interest, fear and possibly shame as the motivating emotions. However, the (at times, unwitting) messages received by the offspring of such parents are that they cannot do things for themselves, that if they get into trouble, the adult is there to rescue them from adversity, that not much is expected of their abilities and that they are, as Vaandering suggests, 'objects of need' of their parents.

The interpersonal impact of snow-plough parenting is that the child experiences the parent as being more interested in having his or her own needs met than they are in the actual *person* of the child. The child will feel as if he is not competent when he is not allowed to try things himself. Furthermore, when a parent – even if it is out of love – solves her child's issues, is overly protective and rescues him from difficult situations, that child may fail to develop resiliency scripts. For instance, shame experienced when failing at a sport or doing poorly on an exam is a natural part of emotional life. It must be experienced to be learned from and to aid in the development of healthy scripts for dealing with life's many and inevitable failures. And finally, if a parent always jumps in and excuses her child, that child may never learn to be accountable for the impact of his behavior on others. Indeed, that parent may well end up becoming a doormat whose child rules the roost without regard for the feelings of the parent (or others) – a serious imbalance in emotional connection that will negatively impact that child's ability to relate to peers and a significant other in the future.

In a workplace, the FOR style of dealing with a worker manifests itself by an out-of-balance ratio between expectations and support. One might hear such comments as 'Poor thing, we can't put too much pressure on this person to perform because they are going through a bad patch'. While at times, this may be supportive and necessary, if it becomes the predominant method of interaction, then shame triggers regularly in both people. The person in authority will have his interest in the worker performing effectively interfered with and much extra work that needs doing. The worker will experience a sense of incompetence instead of a sense of pride in a job well done. Eventually, both people will resort to Compass of Shame behaviors around one another. For instance, someone stuck in *attack other* may well throw tantrums and be scary around people, while the boss may withdraw and do nothing, creating negative emotion in the remainder of the staff. In such an atmosphere, all the relationships become strained and people have difficulty connecting emotionally with one another. This makes collaboration and problem-solving difficult.

WITH (Restorative): High Expectations and High Support

Restorative responses to wrongdoing focus on caring about emotional connections. The caring communicated through the power of being WITH others comes about by showing interest in them and inviting them to be interested in those in authority. This comes about through *authoritative* as opposed to *authoritarian* dealings with those for whom one has responsibility. Such dealings are firm, fair, democratic and transparent. Those in authority act based on a positive sense of self that allows them to permit dialogue with all involved when wrongdoing or mistakes happen. The ability to treat wrongdoing and mistakes as opportunities for personal growth and further education succeeds because of the perception that problematic or 'bad' behavior is not the essence of the person. In other words, when one *does* a bad thing it does not mean one *is* a bad person. (See Chapter 6 for case examples of how this approach applies in situations of spousal abuse.)

When caring about relationships is central to problem-solving, techniques evolve motivated by a desire to maintain an interpersonal atmosphere consistent with the Central Blueprint of all involved. The focus becomes maximizing positive affect and minimizing negative affect while minimizing the inhibition of affect. Dialogue about emotional experience is encouraged and all parties are listened to. The creation of mutual respect occurs, especially when those in authority are comfortable with their role and are, therefore, able to provide strong, but fair boundaries. Shame triggered in these settings simply provides *information* about impediment to positive affect, leading to constructive ways that remove the need for people to resort to Compass of Shame behaviors.

For instance, consider a situation where a student or employee says something offensive to another student, employee or someone in authority. If, instead of a trip to detention or a dismissal without recourse, those in authority sit that person down with whomever he offended to discuss the emotional impact of his words, then the offender will experience appropriate shame and guilt. He will feel that those around him are *interested* in and, hence, WITH him, even though he has done something offensive. The interest in him evidenced by a restorative approach to his actions will prevent him from having to experience his shame in lonely isolation – a state of affairs that causes shame to trigger more shame and a greater need for Compass of Shame defenses to take over. Instead, as he understands his effect on the feelings of the other person and his awareness turns outward toward the damage he has done to the emotional connection with another, the emotions caused by his shame will morph toward that of guilt, as discussed in Chapter 1. With greater awareness of another in situations where the other clearly does not think of one as a 'bad' person who 'should be ashamed of himself' comes the opportunity for reparation of the harm done – perhaps by a sincerely felt apology. With an apology and the forgiveness of the other, the impediment to emotional connection caused by the offensive act disappears. Shame in both people evaporates with the lesson learned that it feels bad to create situations that block the desire of people to be emotionally connected with one another. (More on the biology of how this caring works in the next section.)

Summary

The WITH quadrant of the Social Discipline Window represents the optimal restorative method of supporting growth in the face of the inevitable mistakes and wrongdoing of those in one's care by caring deeply about the emotional connections to others that are so central to wellbeing in all people. It focuses on planning for ways forward not in opposition to but in collaboration *with* wrongdoers. It provides the greatest chance for the minimization of negative feelings and maximization of positive feelings in all involved because those in authority, offenders and victims all have key roles in dealing with offensive acts. Relationships are enhanced and new behaviors asked for with the support provided by everyone. In the WITH quadrant, there is a belief in a person's capacity to change. And it shows!

One might say of the four quadrants: in the TO box, only the adult's (parent, teacher, boss) voice is heard; in the NOT box there is no adult voice; in the FOR box, only the child's voice (with little emphasis on the needs of others) is heard; and in the WITH box, both are heard and the connection and reconnection are at the heart of problem-solving.

A Blueprint for Restorative Healing

Patterned after community customs of indigenous peoples in New Zealand, Canada and elsewhere, one of the major tools of restorative process is the *conference* or *circle*. Conferences (circles) are convened when wrongdoing or community strife creates harm and threatens the wellbeing of either individuals or the community as a whole. Pranis (2005, pp.25–26) described the ethos behind the circle when she wrote:

> ...the foundation of the Circle Process includes several assumptions about the nature of the universe. These assumptions are common in the worldview of most indigenous cultures and are often metaphorically associated with the image of a Circle. These assumptions have been passed from generation to generation through cultural teachings.
>
> One of the most important teachings underlying the Circle Process is the assertion that everything in the universe is connected. This teaching tells us that every action affects everything in the universe, that it is impossible to isolate something to act on it without affecting everything else.

While conferences may take place with only a few people sitting in a small circle or many people, they all begin in an atmosphere of raw, powerfully negative emotions including anger, fear, disgust, dissmell and shame. As detailed eloquently by Abramson in Chapter 3, conferences are designed to be very emotional meetings in order to encourage each participant to express these emotions, to let everyone know how the situation that prompted the conference has affected them emotionally, all the while avoiding direct attacks on others in the circle.

This method is in direct contrast to how most modern cultures currently demand – both directly and indirectly – that people handle strong emotions in their relationships with others. One is supposed to be polite or 'civil' or 'nice' to others, to 'keep a stiff upper lip', to control oneself and not show weakness by being 'emotional'. However, when negative events do take place in one's life, these cultural demands to stifle emotion create a state that Tomkins (1991, pp.13–14) called 'backed-up affect'. This is in direct violation of the rule of the Central Blueprint to minimize the inhibition of affect, and, as a result, cultural rules about hiding emotion significantly reduce one's ability to be attuned to the information provided by one's feelings. Furthermore, just because they are ignored or not expressed, negative emotions do not disappear into thin air; hence, they become *backed-up* and, over time, begin to negatively affect the physical and emotional wellbeing of individuals. It is not surprising, then, that when they finally boil over, these unattended-to feelings often motivate vicious verbal and physical attacks. Nor is it surprising that when people cannot be real with each other about what they are feeling, many seemingly minor incidents cannot be more easily resolved. (This is why the restorative work being done with our young people in schools and other youth organizations – described by Williams in Chapter 7, George in Chapter 9, and Hansberry and Langley in Chapter 10 – to educate them about how to deal with their emotions and their relationships with others is so critical for the emotional wellbeing of all communities.)

Affect Resonance

When a restorative conference has been properly set up beforehand and is managed skillfully by the facilitator (Abramson and Beck 2011; MacRae and Zehr 2004; McDonald 2012; Pranis 2005; Riestenberg 2012; Thorsborne and Vinegrad 2003), the question posed to each person in the circle about how the incident(s) that created the harm affected them will increase the intensity of negative emotion in the room – even if the level of emotion was high to begin with. This is inevitable given the biology of the human affect system. As mentioned earlier, because each affect is an activator of itself, both in the person experiencing it and in others around that person, when one person expresses anger or fear or joy, those around him will begin to feel angry or fearful or joyful. This *affective resonance* is the biologically directed reason why everyone in a circle or at a conference experiences intensification of their emotions and is forced to 'get in touch' with their real feelings about how the incident affected them. This is an important part of the process because emotionally painful incidents often cause people to want to hide their feelings, for both personal and culturally driven reasons, especially if the incident triggered shame and the need to resort to withdrawal scripts on the Compass of Shame.

Affective resonance also provides everyone present with a clearer understanding of what each person is feeling. Even if one wants to reject what others are saying – and they often do in the beginning stages of the process – the open expression of emotion by someone, especially if intense, always triggers similar affects and feelings in others. This eventually opens the door for *empathy* because all people share the same innate affects. Everyone knows fear, anger, distress, shame, disgust, dissmell, surprise, interest and enjoyment. So all people can understand and, if they wish, connect emotionally with everyone in the room.

Another factor contributes to the general increase in empathic connections as the conference proceeds. Since the conference process usually allows one person at a time to speak, there is a built-in mechanism for each person to feel the *interest* of others in what they have to say and for each listener to be interested in what is being said. The sharing of *interest* is a powerful motivator of our first social scripts and the subsequent drive for emotional connections between people. As a result, positive relationships – even between people on 'opposite' sides of the incident – begin to form within the group as a conference moves forward. Emanating from the biology of our species are the values to which Pranis (2005, p.24) refers when she describes a value framework about circles that 'assumes a universal wish to be connected to others in a good way. The values of a circle derived from this basic impulse'. (Note: all 'impulses' are actions motivated by affects, feelings and/or emotions. In this case, the motivator is interest.)

(It is worth noting that there are those for whom and with whom affective resonance is difficult or impossible. This includes people with serious disorders of the affect system, as is seen in depression, and many with personality disorders that cause 'glitches' in the ability to be empathic. In pre-conference preparation meetings, facilitators must assess their own ability to resonate with each participant in order to anticipate potential difficulties later on.)

The Central Blueprint in Groups

In Chapter 3, Abramson presents two examples of conferences and demonstrates how, with remarkable regularity, the emotions of anger, disgust and fear present at the beginning transform gradually into positive feelings that permit those involved to come to an agreement about how to repair the harm done. How highly negative, often antagonist interactions and feelings transform into something positive where agreements can be reached involves a number of factors – all emanating from our mutually shared biology.

As detailed in Chapter 1, to enhance our survival we have evolved a complex central nervous system that continually assesses environmental conditions and what to do about them through the triggering of affect, the analysis of the feelings that arise and then responses that maximize positive feelings and minimize negative feelings. In a restorative circle, each individual's Central Blueprint is at work doing exactly that. In properly managed conferences, it is biologically inevitable, therefore, that undesirable negative feelings will begin to diminish as each individual is motivated to minimize negative affect. In addition, because there is a *pre-established purpose* for the conference agreed to by all – to see how to repair harm done – each person in the room shares, to a greater or lesser extent, some responsibility and interest in achieving that goal.

Affective resonance in group settings creates an emotional environment wherein all members of the group begin to experience similar emotions. This can produce serious negative consequences in certain situations – mob violence, for instance, may being with the loudly voiced anger of a few inducing anger in others; and positive outcomes in other situations – the loudly voiced excitement of a few at a well-attended sporting event inducing excitement in the rest of the crowd. In the properly designed and facilitated setting of a restorative conference, affective resonance and the gradual building of emotional connections amongst those present, and the increased interest in and empathic understanding of one another, lend themselves to the creation of a *community* atmosphere. A community of people in the same room, sharing emotions openly, inevitably leads to a process that recruits the Central Blueprint of each person and directs the group toward a communal motivation to maximize positive affect and minimize negative affect – the minimization of negative affect initially being the most pressing of the two because the process usually begins in a storm of negative emotion. The timely introduction by the facilitator of the question 'What can be done to repair the harm?' opens the door for a community cooperating – sharing an interest – in minimizing bad feelings and arriving at an agreement.

Shame, Harm and Healing

As outlined in Chapter 1, those who experience emotional harm feel unrelenting negative emotions that originate primarily in the affects of fear, distress, anger and shame. To restore wellbeing, those negative emotions must be addressed directly. Restorative conferences bring together victims and their offenders to recruit compelling forces in the caring systems of everyone involved and bring such emotions to the surface. The motivational caring power found in the biology of each person – their affect systems and their Central Blueprints – makes for a process that creates multiple emotional connections and a community experience wherein change is inevitable in everyone as old, rigid scripts are challenged and new ones form. In the chapters that follow, the reader will learn about specific, real-life examples of restorative processes. To help readers better recognize the biologically based changes in the emotions of victims and offenders during conferences and circles, I present here a brief ASP sketch of the process – with the caveat that all people are, of course, unique and bring different healthy and unhealthy scripts into each situation. What is not unique is that everyone brings the same innate affects and Central Blueprint rules into a conference.

(While it is remarkable how many people are deeply moved in positive directions by conferencing, there will always be those for whom the process is ineffective or even damaging. It is beyond the scope of this volume to detail all of the possible causes, but facilitators need to assess ahead of time each individual's level of emotional readiness to engage with the group and to be able to assess any risk to the process or to people already victimized. Many, who are not ready or cannot be convinced that a restorative approach will be effective, will refuse to participate. Others whose shame is very pronounced may exhibit such extreme Compass of Shame behaviors – dangerous *attack other* rage of an intensely hateful nature, *withdrawal* to the point of being unable to communicate, *avoidance* with complete denial about the harm caused by the incident or powerful feelings of suicide from *attack self* – that their participation in the conference would impede progress by the group. In addition, there are those who may have biological depressions or other malfunctions of their central nervous system that preclude normal Central Blueprint functioning and interfere with the capacity for empathy necessary for healthy interactions with others.)

VICTIM DYNAMICS

Because of the helpless, out-of-control feelings experienced during an offense, most victims come to a conference with significant, lingering shame and fear triggered whenever they relive what happened or, in some cases, continues to happen. If, before the conference, there has been no way for them to deal with their shame, they will have resorted to Compass of Shame scripts, and that usually makes matters worse. Depending upon the intensity of the shame, they may have had their relationships damaged by silent *withdrawal* from others, or continue to engage in *attack self* put-downs for having been weak and helpless, or have resorted to heavy drugs or alcohol as an *avoidance* of the feelings and/or carry inside of them intense, hateful *attack other* rage at the offender.

In the emotionally charged atmosphere of a restorative conference, victims are encouraged to express all their emotions when asked, 'How has what happened affected you?' As these emotions are expressed and listened to respectfully by others in the circle, there is a resonating and mutualization of the emotions with many sharing, through verbal and non-verbal cues, that they understand and would feel the same way. The victim experiences this reaction as *interest* in who they – the victim – are and what they feel, which creates a sense of connectedness with those in the room and encourages even fuller willingness to share. This may not occur right away because they may not feel emotionally or physically safe. However, as the conference progresses, interest and a sense of connectedness, coupled with the chance to expose their negative feelings, trigger feelings of *relief* in the victim.

In Chapter 1, I described the social scripts at the core of all motivation for emotional connections (attachments) as arising from the shared interest with others and the shared sense of relief of negative affect provided by others. Conferences, therefore, enhance the earliest attachment scripts that motivate people to want to relate with others, which explains why positive interactions often take place between those who began the process on 'opposite' sides. The effect of this for victims is that they no longer feel alone with their shame and fear, and are therefore even more comfortable expressing those feelings. The relief from backed-up and often 'unprocessed' or repressed negative affect is made even more effective because it is expressed in the presence of the offender, who may now seem much more human and less a person to fear.

Community *interest* in a person is a very powerful force because it resonates with everyone and produces a magnification of that interest. The greater the interest of others, the more one experiences a mutualization of positive affect and a greater sense of wellbeing – an emotional state that permits one to revisit the shame and fear of an incident and develop healthy scripts to deal with what happened. As negative affect in the victim is relieved and the level of interest enhanced, it is no longer necessary that their Central Blueprint focus be solely on minimizing negative affect. There is less need, then, for Compass of Shame scripts that may have been dominating their emotional life and creating harm in their relationships. Conferences initiate a process in all individuals that helps restore the balance of Central Blueprint functioning in both individuals and the entire community – a balanced ability to maximize positive affect, minimize negative affect and minimize the inhibition of affect that is critical to the biology of wellbeing. The ability to forgive, a critical emotional script for true wellbeing, is discussed below.

OFFENDER DYNAMICS

The seminal work of Braithwaite (1989) on *reintegrative shaming* emphasized the importance of understanding the emotions involved in restorative conferencing. His theory and some of his and his colleagues' subsequent work (Ahmed *et al.* 2001) has focused primarily on offender scripts from psychological and sociological perspectives. Their work helps clarify that for shame in conferences to be effective in motivating positive movement forward, it must be reintegrative, not stigmatizing – that is, it must create in the offender shame about his *actions* and not about his *self*. ASP adds to this understanding by permitting one to follow more precisely the emotional dynamics that motivate change during a restorative conference. What follows presents a pattern based on ASP for understanding the emotions of an offender during a conference.

An offender who has admitted to wrongdoing and agreed to participate in a conference brings a variable degree of shame with him into the room. His acts are already exposed as unacceptable to the community. Because he knows he will be face to face with his victim(s) and others, including possibly his own family and people from his world, then, in addition to shame about his past actions, he will also have fear and fear of shame as he anticipates how he will be treated during the conference. Therefore, when the conference begins and the facilitator asks him to describe 'what happened', there is an immediate intensification of his shame. The Central Blueprint directive to minimize negative affect will cause many offenders to initially seek refuge in one or more of the Compass of Shame scripts. They might use:

- *withdrawal* – and refuse to speak or look at others, and/or

- *avoidance* – and blame the incident on others, or minimize the event and/or

- *attack other* – and become angry or give sarcastic responses, and/or

- *attack self* – and say 'I'm stupid' or 'bad' rather than accept real responsibility.

Such responses are clear impediments to the interest others have in hearing what happened from the offender and, therefore, trigger shame, as frustration or impatience or other manifestations of shame, in many of those present. Properly trained facilitators anticipate this possibility and continue to press the offender to tell the group what happened. Once his story begins, the impediment to the group's interest disappears, and interest focuses on the story and the person telling it.

As the offender shares his story and listens to the stories of how his actions harmed others, the presence of shame in him will be obvious as he looks down or off to the side and avoids eye contact with others in the room. In general, this is a sign that heralds a positive outcome because the shame is overt, not hidden behind Compass of Shame behaviors. Others present whose caring systems will eventually be motivated to help reduce his shame will resonate with such shame. Tomkins (1963, p.216) wrote:

> Further, the fact that the other identifies sufficiently with others to be ashamed rather than to show contempt[1] strengthens any social group and its sense of community. Just as contempt strengthens the boundaries and barriers between individuals and groups and is the instrument par excellence for the preservation of hierarchical, caste and class relationships, so is shared shame a prime instrument for strengthening the sense of mutuality and community whether it be between parent and child, friend and friend, or citizen and citizen. When one is ashamed of the other, that other is not only forced into shame but he is also reminded that the other is sufficiently concerned positively as well as negatively to feel ashamed of and for the other.

As an offender experiences the group's interest in him as a *person*, and his own interest in them being interested in him – triggered by primitive attachment scripts motivating him to want to connect emotionally – it will shift his focus from shame about the self to shame/guilt (see Chapter 1) about what he has done and how his actions have caused harm to his victim, as well as his own family and friends. Since his attachment scripts generate an interest in being emotionally connected to the individuals and the community created by the conference process, he will experience shame that his offense is an impediment to his being accepted in that community. This makes it more likely that he will be motivated to restore his connection with the group and, therefore, be a willing participant when the facilitator asks, 'What can be done to repair the harm that has occurred?'

Various dictionaries define *reintegration* as meaning *restoration to a unified state*. Shame and shame/guilt triggered by his offense and the response to it by others in the community act as impediments and cut an offender off from emotional connections with those in that community. Abramson (see Chapter 3) describes how the collective shame of a conference community motivates those present to minimize the shame by working together – using emotional connectedness – to restore positive feelings through mutually arrived-at agreements and

---

1   Tomkins (1992, p.24) viewed contempt as a mixture of dissmell and anger.

reparations. An offender's shame diminishes significantly as he begins to feel welcomed in and emotionally connected with the community. His shame/guilt is partially relieved when the community, especially the victim(s), comes to an agreement as to how he can make amends for the harm he has caused. Offender shame is most fully extinguished when he feels those he's harmed the most have truly forgiven him.

The NOT, TO and FOR quadrants of the Social Discipline Window all represent methods of dealing with wrongdoing that preclude emotional connections of a positive nature with the wrongdoer. Because of this, these methods are not mutual processes and the wrongdoer can never feel a part of the community. Punitive treatment and stigmatization of wrongdoers is essentially an *attack other* way of dealing with the shame created by harm. It triggers more shame in offenders and leaves them no option but to resort to Compass of Shame defenses to minimize that negative affect. They are then likely to deal with the community by attacking others in it, withdrawing from its ethical standards – 'They don't care for me – why should I care for them?' – and avoiding any sense of caring about how their behaviors affect those in that community. In other words, there is a very high probability of them reoffending.

Summary

The community Central Blueprint that evolves during a conference, with the biologically based demand to minimize negative affect, will motivate members of the group to do everything possible to help offenders minimize their shame, since to do so also relieves the shame experienced by everyone through affective resonance. Readers of this volume will encounter a number of stories of offenders and victims working together during and after conferences because of the power of the emotional connections and sense of community engendered by the emotional processes that take place during a restorative conference. A properly facilitated conference awakens the deepest emotions motivating social scripts, and reinforces them in the post-conference sharing of refreshments, in victims, offenders and the others involved.

Forgiveness

In Chapter 5, Katy Hutchison tells the remarkable story of her forgiveness of the young man who murdered her husband and the father of their then four-year-old twins. Something in her scripts – possibly from aspects of her relationship with her father[2] – allowed her to see clearly that the pain of the loss could dominate and define her life, and that of her children, if she did not forgive. Her ability to forgive cleared the way, in spite of many bumps on the road, for her to find a new love relationship for herself, a meaningful career teaching adolescents in schools around the world about the potential life-altering dangers of alcohol and drug use, and a sense of the positive power of restorative practices. It also helped the young man who killed her husband. He eventually joined her in her teaching, once he had served his sentence and after they had engaged in a restorative process. It is his belief that the emotional connection between them that resulted from her forgiveness and their restorative work together helped him avoid a downhill spiral into further drug and alcohol use and the life of a prison-hardened criminal.

In delineating his theory of forgiveness, Enright (2012, pp.14–15) wrote:

> This is the point Gandhi was making when he stated that if we keep taking an eye for an eye, then eventually the whole world will be without sight. In our theory of forgiveness, this happens because love has been withdrawn from people who do not take the time to restore that love within their own hearts. They, in turn, withdraw love from others, which leads to relational disconnection, and on it goes. Are you beginning to see why I have entitled this book, *The Forgiving Life*? It is a life that can restore connections – within the self, with the family, and within and among communities. In a sense, the connections that we formerly had with good people can become broken, and we become disconnected form a variety of other people.

Enright's theoretical position is consistent with and best explained by the biology of emotion proposed by ASP. How? An obvious place to start is with the question 'What emotions create the need

---

2   Hutchison (2013) personal communication.

to forgive?' They are always the emotions that are the source of the greatest vulnerability in people – fear, shame and distress. Essentially, all offenses against us, our loved ones or our communities – from our neighborhoods to our world – trigger one or all of those vulnerable feelings. The shame and fear emanate from and even create more of a sense of helplessness about what happened, which, in turn, triggers even more shame.

Soon after one gets over the immediate shock of the event, most people's anger scripts are also activated and the adrenal glands called upon to produce epinephrine (adrenaline). The presence of anger/adrenaline makes people feel stronger and ready to fight. This significantly reduces shame and fear – an example of the minimization of more vulnerable negative affects by replacement with a less vulnerable negative affect. It is an evolutionary advantage for our species that, rather than stay frozen in fear or shame, we have anger to activate the ability to fight back and survive. This is a case where the Compass of Shame script of *attack other* works to our advantage. However, anger and/or *attack other*, if persisting for too long, disguises the shame and fear. This disrupts one's normal Central Blueprint balance by failing to minimize the inhibition of affect. If unaware of negative affect, one cannot do the healthy work necessary to minimize it. As long as the shame and fear persist, they will, therefore, continue to call for the need to defend against them with anger. This kind of anger fools many theoreticians. They perceive it to be the *only* emotion one must deal with in order to be able to forgive. (This is similar to the mistake made by many who run 'anger management' therapies and neglect the shame motivating the anger.)

Nonetheless, from a physical health standpoint, the constant presence of anger, fear and shame presents great dangers. While it is the normal function of the adrenal gland to respond when stressors threaten us, when those stressors persist and continue to demand adrenal response, there are many negative physical consequences. These range from fatigue and weakness, to immune system suppression, depression, hormone imbalances, low sex drive, decreased ability to handle stress, poor memory and more (Wilson 2001).

From an emotional health standpoint, the persistence of fear, anger and especially shame act as impediments to emotional connection.

Regardless of one's definition of love – and there are many – emotion is clearly at its core. Impediments to emotional connection can only serve to block love. As has been discussed earlier, healthy emotional connection with others involves the sharing and resonating back and forth of the positive emotions of interest and enjoyment. The presence of negative affect makes it more difficult to experience positive affect (Tomkins 1962). For instance, if something that happened at work causes you to feel distress or shame or anger, it is much more difficult for you to enjoy yourself or maintain interest in things when you go home. This will interfere with your desire and ability to relate to your family.

The central emotional problem that begets the need for forgiveness is the presence of unremitting fear, shame and anger that can linger long after an offense and create backed-up affect. The Central Blueprint then gets out of balance, and behaviors that minimize negative affect become the major goal of that person's life. This robs one of the flexibility to maximize positive affect, compromising overall wellbeing. It is a state of affairs that leaves a person caring more about the self than others because the self seldom feels good. I liken this to the experience of being ill with a viral influenza. People feel so achy all over and miserable that they naturally turn inward because their distress is so intense and they can only focus on their misery. The high level of distress caused by serious illness – or the presence of high levels of any of the other negative affects – becomes an impediment to positive affect and to emotional connection. All one's relationships suffer when one is too self-absorbed. Once the illness finally remits, people are again able to experience positive affect and relate to their loved ones. Such is not the case when victims retain unaddressed, unmanageable fear, shame and anger. Matters are even worse if their shame is strong and they respond with angry *attack other* that leads to the thoughts and behaviors of revenge (see Chapter 1). The 'need' for revenge produces actions – often with terribly bad consequences for communities – or obsessions that usually generate more shame – with equally bad consequences for that person's wellbeing.

All successful methods of forgiveness must necessarily provide a means for the relief of backed-up fear, shame and distress – when they work, anger dissipates naturally as there is nothing left to trigger it. Forgiveness is not an obligatory component of restorative conferencing. The group gathers to help manage the *harm*, eventually asked by the facilitator, 'What can be done to repair the harm?' not 'Can we all forgive each other?' But successful reduction of harm means that fear, shame and distress diminish to a greater or lesser extent. There are, of course, many methods used by people to rid themselves of negative affect, ranging from the spiritual to the hundreds of psychologically based therapeutic modalities. In addition, there is a growing literature on forgiveness – for example, *The Forgiving Life* by Enright (2012) referenced above. In general, however, none of these methods involves direct interaction between victims and offenders, as do the restorative practices discussed in this volume.

The marked advantage of using techniques that place victims and offenders in restorative interactions is that it provides a community setting where the greatest caring of all involved can take place. It uses the natural biology of emotion to its fullest. It intuitively recognizes that the neurological wiring of human beings motivates us to maximize our own wellbeing. That wiring makes way for the early interactions with caregivers to initiate the interpersonal scripts central to wellbeing – relationships with others become the major source of our ability to maximize good feelings and minimize negative feelings. We are motivated to be social beings because of those feelings and the capacity for empathy that arises from them. To feel that one who has caused us harm will listen to our feelings – no matter how intensely they are expressed – reduces our sense of helplessness and shame and fear. To feel that one who has caused us harm cares enough that we felt harmed to engage in reparations for our harm reduces our sense of helplessness and shame and fear. To share these feelings with a community of others amplifies the power of such feelings as the entire group moves toward maximizing positive affect and minimizing negative affect. Victims experience such a strong sense of relief from the reduction of anger, fear and shame that they become more open to empathy with their offenders. Offenders become 'real people' to them, not mysterious monsters whose motivations are unfathomable. It is no wonder that spontaneous feelings and acts of forgiveness often arise during and after restorative conferences. Restorative practices provide the ultimate motivational settings for forgiveness: people just plain feel better and not forgiving would require them to hold on to their shame, fear and anger – a violation of one of the guiding principles of wellbeing: the minimization of negative affect.

Conclusion

The power of the indigenous traditions that have led to the 'development' of restorative conferencing is that they intuitively recognize, honor and make potent use of the essential humanity of offenders, victims, those in authority and the communities that embody them. Each human life is treasured, along with the emotion that accompanies and makes rich the life of each individual. Blessed with affects, feelings and emotions that teach us how to care well for and with each other and for our own wellbeing, we only need listen. ASP has not invented anything new. Its theories simply provide a clearer path to understanding self and other. The chapters that follow recount stories of how such understanding aids in the process of restoration.

References

Abramson, L. and Beck, E. (2011) 'Using Conflict to Build Community: Community Conferencing.' In E. Beck, N. Kropf and P. Blume Leonard (eds) *Social Work and Restorative Justice: Skills for Dialogue, Peacemaking and Reconciliation.* Oxford: Oxford University Press.

Ahmed, E., Harris, N., Braithwaite, J. and Braithwaite, V. (2001) *Shame Management Through Reintegration.* Cambridge: Cambridge University Press.

Bianchi, H. (1994) *Justice as Sanctuary.* Bloomington, IN: Indiana University Press.

Braithwaite, J. (1989) *Crime, Shame and Reintegration.* Cambridge: Cambridge University Press.

Coloroso, B. (2003) *The Bully, the Bullied and the Bystander: From Preschool to High School – How Parents and Teachers Can Help Break the Cycle.* New York, NY: HarperCollins.

Enright, R. (2012) *The Forgiving Life: A Pathway to Overcoming Resentment and Creating a Legacy of Love.* Washington, DC: American Psychological Association.

Grille, R. (2005) *Parenting for a Peaceful World.* Woollahra, Australia: Longueville Media.

Kelly, V.C. (2012) *The Art of Intimacy and the Hidden Challenge of Shame.* Rockland, ME: Maine Authors Publishing.

McDonald, J. (2012) 'Best Practice in Restorative Justice Conference Facilitation: Some Big Ideas.' In J. Bolitho, J. Bruce and G. Mason (eds) *Restorative Justice: Adults and Emerging Practice.* Sydney, Australia: Institute of Criminology Monograph Series.

MacRae, A. and Zehr, H. (2004) *The Little Book of Family Group Conferences, New Zealand.* Intercourse, PA: Good Books.

Pranis, K. (2005) *The Little Book of Circle Processes.* Intercourse, PA: Good Books.

Pranis, K., Stuart, B. and Wedge, M. (2003) *Peacemaking Circles: From Crime to Community*. St Paul, MN: Living Justice Press.

Riestenberg, N. (2012) *Circle in the Square: Building Community and Repairing Harm in School*. St Paul, MN: Living Justice Press.

Thorsborne, M. and Blood, P. (2013) *Implementing Restorative Practices in Schools: A Practical Guide to Transforming School Communities*. London: Jessica Kingsley Publishers.

Thorsborne, M. and Vinegrad, D. (2003) *Restorative Practices in Schools: Rethinking Behaviour Management*. Queenscliffe, Australia: Inyahead Press.

Tomkins, S. (1962) *Affect Imagery Consciousness. Volume I: The Positive Affects*. New York, NY: Springer.

Tomkins, S. (1963) *Affect Imagery Consciousness. Volume II: The Negative Affects*. New York, NY: Springer.

Tomkins, S. (1991) *Affect Imagery Consciousness. Volume III: The Negative Affects: Anger and Fear*. New York, NY: Springer.

Tomkins, S. (1992) *Affect Imagery Consciousness. Volume IV: Cognition: Duplication and Transformation of Information*. New York, NY: Springer.

Vaandering, D. (2010) 'A Window on Relationships: Enlarging the Social Discipline Window for a Broader Perspective.' Paper presented at the 13th World Conference of the International Institute for Restorative Practices, Hull, UK. Available at www.iirp.edu/pdf/Hull-2010/Hull-2010-Vaandering.pdf, accessed on 15 May 2013.

Wachtel, T. (1999) 'Restorative Justice in Everyday Life: Beyond the Formal Ritual.' Paper presented at the Reshaping Australian Institutions Conference: Restorative Justice and Civil Society, 16–18 February. Canberra: Australian National University. Available at www.iirp.edu/article_detail.php?article_id=NTAz, accessed on 14 September 2013.

Wilson, J. (2001) *Adrenal Fatigue: The 21st Century Stress Syndrome*. Petaluma, CA: Smart Publications.

Zehr, H. (2005) *Changing Lenses: A New Focus for Crime and Justice (3rd edition)*. Scottdale, PA: Herald Press.

Part 2
The Theory in Action in Communities and the Criminal Justice Setting

CHAPTER 3

Being Emotional, Being Human

Creating Healthy Communities and Institutions by Honoring Our Biology

Lauren Abramson

Introduction

In Chapters 1 and 2, readers of this book have been given the gift of a clear and cogent overview of the biology of emotion and the reasons why understanding such is so important for restorative practices. Vernon Kelly outlines the pioneering work of Silvan Tomkins, shining a specially focused light on shame. In this chapter, cases from Baltimore's Community Conferencing Center (see www.communityconferencing.org) will be used to provide readers with a 'feel' for the flow of the full range of innate affects and emotion during the community conference process, with a special emphasis on how the level of emotionality in conferences helps to transform conflict and build community. Discussion of how an understanding of emotion can help build the skills of restorative practice practitioners follows.

Background

For the last two years of his life, I had the honor and pleasure of working with Silvan Tomkins. His thinking was broad, deep, insightful, and truly brilliant. Sadly, Tomkins's work was largely ignored by the field of psychology for many decades, and remains incompletely 'mined' for the many gems it holds for those willing to do a little digging. Interestingly, though, the field of restorative justice provides a remarkably welcome home for his work and for affect theory, and may very well be the springboard for a renewed appreciation of the power of this theory – and for our quest to understand, as Tomkins put it, 'what makes human beings tick'.

I believe that Tomkins would be in awe of restorative practices. They not only allow but encourage human beings to be fully *human* – which, for him, meant being deeply emotional, mindful, and social. This is built into our biology. And restorative processes create, by design, such a safe and inviting space – sometimes more like an alchemist's cauldron – to be human in these precise ways.

Instead, and much to our peril, industrialized societies have leeched many of the opportunities to be emotional (and thus, to be fully human) out of so many aspects of our lives. In many US schools, curricula are so focused on rote learning of reading and math skills that any deviations – for vital learning opportunities through play, art, physical education, or relationship/conflict management – not only fail to exist but are discouraged. The Bush-era 'No Child Left Behind' legislation compounded the problem with the mandated and narrow focus on standardized testing. Similarly, in US courts, the focus is on punishing the offender and keeping the victim removed from the justice process, leaving a society with a growing and angry population of incarcerated and formerly incarcerated (disproportionately minority) individuals, and victims who often feel alienated from and further victimized by the criminal justice process. And in our neighborhoods we live our lives indoors, isolated from neighbors and insulated by the comforts of air conditioning, television, internet, and video games. Conflicts are typically resolved by calling the police, not by talking with the neighbor.

Thus, and for other complicated reasons, we are now plagued with increasing levels of violence in its many forms, with few opportunities to address them ourselves. Instead, we rely on experts – principals, police, lawyers, and judges. Fortunately, restorative practices offer us a way *back* and *in* to our biological (socio-emotional) nature, and thus *forward* to a more emotional, thoughtful, collaborative, and socially connected human future.

Affect and Conflict Transformation

I came to conferencing not as someone who worked in criminal justice, or education, or law enforcement. Instead, I came with a background in neuroscience and animal behavior, and as a scientist learning about the effects of emotions on health and illness. For years I had studied the biological nature of emotions, and the physiological consequences of suppressing them. Additionally, as a clinician in a behavioral medicine clinic, I had also seen the suffering that stemmed from people having to put a lid on their feelings – suffering that manifested in all types of physical ailments (bowel disorders, jaw problems, heart-related issues) and interpersonal difficulties (stressed personal relationships at home and at work).

What so excited and heartened me about conferencing when I first heard about it from Australian David Moore at the annual meeting of The Tomkins Institute (see www.tomkins.org) in 1994 was that the process not only allows for but *encourages* a great deal of expression of really tough emotions – among a group of people who are usually really angry with each other, and who otherwise would probably never (want to) be in the same place to talk with each other. What an amazing opportunity this is for people to be healthy *on an emotional level* with each other! And even better, they could do all this within their own communities, and really own the process and the outcomes – without an expert telling them what to do.

Theory

What I have witnessed now, over the past 15 years, are literally hundreds of community conferences where people have been able to transform their rage, disgust, and terror into some remarkably positive feelings about each other and healthy ways of moving forward. Tomkins's (1962, 1963, 1991, 1992) work on affect and emotion, I believe, helps explain so much of the power of conferencing and other restorative justice (RJ) processes. Tomkins's basic theory is very simple at its core:

1. Human beings are born, hard-wired, with a set of affects. They are innate.

    a) Tomkins drew from Charles Darwin's 1872 book titled *The Expression of Emotions in Animals and Man* for the foundation of his ideas.

2. Our affect system is the primary system that motivates human beings.

    a) We need emotions to survive, and each one motivates us in a particular way to help us survive.

    b) When Tomkins said in the 1950s that the emotions were the primary motivators in human beings, he was standing in direct opposition to the prevailing thought of the time. Freud said that the drives were the primary motivators. But Tomkins would easily point out the primacy of emotion over drives (e.g. sex, hunger, sleep) with questions like 'What wins out if you bring fear to the bedroom?' Or, 'If a mathematician is completely absorbed and interested in solving a math problem, how much will s/he sleep and eat?'

    c) We are born with nine innate affects, and each one motivates us in a particular way that helps us survive. Darwin said that the most important function of emotion was a 'preparatory' one; emotions *prepare* us to act in ways that maximize our survival. With anger, our heart pumps blood to our muscles, our teeth are bared, and our pupils constrict, all of which prepare us to *attack*. With interest, our eyes widen, our adrenaline increases slightly, both of which prepare us to *engage*.

Table 3.1 shows how each innate affect motivates us.

TABLE 3.1 How the affects motivate us

Affect	Motivation
Dissmell	'Stay away!' (avoid)
Disgust	Get rid of it (escape)
Fear	Run
Anger	Attack
Sadness	Comfort
Shame	Seek to restore
Surprise	Stop. Look. Listen
Interest	Engage
Joy	Affiliate

3. While the affective response is hard-wired and is experienced very quickly, we learn over time to experience and respond to these affects in different ways. These are emotions.

    a) Affect is biology. Emotion is biography.

Thus, according to Tomkins, we have six negative affects, one neutral/orienting affect (surprise), and two positive affects. That does not mean that some affects are 'good' and some are 'bad'. They all help us survive!

A few words about two of these affects, dissmell and disgust, for which Tomkins had particularly powerful insights. Tomkins referred to dissmell and disgust as *drive auxiliary* responses, because they are connected to the drives of smell and taste respectively. Disgust derives from *gustation* and protects us when something was thought to be good and 'taken in', but turned out to be bad and needed to be spat out or vomited. Think of the tuna salad that you ate that was left out in the sun a little bit too long. This is a protective *escape* response.

Tomkins distinguished disgust from the *avoidance* response elicited when something smells bad. Since there was no word for this, Tomkins made up the word 'dissmell'. Both disgust and dissmell can be elicited in the psychological domain. Think of a time when someone offered up a bad idea and the response was 'That idea really stinks!' Everyone knows that the idea in question will be kept at bay and not 'ingested'. It means that the closer something gets to the dissmeller, the more noxious it becomes. Dissmell is an *avoidance* response.

Tomkins's understanding of shame also merits further explanation. He called shame an *affect auxiliary* because he felt that it comes about only in the presence of a positive bond/connection (positive affect of interest or joy) and when there is a perceived *barrier* to that positive bond. Think of the loyal dog that gets kicked by the human who it loves. Shame is that slumped, deflated look. However, the motivation that comes with shame is a wish to *restore* that bond/connection. Thus, a person who is shamed is much more positively inclined toward the other than someone who is disgusted by the other. With shame, they will want to reconnect; with disgust they will judgingly reject and avoid that person.

Table 3.1 lists the affects in a particular order, from the most negative to the most positive. This is done deliberately because I have seen over and over again that this fairly accurately describes the general flow of affect and emotion during a community conference.

Case Studies

The following two case studies from the Community Conferencing Center in Baltimore, Maryland are shared to demonstrate this flow of emotion within a community conference. I hope that these cases will accomplish the following:

1. Illustrate the vital role of biology and emotion in conflict transformation.

2. Demonstrate more specifically how emotions tend to flow in community conferences from the most negative through to the most positive in the course of conflict transformation.

3. Highlight for practitioners what a powerful force emotion is in their work.

Context: Community Conferencing in Inner-city Baltimore, Maryland, USA

First, however, I offer some context for the community conferencing work we do in Baltimore. Millions of people worldwide have seen the popular HBO series called *The Wire*, which depicts the immorality of the drugs war from a variety of perspectives, including neighborhoods, government, law enforcement, education, and the media. The series is based on, and in, Baltimore, Maryland. As accurate as this depiction of inner-city America may be, we have another story to tell about Baltimore: one in which thousands of residents, in disinvested and crime-ridden neighborhoods, are able to deal with very difficult crimes and conflicts themselves, in their own neighborhoods, because they have been provided with a well-designed, inclusive, and non-institutional structure to do so.

Since 1998, the Community Conferencing Center in Baltimore has been using the community conferencing (CC) process to allow residents to collectively address crimes and conflicts themselves within their own neighborhoods. As of 2013, more than 15,000 inner-city residents have successfully resolved their crimes and conflicts using CC, and hundreds of young offenders have been held accountable for their harmful actions without going through the court system. More than 95 percent of the CCs have resulted in *effective* agreements, reoffending rates are 60 percent lower than those for court, and all of this was accomplished at one-tenth the cost of court.

The Process

The process we use is the deceptively simple and effective structure for a conversation that was shared with us by our Australian colleagues, adapted from the Māori Family Group Conferences (FGCs) in New Zealand. Everyone who is involved in and affected by the incident/conflict is invited to attend, along with their supporters. In this way, the entire *community* of people affected by the situation is part of the process. Before a CC, every participant is made aware of how the process works and decides if they would like to participate. In the circle, the facilitator guides the group as they hear about and discuss the following three questions:

1. What happened?

2. How have people been affected?

3. What can be done to repair the harm and prevent it from happening again?

We follow a script, but only as a guide that helps the participants move through the past (what happened), the present (how are people affected by what happened), and the future (what can be done to make this better), in emotionally meaningful ways.

The following case studies – one school-based sexual harassment incident and one neighborhood conflict – are followed by a discussion of the flow of affect in that conference, and how we use this information in developing facilitator skills.

CASE STUDY: SEXUAL HARASSMENT IN A MIDDLE SCHOOL

Mr C had not slept a full night since the incident at his daughter's school when, in the cafeteria line, one 12-year-old boy took his friend's hand and put it on his daughter's breast. She immediately ran out of the cafeteria, hysterical, in tears. Both boys were suspended for 25 days. One had already been transferred to another school.

The Community Conferencing Center was referred the case by a case worker at the office of suspension services at school headquarters. The case worker indicated that the father was extremely angry about this, and was keen to also press charges against the boys. After an extensive conversation with him, she said he was willing to try a community conference before calling the police.

The facilitator contacted everyone, and the conference was set up for two days following the referral. Ten people attended the CC at the school, which was two weeks after the incident. Participants were: Mr C, his daughter RC, her mother; K, the boy who instigated the incident, his mother L; the other boy M, his aunt N; the principal and the assistant principal, and the suspension office worker.

As they all sat in the circle, K and M started the conference by telling the story of what happened. K slouched in his chair and seemed unrepentant. In contrast, M was meek and very remorseful as he told what happened. The girl, RC, then told everyone how upset she was about it. Then her father, Mr C, chimed in loudly with all of his anger, leaning forward and saying to the boys, 'This has been terrible. I'd really like to have you both arrested, but we'll see if this meeting does anything. I haven't slept very much since this occurred. So tell me this, because what I really want to know is: Did you *target* my daughter or was this just some stupid thing you decided to do?'

They both replied, independently and quietly, that it was just a stupid last-minute thing. K remained slumped in his chair with his arms crossed.

RC's mother was also outraged. With pain and urgency in her voice, she asked them: 'How would you feel if someone put their hand on YOUR sister's breast? Or how about your MOTHER's breast? Or how would you feel if I put my hand on YOUR private parts?' They sheepishly answered that they would not like it. M added, 'Not one bit.'

Everyone else took their turn to say how this incident affected them. The assistant principal was especially angry that K did not seem like he was 'getting it' at all, sitting all slouched in his chair, avoiding eye contact with his head down.

At this point, K's mother piped in: 'He may look like this now, but he's been crying at home about this.'

There was a silence. That comment made people think. What do we teach our boys about expressing difficult feelings? They learn that it's not manly or OK to do so. Maybe there is another side to K we're not seeing.

Mr C chimed in impatiently: 'You're just not realizing how much damage you've done here.'

Soon after, tears began streaming down K's face.

Everyone sat for a moment in silence, looking at K.

Then Mr C leaned forward again in his chair, and with a much softer (but no less insistent) tone he said to K, 'Son, you just don't realize the consequences of what you're doing, because if you keep doing this kind of stuff you're going to end up in jail, and I don't want that to happen. There are too many African-American males in prison, and I don't want that to happen to you. I want you to make the most of your life. I love you, son.'

Tears welled up in everyone's eyes.

Mr C continued: 'What I'd *like* to see happen is that you boys return to this school and have your role to be to protect the girls in this school.'

The facilitator turned to the principal, who said that she had not had any previous problem with these boys, and she would welcome them back, but it was out of her hands at this point. Suspension services would have to approve it. The worker from suspension services was also in the circle, and without hesitation she said it would be fine.

K's mother was thrilled as she'd no longer have to transport K to his new school, which was miles from this school and required him to take two buses and over an hour to get there. M's aunt then asked how M was going to make up the work he had missed those three weeks he was out of school. The principal was shocked and disappointed to learn that M had not been receiving lessons at home.

Both of the boys apologized to RC. She accepted their apologies and said that she was OK for them to return to school so long as the boys agreed it was all over and that they would not talk about it with *anyone*. They agreed. The principal, the suspension services worker, K's mother and M's aunt all commended RC for her courage to speak up for herself. She smiled broadly when she heard these compliments and words of support.

Mr C said that he would like to check in on the boys to see how they were doing. They said they would like that. For the rest of that year, Mr C checked in on those two boys every two weeks.

There were no incidents from either of the boys for the remaining eight months of the school year.

What was the impact of this 45-minute CC? A middle school girl regained a sense of safety, dignity, and comfort in going to her school, and learned that she was respected for coming to the CC and speaking up for herself. Two boys were not arrested; instead, they returned to school halfway through their suspension; one had slipped through the cracks and may have had difficulty getting his place back in his grade. One mother was spared having to provide transportation for her son to a new school that was miles away. A father now has a caring relationship with two boys he had wanted to be jailed, and a mother can be proud of her daughter's courage. A middle school now has two boys who look after and stick up for the girls in the school. A principal and assistant principal now know about an effective way to handle serious incidents without kicking students out of school. A community of ten people now know that they can resolve a very difficult matter themselves, and they all learned how to better care for each other. And a father can now sleep through the night.

Table 3.2 illustrates the expression and flow of emotion during the sexual harassment conference.

TABLE 3.2 Expression and flow of emotion during the sexual harassment conference

Conference participants	Beginning	End
Girl, RC	Fear	Relieved
Girl's father, Mr C	Rage	Relived, happy, interested
Girl's mother	Anger	Relieved
Boy 1, K	Flat, then sadness	Relieved
Boy 1's mother, L	Sadness	Relieved

cont.

TABLE 3.2 Expression and flow of emotion during
the sexual harassment conference *continued*

Conference participants	Beginning	End
Boy 2, M	Shame	Relieved, happy
Boy 2's aunt, N	Anger	Relieved, happy
Principal and assistant principal	Anger, distress	Happy, relieved (that the boys would come back to the school) Distress, shame (at failure of one boy to get home assignments that he should have been getting)
Suspension services worker		Happy

CASE STUDY: NEIGHBORHOOD CONFLICT WITH 75 CALLS TO POLICE FROM THREE HOUSES

Two weeks after a police lieutenant had participated in a CC that resulted in a remarkably positive outcome for an ongoing neighborhood conflict in her district, she decided to use CC for a situation that had become the bane of her existence. Three families on the same block had made 75 calls for service due to ongoing feuding. Despite the fact that the families had been to court four times due to several fights – some of which involved a knife and one of which involved a gun – the situation remained unresolved. In fact, it was escalating.

So, on the Friday after Thanksgiving, at 3 p.m., she called to ask for a facilitator to do a CC. She told the facilitator that she had already dispatched her officers to go to each of the three homes – not to make another arrest, but to pick up the residents and bring them immediately to the local fast food restaurant. She wanted the CC facilitator to meet them at the restaurant in a half-hour.

The facilitator showed up and saw the residents sitting with the police officers and the lieutenant. The facilitator explained that a conference could not take place right there and then, because preparation needed to take place, and she needed to find out who else might need to attend the conference. Everyone understood. She then started asking the neighbors about the conflict. Despite the fact that the police were right there, another fight started. Clearly, this was a volatile group! Still, everyone agreed to attend a CC the following Tuesday evening. It would take place in the basement meeting room of the local library.

Each of the three families showed up, as did the three police officers who had responded to the dozens of calls for service over the past year. The conference began with one neighbor talking about what had been happening over the past year. It quickly became clear that no one was quite sure how it all started. Through a fair amount of yelling, the neighbors finally figured out that it began about a year ago when one of the girls made a mean comment to another girl about her clothes. The officers sat impatiently through this discussion with their arms folded tightly across their chests. One officer, slumped in his chair, finally blurted out, 'This is ridiculous. Can't we just get to what's going to be done to fix this?'

The facilitator reminded him that everyone first needs to have a chance to say how they have been affected by this situation before anyone talks about solutions. At that point one of the men started yelling at the officer. He was angry because a few months ago, his neighbor had punched him. Despite the fact that *he* called the police, *he* was the one who ended up being arrested by this officer. 'How is it that *I* call the police, but I end up being taken down to booking?' The officer sat up and replied, 'Sir. When I arrived at your house, I got out of the car and saw you hit your neighbor. I am required, *by law*, to make an arrest if I witness an assault.' The man was completely taken aback. Stunned, he said quietly, 'Oh. I didn't know that.'

The group went on to discuss the various fights they had had, yelling and angry about all time off of work they had taken for court, and all of the fear and anger they had because these fights were becoming increasingly dangerous. At one point, things got so heated that the security guard from the library came in to find out if everyone was OK. 'We're fine,' the facilitator assured the guard.

Then, in the midst of the heated conversation, one of the mothers burst into tears. Everyone in the circle looked at her. 'You know,' she said, her voice shaking, 'I just realized something. My cousin was killed last month over something as stupid as what we're fighting about. And if we keep this up, someone in this room is going to get killed.'

Everyone stopped. The sense of deflation of all the anger in the room was palpable. Everyone realized that this woman was right.

Unless they did something about this ongoing feud, someone would die. The facilitator let the silence linger for many moments, and then she asked, 'So, what would you all like to do to resolve this?'

The mood was much lighter as they all agreed that they would stop the fighting, stop the nonsense, and begin to be nice to each other. The girls agreed that it had all been over for quite some time, but that the adults had kept the conflict going. Everyone agreed to a potluck dinner together within the coming week. One man requested that no one bring turkey since he was tired of having turkey for Thanksgiving, and they all laughed and agreed. They signed the agreement and everyone went to the side of the room to enjoy refreshments. The neighbors and police all shared handshakes and hugs.

Calls to the police for those three homes were monitored for the next two years. There were no more calls to police from any of those families.

Table 3.3 illustrates the expression and flow of emotion during the conference.

TABLE 3.3 Expression and flow of emotion during the conference

Conference participants	Emotions: beginning	Emotions: middle	Emotions: end
Neighbor woman 1	Rage, fear	Sadness, shame	Relieved, happy
Neighbor man 1	Rage, disgust	After hearing why he was arrested, shame at realizing where this would lead to	Relieved, happy
Neighbor teenager 1	Fear, anger	Shame	Relieved, happy
Neighbor woman 2	Fear, anger, disgust	Shame	Relieved, happy
Neighbor man 2	Anger	Shame	Relieved, happy
Neighbor teenager 2	Fear	Shame	Relieved, happy
Neighbor man 3	Anger	Shame	Relieved, happy
Neighbor woman 3	Anger	Relieved, happy	
Police officer 1	Anger, disgust	Surprise	Relieved
Police officer 2	Anger	Surprise	Relieved, happy
Police officer 3	Sadness	Shame	Relieved

Case Analyses: Understanding the Flow of Emotion

Both of these cases illustrate how the conflict was transformed as the flow of emotion moved from the negative emotions that generated conflict through to the positive emotions that promoted cooperation. So how does an understanding emotion help us understand the process of conflict transformation?

When people come in to CCs, they typically are feeling the emotions that motivate them to be in conflict with one another. This is illustrated in Table 3.4.

TABLE 3.4 Emotions that motivate conflict

Emotion	Motivation
Dissmell	'Stay away!' (avoid)
Disgust	Get rid of it (escape)
Fear	Run
Anger	Attack

In the school case, Mr C was so enraged he had not slept well since the incident with his daughter. His daughter was terrified, as were the two boys who had harassed her. In the neighborhood case, the residents and the police were incredibly angry and frustrated with each other, and somewhat disgusted with the police (and vice versa).

However, once the conference participants heard 'what happened', and began to share and listen to how they had each been affected by the incident, the tears began to flow. The motivation that comes with sadness begins to soften the distance between people as they show a level of vulnerability with their tears (Table 3.5).

TABLE 3.5 Motivation that comes with sadness

Affect	Motivation
Sadness	Comfort

While sadness is, indeed, still a negative emotion, it is not as toxic to experience (for self or others) as the emotions of dissmell, disgust, anger, and fear. It is very punishing to experience rage or terror or disgust for extended periods of time. When conference participants begin to cry, however, there is usually a softening within the circle. Distress motivates us to seek comfort and thus begins to bring us closer to others.

People feel more open and inclined to listen and to reach out. In the sexual harassment case, when participants looked at the boy who was slouching with his arms folded and saw the tears streaming down his cheeks, the yelling stopped.

At this point, something very particular often happens during many conferences; it is a very special emotional shift. We never know when it will happen or how it will happen, or who might initiate it, but someone says something that takes all of the heat out of the conversation. In the neighborhood case, it was when the woman shared the story about her cousin who was killed, and realized that they were headed for a similar outcome. In the school case, it was when the father of the girl, seeing the boy cry, leaned forward in his seat and told the boy he did not want to see him go to jail, that he wanted him to make the most of his life, and that he loved him. At that point, in both conferences, there was a sense of deflation in the circle, as everyone felt a certain amount of shame about the situation in front of them.

A First Nations woman once referred to this as 'a moment of collective vulnerability', in that everyone in the circle awakens to a feeling of collective responsibility for what is happening. Thus, shame may be felt not only by the 'offender' but by any number of people sitting in that circle. When there is that feeling of shame, people are motivated to restore (or build) a positive connection with others (Table 3.6).

TABLE 3.6 Motivation to restore

Affect	Motivation
Shame	Seek to restore

At this important emotional shift, the facilitator then asks, 'So, having heard all of this, what would you all like to see come out of today's meeting to make things better?'

In the neighborhood case, this shift, this moment of collective vulnerability, happened when the mother connected this conflict with the recent death of her cousin.

In the sexual harassment case, this moment occurred when the father of the girl wanted the boy to realize the consequences of his behavior and to make the most of his life because he loved him. At this point everyone was in tears, and everyone wanted to try to make things better – for everyone, not just the girl.

Once this moment of collective vulnerability, deflation, and collective shame occurs, the emotional tone of the conference shifts from the negative emotions, often momentarily, to the neutral emotion of surprise (reorienting) (Table 3.7).

TABLE 3.7 The neutral emotion of surprise (reorienting)

Affect	Motivation
Surprise	Stop. Look. Listen

In the school case, the father is surprised to hear himself say that he would actually like to be a mentor for these boys. The neighbors, in the police case, are shocked to realize that they need to get their act together before there is a murder.

And this is when the group, interested in each other and in their own wellbeing, comes up with their agreement. But they are coming at this task feeling relieved and good about each other, rather than feeling angry and vengeful (Table 3.8).

TABLE 3.8 The emotions of feeling good

Affect	Motivation
Interest	Engage
Joy	Affiliate

The neighbors immediately shared apologies and promises to be kind to and supportive of each other. They each struggled with raising teenagers, and decided that they could really help each other out in that regard. They also planned to have a dinner together.

In the school case, the girl was happy to have received the apologies from the boys and the compliments from the adults. The father extended his love and care to the boys and offered to be their mentor. The boys were relieved to be able to go back to their school, to avoid jail, and to have the girl's father as a new mentor. And the principal and assistant principal were very happy to know that these boys were going to be back in school and have a supportive male in their life at school.

In addition, once the agreement was worked out and signed, everyone was invited to enjoy refreshments. But the more important purpose of this time is so that they can enjoy each other, exchange phone numbers, and feel good about their accomplishment and new connections. The formal process is over and the informal process over food extends opportunities for healing moments.

Using an Understanding of the Biology of Emotion to Build Facilitator Skills

In our facilitator training workshop offered at the Community Conferencing Center, we infuse the 22-hour training with information and discussion about the biology of emotion, and the role of emotion in conflict transformation. We encourage facilitators, over time, to deepen their awareness and understanding of emotion with particular attention to two locations: (1) the expression of emotion within the circle, and (2) the experience of emotion within themselves as they facilitate.

Expression of Emotion within the Circle

We feel that one of the important roles of facilitators of CCs is to allow participants the full expression of their emotions. This does not mean that participants can attack one another when they are furious. It does, however, mean that they can fully express the depth of their feelings, whatever those are, with guidance that they share how they have been personally affected by the situation (as opposed to insulting someone).

We want our facilitators to fully appreciate that, just because we have negative and positive emotions, this does not mean that some emotions are bad and some emotions are good. They are *all* important in the sense that they motivate us in particular ways that help us survive. When we continually 'put a lid on our emotions', they make us physically ill, and they negatively impact our relationships.

CCs and other restorative practices are among the few processes where we are encouraged to be emotionally healthy with each other. Thus, we want facilitators to appreciate this important dynamic of the work. Some of the facilitator skills that are helpful in this regard include:

- being grounded in the understanding of the vital role of emotion in the process, and not to 'short circuit' this part of any conference

- not being afraid of the expression of strong negative emotions

- remembering to prompt participants to share how they felt at different times, and to share how they are feeling now about the situation

- deepening awareness of one's own emotional responses to emotion.

Facilitators' Awareness of Their Own Emotions

Most of us are not used to convening a meeting where a lot of people sit in a circle and end up yelling, crying, laughing, pouting, and so on. Just the thought of it makes many people uncomfortable.

We take a great deal of time during facilitator training to discuss and experience the emotional aspects of the conferencing process so that facilitators in training will be more aware of what to expect during the conferences. If they can expect a lot of strong emotions, they will be less likely to be surprised and/or afraid of them when they arise, and will be less likely to do the various things that facilitators can do overtly or subtly to dilute the expression of emotion during the conference. For example, some facilitators who are not comfortable with the emotion being expressed may interrupt the person by asking them another question, or they will redirect the conversation to another person.

Many facilitators are not aware of their own emotional responses, and thus are not fully aware of why they make the move they do as a facilitator in any given point. The pattern presented in Table 3.9 can be a helpful tool to engage facilitators in reflecting upon and becoming more aware of their own emotional responses to emotion.

TABLE 3.9 How I feel about different emotions

Emotions	In myself	In others
Joy		
Interest-excitement		
Surprise		
Shame		
Sadness-anguish		
Fear-terror		
Anger-rage		
Disgust		
Dissmell		

Over the years of training hundreds of facilitators, it has been very common for people at the end of the training to say, 'I really love this process and this work, but I don't think I can do it.' People share a variety of reasons why, but the most common ones are that (1) the person recognizes that they want to be more in control of what people do, or (2) they feel very uncomfortable with people expressing their anger. The latter may be a particular issue in American culture. There are many cultures that are far more comfortable with the expression of anger (e.g. many Mediterranean countries).

Still, there is probably something about facilitating circles that will be uncomfortable for most of us. What we invite our facilitators to do, if they choose, is to be willing to unlearn their own patterns of responding and to step into their own insecurities and discomforts, in service of providing a 'clear' space for people to do the very best they can to resolve their own conflict.

Several people who have been willing to step into this challenge have noticed remarkable changes in themselves. One facilitator, a high school teacher, shared during a facilitator skill-building session that he had been an introvert his whole life, and after facilitating conferences for several months he re-took the Myers–Briggs personality test (which measures relative levels of introversion–extroversion as one of four personality dimensions) and found that he had moved more toward extroversion. Another facilitator, a school police officer, said that once he realized that he didn't have to control people's emotional outbursts, and that he did not have to be responsible for the outcomes of the meeting, he 'felt 20 years of anger just melt away'.

The importance of creating a space for facilitators to reflect on their own experiences with and feelings about facilitation cannot be underestimated. Our office space is deliberately set up primarily as an open space (with knee walls which give some privacy to the facilitators), so that co-workers can easily and spontaneously share their concerns and feelings about anything that arises. If a facilitator wants more in-depth support about something, they can always call a 'campfire', and everyone knows to drop what they are doing and come sit in a circle and talk something through. In addition, our volunteer facilitators are invited to quarterly skill-building and reflection sessions.

There are many ways to reinforce, nurture, and support facilitators so that the emotional aspects of this work are duly honored. We take every opportunity to do that, whether it is in the form of skill-building, debriefing, support, staff coffee hours, or facilitator fun days.

Conclusion
Creating Institutions that Honor Who We Are as Human Beings

Affects *just are*. We have them. They are built into our biology. And conflict is inevitable. We are social beings. Our hope is that we will come to fully appreciate that it is folly – if not dangerous – to deny our emotions. Once we do that, we can find ways to create structures within our communities, our schools, our workplaces, and our justice systems that allow us to be fully human and to express our emotions.

To paraphrase Winston Churchill: we are shaped by the institutions that govern us. Restorative practices provide elegant and effective structures for conversations that allow us to be emotional. As we begin to weave these structures into the workings of all aspects of our daily lives, we will shape and reshape our institutions – and, in turn, our cultures – into ones that nurture healthy, safe, caring, connected, and resilient communities.

References

Tomkins, S. (1962) *Affect Imagery Consciousness. Volume I: The Positive Affects.* New York, NY: Springer.

Tomkins, S. (1963) *Affect Imagery Consciousness. Volume II: The Negative Affects.* New York, NY: Springer.

Tomkins, S. (1991) *Affect Imagery Consciousness. Volume III: The Negative Affects: Anger and Fear.* New York, NY: Springer.

Tomkins, S. (1992) *Affect Imagery Consciousness. Volume IV: Cognition: Duplication and Transformation of Information.* New York, NY: Springer.

CHAPTER 4

Restorative Practice in a Policing Environment

Understanding Affect Will Help

John Lennox

Introduction

Policing is an occupation that is at once complex and simple, an occupation that places a police officer in situations which bring out the best and worst in people – and that includes the police officer. In this chapter, writing about the daily work of a practising police officer, I hope to describe the range of cases I have been involved in and the nature of the emotional harm that the incidents have caused.

Police officers, as I came to realize, are daily confronted with situations that cause them to become keen observers of human emotions. This was certainly true of my police experience of more than 30 years of service. I was dealing with situations where other people were displaying a range of emotions that were challenging, and for which I had not received adequate training. I was trained in the law and knew my powers and duty as a constable but was reliant on my own life experience in dealing with those emotions. How was I to deal with advising a person of the sudden death of a loved one, to deal with a couple in the midst of a violent domestic situation, to deflate a violent confrontation between intoxicated males? With experience, I found out. What did help me was my previous service in the Army. Leadership training instilled in me the need to be fair, firm and friendly to subordinates if I was to command respect and receive a willing response to an order.

Every contact a police officer has with a citizen involves a range of affects from positive to toxic, and, more often than not, negative. The nature of policing by and large includes daily contact with people who are victims or who have offended in minor ways, to people involved at the much more serious end of the spectrum. Normally, the officer will not know that person's life story, how their emotions have been scripted by that life experience or what their response will be. A simple traffic stop, where an officer intended to caution the driver, can, in some instances, trigger an outburst of anger-rage and lead to the arrest of the driver for offences against the officer. The officer, later, is left relating the story to his colleagues of the 'yobbo who went off in his face' over a minor matter and was eventually arrested after a struggle!

Police officers themselves also bring to their profession their own life experience, which, if not reflected upon, can sometimes draw them into a situation as a person involved in a problem rather than a person who is there to help provide solutions or take control. There will, of course, be situations where an officer will have an empathic response, and he or she may allow his or her humanity to show particularly in crisis situations where there is distress or fear in another.

My 'patch' at that time, and for the next 18 years, was primarily a government, low socio-economic housing area with high unemployment and families who had mostly at some point been in trouble with the law. Prison was not a deterrent but an occupational hazard, a place to catch up with friends and a place where you got three meals a day. Use of alcohol and drugs was prevalent and this led to high rates of family violence and young people disengaged from school. The media repeatedly reported on events, crime and social ills in this community in a negative way that increased their sense of shame and stigmatization. Our suicide rate was abnormally high, as was the use of violence to resolve problems.

It was not until I learned of Silvan Tomkins's affect theory in 1995 (Demos 1995), as part of a training session in restorative practices, that I made sense of my observations and experiences. What really became apparent to me was how humans react to shame as postulated in Donald Nathanson's Compass of Shame (Nathanson 1992). Suddenly I could make sense of all my observations and experiences. When subsequently dealing with people, I would explore their stories so I could better understand their responses to an event that had triggered the response. I read, re-read and digested

Nathanson's writings to get a grip on affect theory. As a result of my experiences and with my initial training in restorative justice, I jumped into practice and set out on a journey.

I also came to realize that the pervading attitude of the police, when a person had offended, was arrest, charge and let the court decide. This attitude was, in most instances, unhelpful in bringing about a change in people's behaviour. In fact, as my understanding of affect theory grew, I realized that in the majority of cases, it made people's behaviour worse and, as a consequence, the community at large suffered. This thinking changed my approach to policing my community. I began to build relationships with any and all organizations working in the community and supporting and encouraging individuals from the community who showed leadership that could assist in bringing about change of the culture. This did not mean I stopped arresting where required, but I developed a more relational approach that allowed individuals to make choices about what that arrest would look like. The evidence of the merits of that approach was most apparent in the fact that my home telephone number was listed in the telephone directory and, over the 18 years, I only had three annoying calls out of the many hundreds of calls from people in the community who were looking for help, advice or to provide me with information.

The Compass of Shame

I well remember several cases involving toxic shame experiences, best explained by the Compass of Shame described in Chapter 1.

Attack Self

There were young people commiting suicide for reasons as diverse as a girlfriend leaving, sexual abuse by a father and a 17-year-old who had been shamed when his father, following an altercation, slapped him across the face in front of other men in a public bar. He had told a friend before he shot himself that he was so ashamed that he had been slapped like a boy rather than being punched like a man.

I recall other adults, who were prominent in community, who commited suicide after being charged with sexual offences against young children or other serious crimes when these became public; and one particularly sad case of a teenage girl who shot herself for reasons unexplained. She was a high-performing student, had modelling work and was positioned to make a contribution to the community. I suspected the probable cause, but was not able to substantiate that for the coroner despite discreet enquiries with school friends. Several years later the brother of the deceased girl also committed suicide by jumping from a cliff. He had been stealing for some time and using scheduled drugs from his employer. The note he left subsequently led to the arrest and charging of their father with sexual offences. He did not make it to court as he, too, shot himself. I suspect that, as Vernon Kelly mentions in Chapter 1, the teenage girl responded to her confusion and shame by *attack self*. Her brother's response was initially *avoidance* (avoidance with drug use) but later *attack self*, and their father, who held a responsible position in the community and also in the public service, responded by *attack self*.

Another poignant memory was attending to the sudden death of a man who had committed suicide using a shotgun. There was no identification on the body but the nearby motor car led to my going to a residence to make enquiries. I knocked on the door and when it opened a woman momentarily looked surprised but immediately began to assault me, screaming, 'You have killed him.' I, too, was surprised and startled at this apparent unmerited outburst. This was almost immediately followed by anguish that I had only previously experienced at another suicide. I gently took the sobbing woman inside where I noticed a wallet, wedding ring and note on the kitchen bench. I discovered that her husband had been interviewed and charged in relation to matters involving a young boy in another police district. Her husband had told her he was innocent. On her return home just before I arrived, she found the objects on the bench. Both, I subsequently discovered, had discussed the matter the previous evening and the impact the court appearance would have on his employment and family. Their shared anticipation of shame had played on both their minds and led to this outcome. My empathic response and understanding of her affect subsequently developed a positive relationship and later involvement with the family as the children passed through their teenage years.

Many a time in situations of repeat family violence, I would suggest to women that they should leave the violent relationship only to receive a response like 'I can't, and anyway who would want me?' In their self put-downs, they revealed not only their inner feelings of shame (*attack self*) but also their sense of powerlessness.

Attack Other

There were those families whose members were generational offenders, and whom the community stigmatized to the point that they *attacked other* through further criminal activities. They were often seen in news reports leaving court with a covering over their head (*avoidance*) or alternatively giving the public (through the news camera) the proverbial raised-finger salute (*attack other*). They were, because of the stigmatization, excluded from the community and regarded as outcasts or outlaws.

Family violence was, as I mentioned above, a prevalent social problem. I have no doubt that it was as a result of observed and learned scripts in families that did not have the skills to communicate and negotiate solutions to intra-family problems. When problems arose, it generally revolved around money. Unemployment payments from the government quickly disappeared on cars, alcohol and drugs, particularly for males. Understandably, this provided them with some interest and enjoyment in an otherwise bleak future. These interests inevitably led to breaches of the law and monetary penalties from the courts. They also led to disputes with wives and partners over lack of money for rent, utilities and food for families.

The male's inadequacy as breadwinners highlighted in an intra-family dispute would engender anger and *attack other*, which was normally directed at the wife or partner but could also include the dwelling. I recall most every home would have holes punched in plaster walls or internal doors by angry males. Police attendance would often trigger a further attack on the officers. I never felt that this was personal but rather an attitude that the offender had to demonstrate to the neighbours that it 'took four coppers to arrest me'. Given my longevity in the community, I found that I could reverse this sense of shame by making it clear that an arrest would occur and to walk out like a man would not upset their children but would demonstrate to the neighbours they were in control of their own arrest. This usually worked.

Avoidance

There were many in this community who used *avoidance* by simply resorting to the readily available alcohol and illicit drugs, the use of which was extremely high. In fact, the community had the highest drink-driving conviction rate in Australia at that time. The whole community was so stigmatized by the media and wider community that they avoided using their telephone numbers on job applications as the prefix immediately identified where they lived. Employers would, judgementally, place all in this community in the one basket. To obtain a call back, young people and their families would use telephone numbers and addresses of friends and relatives in other suburbs on a job application.

CASE STUDY: ARSON

After a few years with some conferencing practice under my belt, I was approached by my senior officers in relation to a file from another police district. This was in respect to four young boys who had caused extensive damage when they set fire to a school. The offence had been committed in October 1998, and whilst all of the boys had admitted being present at the time of the offence, none had admitted actual responsibility.

As restorative practice was relatively new and not yet held in high regard by my police department, the investigating detectives saw the matter as being very serious and had referred the file to the State Prosecutor for consideration. Subsequently, the file was returned to the police department with the advice that a Supreme Court prosecution was unwarranted. After much delay the file ended up in my lap.

What to do?

After digesting the file I found that I had four boys, two of whom were brothers, Bill, 14 years old, and Ben, 12, John and his friend Chris who were both 13.[1] They had been charged with arson, setting fire to vegetation and injuring property.

---

1   All names in this case study have been changed to protect the identity of those involved in the conference.

The Facts

Bill, the older boy, had gone to the school and broken a window in the kindergarten classroom on a Friday. He had returned to his home where he met his three co-offenders and together they had discussed how they would set fire to the school. Together, they all returned to the school and disconnected the public address system, believing it was connected to the alarm system. The next day, Saturday, they returned to the school and, after spray-painting some graffiti, they set fire to some vegetation. This fire was attended by the fire service. On the Sunday, some accelerant was acquired and hidden, and the four boys resolved to meet later that evening at the school and set fire to it. A pact was entered into that if a member of the group failed to turn up, he would be punished by the others.

That evening, armed with weapons to protect them, Bill, Ben and John went to the school and attempted to start a fire in a storeroom. When this failed, they started a fire in the classroom through the broken window. Chris arrived at this point but quickly decamped with the others when the fire alarm was activated by smoke. Fortunately, due to the gusty wind conditions, the fire service was revisiting the school to ensure the previous day's vegetation fire had not flared up, and their timely arrival minimized the damage. The four boys had fled and spent the night sleeping out. Bill assaulted Chris for turning up late. All the boys were first approached by the police on the following Tuesday.

I decided that, as it was now April in the following year, I should, in the first instance, visit the primary school where the offence had occurred. This proved fortuitous as on entering the kindergarten classroom I immediately experienced *dissmell* (see Chapter 1). The smoke from the fire had permeated the straw roofing material and now, six months later, the smoky smell was still very strong. Then and there I made the decision to hold the conference in the classroom as I felt the affect of dissmell would trigger emotional memories of the crime and its effect on the participants.

Before becoming involved with conference preparation, I sounded out the class teacher and the school principal. My conversation with the teacher, Christine Smith, revealed that the fire had caused much distress and shame to the young children in her class whose year of work had largely been destroyed by fire, smoke and water. Christine, too, was noticeably angry as the boys were all former students of the school, and she was at a loss to understand why they had picked on her classroom. From the principal, Kate Munday, I was able to get some understanding in relation to the boys and their family situations. Kate was very angry that the offenders proved to be former students and was initially unhappy that the police were not sending the boys to court. However, she accepted that a conference was to be held and was looking forward to that as she wanted the boys to pay back for the harm that they had caused. On discussing this with her, she indicated that she thought the boys, notwithstanding their age, should make some financial reparation.

Conference Preparation

I began the pre-conference preparation by interviewing the others whom I identified as being affected by the ripples that emanated from the crime.

THE PARENTS

The parents of Bill and Ben were Dennis and Barbara Brown. The family had recently relocated to Tasmania from interstate as Dennis had been transferred by his employer. During the interviews with the school staff, I received advice that Barbara habitually left her husband to deal with any issues relating to their children and would often return to her own family (*avoidance*) until Dennis had resolved any crisis. Dennis was quiet but a solid type of a man. Both boys were intelligent and, when in trouble, would either deny or lie about their behaviours (clearly avoidance behaviours).

The parents of Chris were Marea and Paul Jones. They had been separated for some years but shared the parenting of their children. Marea's father, David, resided with her and her other child, Peter. Marea was highly emotional and very upset that her son had been assaulted by Bill and was still being threatened by the other three boys.

John's parents were also separated. His mother, Jane May, had a new partner, Richard. Jane was suffering from depression and had little control over her son, who was, at the time, residing with his grandmother, Rita. Richard took no part in the parenting of John and neither did his biological father, Robert. As a result, John was truanting from school, believed to be using cannabis and had been suspended from school for setting fire to a book in class. An intelligent boy, he had been the first to confess to the offences. Like a lot of young males I was in contact with in these family circumstances, the lack of a supportive male role model as they passed through puberty was a contributing factor to offending behaviours. My experience was that on separating from a family, a male generally was more interested in the new female in his life. As a result, he was neglectful of his responsibilities as a father and oblivious of the rites of passage that sons needed with their father.

Each family had enrolled their children in different high schools but the boys had maintained their friendship.

The other participants I interviewed and invited to the conference were an education department social worker, Brian, who was supporting both the school staff and two of the families. I interviewed the senior fire officer, Barry Tones, who had attended the fire; the investigating detectives, Greg Adlard and Paul Buckingham; the school maintenance officer, Michael O'Brien; and lastly Brian Banks, the neighbour who lived next door to the school and was both a member of the school's parents and friends association and the person who had observed the fire and reported it.

Also present was a teacher colleague, who was also a trained facilitator. He and I were mentoring each other and providing feedback on our facilitation with the view to honing our skills.

The Conference

The day of the conference arrived. I had the room set up and my seating plan (chairs in a circle) arranged. Not unexpectedly, two participants did not attend. Barbara (the mother of Bill and Ben), true to form, had gone home to her parents. Robert (biological father of John) rang at the last moment to advise me he was not coming. Unexpectedly, the kindergarten teacher, Christine, advised me she would not be able to participate. She was clearly distressed and indicated she would not be able to handle the conference. I sensed that her previous anger was now so unrelenting that she had become anguished. I also sensed she might have been fearful of facing the boys and perhaps breaking down in front of them.

I decided to leave the three empty chairs in the circle.

As people arrived, I progressively seated the participants in the circle. I started with the opening script, after which I began with Chris who was seated between his parents, with his grandfather and brother flanking them. I felt he was likely to be more honest. Head down, he began to explain what had occurred. As his story came out, his mother, Marea, took his hand and began to cry. His account of the offence began to drift obviously from the facts that were, at that point, still largely unknown to the adults present. As it turned out, this was because of shame avoidance, as he tried to blame the others. The other boys, though, did not want to be seen in a bad light by those present and be further shamed. They indicated they wanted to object to aspects of Chris's account. I allowed the conversation between them to flow, and their shared memories finally exposed what had happened, and the boys, through their shared storytelling, took ownership of their behaviour. Ben took responsibility for actually lighting the fire, a surprise to his father.

I then invited the principal, Kate, to talk about the impact the offences had had on the school, the children whose classroom had been affected, and the emotional impact the offence had upon Christine Smith, their teacher. Kate was still very angry towards the boys, particularly as all had been former pupils. None of the boys was able to answer her repeated question, 'Why?' The boys simply sat with head down, silent to the question. The accusing question left them lost for words, their shame apparent to all.

Progressively, I introduced the stories of harm from the others involved in the ripple effect of the offences. Brian Banks, the parent and friends association representative, and Michael O'Brien, the maintenance officer, both expanded upon the impact of the offence, as did the fire and police officers. They also were alarmed that the boys went armed and asked of them the reason for being armed. Again the boys hung their heads in shame and replied 'dunno'.

The Jones family were next to speak and all, not unexpectedly, were very supportive of Chris and spoke of his positive attributes. Marea was upset that her son had been intimidated by the others and became quite emotional and began to cry. I could see that this was causing an empathic response in Chris as I could see his eyes watering up as he watched his mother's distress.

The May family were next to speak, and Jane was quite open about all the issues confronting her family, her depression, John's father's lack of support (including his non-attendance at the conference), John's cannabis use and problem behaviours at high school, and her lack of control over her son. Her partner, Richard, corroborated Jane's story and added he felt powerless as any attempt by him to have input into the blended family's wider issues created problems between him and Jane.

I was discreetly scanning the faces of those affected by the boys' behaviour as the first two families spoke. Their interest was apparent on their faces.

I then began to draw from Dennis Brown how he had been affected by his sons' behaviour. He too was forthcoming on the internal family issues. He became very emotional and at times struggled to express his feelings in words, but his body language spoke of distress. He indicated his disappointment in his sons' behaviour and their failure to take responsibility, not only to the police but also to him. He apologized to the school and to the Jones family for the assault and intimidation of their son by his children. He assured them it would not happen again.

I felt that this was the tipping point for most of the victims who were empathizing with the families. The exception was Kate Munday, the principal, who remained silent. I have since reflected on many occasions about what was motivating her. What was her life experience that blinded her to the evident emotions in others and prevented her from forgiving these four young boys who did a dumb thing?

I then asked the boys what they could do to put things right, making it clear that it was not the responsibility of the parents. All indicated they were sorry for the hurt they had caused the school and their families. Kate Munday stated that she could not accept their apology and was looking for a more substantial sign that the boys understood the harm they had caused to the school community. The boys, led by Chris Jones, suggested they could pay some money to the school, and Ben Brown offered $100. Kate Munday, in light of the seriousness of the crime, suggested it was not enough, and others joined the conversation on what was reasonable given their age. The boys' families indicated that all the boys had the ability and opportunity to earn money by doing chores within their residential communities. After some negotiations, the amount was fixed at $670 to be paid over 12 months. At the suggestion of the fire officer, Barry Tomes, the boys all agreed to attend the fire station and complete a tour of his station and develop some understanding of the dangers faced by fire officers.

The conference then adjourned to 'break the bread'. This part of the restorative conference is a most important stage of the process. It is the less formal part and is where the healing is confirmed and the offenders reintegrated into their community of care. The participants are able to share food and drink, and it symbolizes a new beginning. In my experience, the person(s) harmed and the offender(s) shake hands and often hug each other.

I watched the interactions between the young people and the adults and, with one exception, all were positive, and relief was clearly visible on the boys' faces. The exception was the principal, Kate Munday, who remained on the edge of the celebration. I approached her and we spoke. She felt she was unable to approach the boys or forgive them and was not able to articulate her reasons for not accepting their apology.

For some time after the conference I would regularly meet Marea Jones in the street and hear how well her son, Chris, was doing. The other boys, to the best of my knowledge, have not reoffended.

Conclusion

My work as a restorative practitioner today is founded on the principles I learned in the Army: being fair, firm and friendly, and listening to people's stories so I can understand their affective response and why they might be behaving in a particular way in the moment. It is all about affect.

In my view, understanding ASP is important and should form part of police training. I was fortunate that this view was supported in Tasmania Police. The training of police recruits in basic affect theory and in the objectives and principles of the Tasmanian legislation the Youth Justice Act 1997 – which included two levels of restorative conferencing – became part of all recruit training. The relevancy of that training was often mentioned to me by other officers with whom I had contact after post initial training. Quite often, advice was sought not only about young offenders but also about how the officer might approach an intra-family situation involving his or her own children.

The other important thing that has guided me since I was 17 years old is the need to model that which you preach:

No printed word, no spoken plea,
Can teach young hearts what men should be
Not all the books, on all the shelves,
But what the teachers are themselves.

Anon

References

Demos, E.V. (ed.) (1995) *Exploring Affect: The Selected Writings of Silvan S. Tomkins.* Cambridge: Cambridge University Press.

Nathanson, D.L. (1992) *Shame and Pride: Affect, Sex, and the Birth of the Self.* New York, NY: W.W. Norton.

CHAPTER 5

Forgiveness

Katy Hutchison

Introduction

In June 2009 I was honored to speak on a plenary panel with Barry Stuart and David Gustafson at the Second Restorative Practices International Conference in Vancouver, BC. Barry is a retired Chief Judge from the Yukon and is internationally known through his training, teaching, writings, and involvement as a mediator, negotiator, and facilitator. David is the co-director of Community Justice Initiatives, an adjunct professor in Simon Fraser University's School of Criminology, a therapist in private practice, and a registered clinical counselor. The title of our address was *Rivulets, Confluence, Rivers and the Sea of Hope*. Before a room filled with experts in their field, David described an image of the important work done by restorative practitioners in education, justice, workplace conflict, and government, each in their own stream. He asked us to imagine the confluence of that work into one river, and the resulting powerful surge of water traveling towards a Sea of Hope.

I was momentarily troubled by the metaphor. This was not a river I had chosen. I did not get carried by a current from a calm stream of chosen study or practice. Rather, I was thrown into the rushing river through circumstances beyond my control. Keeping my head above the water was essential to my survival. Restorative justice became my life jacket and connected me to the practitioners I am humbled to swim alongside towards that Sea of Hope.

Murder

Fifteen years ago my husband, Bob McIntosh, was kicked to death while trying to break up an un-chaperoned, out-of-control house party hosted by the son of a vacationing friend. While there were two hundred young people in the home at the time, no one would step up and give the police the information they needed to move forward with their investigation. A five-year silence shrouded the small town in which we lived. I moved back to the community I had grown up in with my children, five-year-old twins – a son and a daughter. Finally, following a complex undercover investigation, an arrest was made and a young man by the name of Ryan Aldridge was charged with my husband's murder.

For ten years I have shared the story of Bob's murder and its aftermath in the hope of preventing similar senseless tragedies. I talk to school children about bullying and codes of silence. I speak to parents about the social responsibility issues surrounding large gatherings of youth, alcohol and other drug use. I speak to educators about the transformational power of restorative practice. I speak to victims about moving through trauma toward healing.

The sharing generates deep conversation, and I am asked the same questions by children and adults alike. The best I can do is to explain what has been true for me, the choices I made from my gut and my heart, and how the story continues to play out. Creating a safe space through storytelling has encouraged others, many others, to share their own stories of harm and healing in return. While connecting carefully around the unique aspects of our experiences, commonalities invariably emerge, and I am left asking for a more scientific explanation for how harm and our responses to it impact us. Affect script psychology (ASP) provides just that, giving me a 360-degree understanding of why the path we chose took us where we needed to go.

Managing in the Aftermath

The starkest recollection I have of the early hours following Bob's death were the absolute clarity and immediacy of my reactions. Standing in the emergency room watching the medical staff desperately trying to resuscitate him, I was firmly focused on figuring out what I needed to do to get past the traumatic scene which unfolded before me and maintain a sense of control. It was what my esteemed friend Vernon Kelly describes in Chapter 1 as the 'too big, too loud and too fast' stimulus of the chaos in the emergency room triggering my fear-terror affect. I do not recall having to deliberately place or hold myself in that mindset; it felt primal and automatic. Nor did I feel confused or overwhelmed; the 'simplification' Kelly refers to caused me to stay dialed into the negative affect. The 'feeling' part emerged later.

I recall a strange, out-of-body feeling of calm and sense of purpose as I was told Bob was dead. With little awareness of what was going on around me, I zeroed in on exactly what I needed to think about in order to move forward. A mother's powerful interest in her children's wellbeing and possible reactions to the tragedy gave me a singular, clear focus at that moment. I had to go home and be with them.

The plainest of language was required to explain to my son and daughter that their father was dead. Their reactions gutted me. One wanted breakfast. The other cried when I poured milk in their bowl and admonished me for not remembering they preferred their cereal dry. Why were there so many adults in the house? Why was the phone ringing incessantly and where was Daddy again?

A close and loving family life was central to all our young children knew about the world. In the early days following Bob's death, much stood in the way of their interest and enjoyment. Distress, anger, and shame affects were triggered for me and for both of them, and have continued to emerge intermittently and uniquely over the last 15 years as the aftershocks of the trauma are felt.

We all received counseling in the weeks that followed. Utilizing eye movement desensitization and reprocessing therapy (EMDR), the clinical psychologist sought to reduce the impact of the trauma and develop adaptive coping mechanisms. (I have since learned that the mechanism by which EMDR provides relief involves the continual triggering of the positive affect of interest by use of a stimulus – touch, light or sound – that alternates to engage the right then left side of the brain. This allows the traumatized person to contact their negative emotions that might otherwise be suppressed, without becoming overwhelmed.)

The day after Bob was killed, I found myself standing on my doorstep dealing with the media. The first reporter to arrive asked me what I wanted to see 'happen' to the person who killed my husband. At that moment, I realized what was so clear in my head and heart was not going to translate into the hatred and vengeance the public was hoping for. I felt sick. I wanted to know that whoever killed Bob was going to be OK. I wanted to understand how my community had failed him or her, enabling such violence to be unleashed. I felt responsible. I cared deeply that the family on the other end of this senseless tragedy was going to be taken care of. It was not what anyone expected to hear on the six o'clock news.

The reality was straightforward to me. My children had lost their father, and I did not want them to lose me in the process. If I reacted the way society seemed to want, what kind of parent was I going to be? The spilling over of our story into the public domain and the resulting potential for something awful to be made even worse galvanized me. I resolved to hold tight to my beliefs and refused to settle for simply being a victim. My Central Blueprint led me to consciously look for a gift amidst the devastation of Bob's death. I instinctively felt if I gave in to the hate, rage, and vengeance of *attack other*, it could dominate my life, as it did to my community.

The murder hung like a dark cloud over the small town we lived in. As time wore on and the police investigation went undercover, the reaction from the public was increasingly negative. The lack of answers and suspicions regarding suspects and witnesses polarized the community. The media persisted to portray the local youth as dangerous, impacting tourism and real estate sales. Some friends, especially those who had been with us the night Bob was killed *withdrew*; several suffered depression. Others *avoided* the situation, masking their feelings of pain with substance use.

I became the target of considerable judgement for choices I made after the murder. There was nothing I could do about what had happened to Bob, so I turned my energy to creating as much stability and normalcy for my children as possible. I hired someone to replace me in my job and helped get them trained to look after my clients. I listed our house and began the process of moving us back to my home town. Keeping my interest focused on moving forward restored my sense of control. My decisions became the subject of public scrutiny, and I can only assume people responded from a place of *fear* in the aftermath of the trauma. It amazed me how quickly someone would say, 'If I were in your shoes...' You just cannot know what it really feels like until you get there, and there is definitely no instruction book.

Now, having the benefit of understanding something about the biology of emotion, I feel more empathy for those around me who lived through Bob's murder. They were caught up in the shame generated by the fear and helplessness of not knowing who amongst them had committed the act. Each dealt with the shame by resorting to their usual defense – some silently withdrew, some raged and attacked, some rationalized and avoided, and some even blamed themselves with *attack self*.

I had never knowingly met a murderer, and struggled to conjure up an image of a person capable of killing someone. During the five years of silence, the idea of the person responsible for Bob's death remained abstract. The face I clearly imagined, however, was that of their mother. Somewhere in my community was a woman tossing and turning in her bed because something had happened to her child. Perhaps she had no idea what that something was, but surely her son or daughter's behavior had not been the same since the night of the murder. Was she frightened or distressed like I was? Could we be suffering a kind of parallel experience? I found myself wanting to comfort her and imagined her reciprocating.

A New Life

We built a new life for ourselves after leaving the community. I worked hard on keeping my heart open to nurture our children and grew accustomed to letting the grief wash over me in waves. I was determined to not find myself in the same place my mother had many years before when my father was diagnosed with cancer. Her coping strategy for the fear and anger triggered by his illness and eventual death was alcohol. The ripple effect of that choice reverberated dangerously through my family.

I came to believe that the grief was never going to completely disappear. It gradually found its way into a place close to my heart where most days it was manageable. On the days it overwhelmed me, I learned to be gentle with myself. I would succumb to the feelings, trusting they would move through me and not get stuck. I also learned that it was possible to fall in love despite the grief and began a relationship with Michael, my lawyer, in the weeks and months after Bob's death. For many months I had been consumed by managing the emotions associated with the negative affects of fear, anger, and shame. Michael's presence created an environment of *excitement* and *joy*; it was an easy decision to accept his proposal and we were married.

Our children were eager to recreate a two-parent family and they accepted Michael easily. They soon referred to him as 'Dadoo'; when I questioned the nickname, our daughter explained it was French for 'Dad number two'. Kindergarten started shortly after we moved. The sense of community, routine, safety, and belonging contributed to an abundance of positive affect, and the formation of strong attachment 'scripts'.

We all experienced different triggers for grief, and at different times. While I had become adept at managing my own process, I found it more challenging supporting the children as their sadness in turn triggered feelings of anger for me. These situations made me appreciate having a support system and community that were not a part of Bob's death.

The years of silence were filled with a myriad of emotions woven through the new life we were working hard to create for ourselves. The children's understanding of the trauma grew as they matured; their questions became the subject of many dinner-time conversations. We talked about what it means to feel safe, accountability, punishment, and feeling labeled as victims. The relentless silence and burden of not knowing what happened to Bob triggered the affect of anguish for all of us. Both children expressed a need for the truth to be uncovered and also to be assured that the person who had killed their father was going to be all right. They had an innate sense of caring and were frightened by the notion that the punishment that may eventually be handed down may do more harm than good. Their insight intrigued me, and I was motivated to learn as much as I could about the other end of the justice system, a part I had no experience with.

Five years after Bob's murder the police concluded their undercover investigation and asked the Crown to lay charges against a young man, Ryan Aldridge. An officer called to inform me and to give me a few days to prepare for what was to come. I felt so sad for all the people attached to this story, many of whom I did not even know.

Overwhelmed by a need to participate in whatever justice was going to look like, I asked the police if I could be there at the time of the arrest. They were stunned by my request. Why would I want to meet the man who killed my husband? I should let the 'system' do its job.

While I respected the justice system, I explained a need to look into Ryan's eyes, to see him as a person. I wanted to be able to ask the difficult questions about what had been going on in his world that enabled him to take someone's life. I needed him to know how devastated we were. I also had to know he was going to be OK. I understood enough about the legal system to know that what lay ahead was a process laden with procedural formality. The focus would be complex interpretation of the criminal code rather than answers to my children's questions about what happened to their father. It was my job to advocate for my children, so who better than me to ask those questions?

While arranging a meeting between a suspect and family member of a homicide victim is generally beyond the duties of police detectives, it had the potential to build a stronger case if a confession was a part of the outcome of such a meeting. Initially, a video was made of me having the conversation I felt the need to have with Ryan. I told him about Bob, wanting him to know about the person he had killed. I told him how hard we had worked as a family to counter our distress, fears and anger. Now it was time for Ryan to do the work and address the affects he was surely experiencing in the aftermath of his actions.

After the video was shown to Ryan, he broke down. The images of the family Bob left behind prompted him to reiterate the confession made during the undercover investigation. Ryan asked to see his mother. Then he asked to see me. The police sent for me, and 16 hours after his arrest we met face to face. I think part of me expected some kind of monster to walk into the room in which I waited – not a young man who could have been my nephew, my younger brother, a neighbor. Overwhelmed by the enormity of the arrest and facing me, Ryan slumped over in his chair sobbing. It was all I could do not to move towards him and give him a hug; he looked like he needed that more than anything at that moment. Before me was the son of the woman I had envisioned for the last five years. I hated what he had done, but I could also feel the ripple effects of the devastation his actions had in every direction. Little beyond a further confession came out of that meeting. I implored Ryan to plead guilty so our families could avoid sitting through a trial. He agreed. Though I had never heard the words *restorative* and *justice* in the same sentence, this had been exactly that.

A Restorative Encounter

Not knowing what would happen behind bars to support Ryan's rehabilitation, I approached David Gustafson and Sandi Bergen at Community Justice Initiatives in Vancouver about the prospect of a properly facilitated restorative process. I felt the initial meeting could be the start of a much deeper conversation, and, if Ryan was willing, we would require help to do that safely. A year into his sentence we met again, spending a full day together. There were many tears shed, many long silences, but ultimately an opportunity to find some humanity around a situation that had been anything but.

During our first meeting, Ryan told me he acted out of anger the night he killed Bob. When we met again with an opportunity to connect more fully, I witnessed Ryan's shame. He described a childhood characterized by being teased and bullied, eventually becoming a bully himself. His parent's divorce left him angry and feeling unsure of where he belonged. The loss of a close friend in a drink-driving crash and not understanding how to grieve in a healthy way confused him. He experienced virtually all of the shame moments described in Chapter 1, and his early behavior belonged in the *avoidance* and *attack other* scripts of the Compass of Shame. The stuffing down of the feelings Ryan had about his experiences, his bullying behavior, and his choice to not cultivate supportive relationships contributed to these scripts. Later, following Ryan's brutal act of violence that took Bob's life and the silence that ensued, he moved towards *withdrawal*, *avoidance* and the *attack self* poles of the Compass of Shame. He pulled away from his family and friends, struggled with depression, substance abuse, and seriously contemplated suicide.

When politicians speak of 'getting tough on crime', such a transformational and healing encounter is not what they are talking about. Building bigger prisons to be filled with an increasing population of offenders for longer sentences is a prescription meant to make communities feel safe. It is a political strategy that focuses on the breaking of laws and punishment but does little to address the repair of the relationships that are damaged when harm takes place. Our meeting achieved this. Together we did the tough work. Without that opportunity to connect around our brokenness, to help each other along the healing journey, Ryan is sure he would have slipped into the dysfunctional sub-culture of the prison, succumbing to drug use and likely reoffending. I worry the societal pressure to have dealt with Bob's murder with hatred and vengeance would have compromised my ability to parent well and have a life of purpose. Ten years after the fact, I can look back and say confidently our choice to work together toward healing changed the trajectory for both of us. For that I am grateful.

Forgiveness

Invariably, the conversation turns to what I have come to refer to as the F-word: forgiveness. It is imperative to point out that restorative practice and forgiveness are mutually exclusive concepts and there must never be an expectation that one suggests the other. Some may suggest that even discussing forgiveness in the context of restorative practice is dangerous. I believe that it is helpful to develop some literacy and understanding around the concept of forgiveness so that practitioners are able to help those they work with through any thoughts or concerns they may have around the issue.

Bob's murder devastated me, but I was frightened more by what I saw in broader terms globally with respect to horribly bad decisions erupting from alcohol- and drug-fueled gatherings than the specifics of this senseless crime. As humans, we are capable of unspeakable harm. While I had not been exposed to the violence that some of the youth in my community seemed to be engaged in, my own generation made its share of poor choices. It seemed a more healing path to get busy and involve myself in being a part of the clean-up, instead of compounding the situation by disengaging through my own shame. We had lost Bob; nothing would bring him back. I hated what Ryan did, but I could not hate the person. I wanted Ryan to create something good with his life. Offering my forgiveness was my way of trusting him to do just that. Who better than me to ask him to do something of value with his life?

I am often asked the question 'How could you?' It is assumed I engaged in a deliberate, higher-order process to get me to a place of forgiveness. My response may disappoint those looking for directions for some kind of spiritual revelation. It simply did not *feel* that way for me. It was organic, dynamic, and practical. It is what I would hope someone would do for my children, or for me. Forgiveness was my way of giving up hope of a better past and giving me permission to create a hopeful future. People wonder if it would have been as straightforward if Ryan had not been remorseful. I'm not sure. But I do know that forgiveness was for me before it was for anyone else.

No expectations were placed on those close to me to support my decision to forgive. I had experienced enough judgement to know I had no right to expect others to feel the same way. My choice to forgive ended some friendships. Harm is a messy business, and there is no way to tie it all up with a bow. For my closest circle, though – Michael and our children – my forgiveness of Ryan freed me to give them the best of me as a wife and mother.

Forgiveness is not a 'one-off' offering. It is a dynamic process I find necessary to revisit occasionally. Just as grief endures, my willingness to embrace forgiveness gets tested. When our children turned 16, 11 years after Bob's murder, my husband Michael legally adopted them. We wanted to wait until they were old enough to have a part in the decision and the ability to understand what it meant. They signed the papers on their birthday. Michael wrote them each a deeply touching letter describing the passage of time and what it meant to him to parent them.

Bob had given us matching diving watches on our first wedding anniversary and I had held on to them to pass along for this special birthday. Later that day, while I was volunteering in the school cafeteria, our son approached me at the counter. He was looking down at his new watch and quietly asked me if Bob had been wearing it when he was killed. He had. I had never considered that fact and immediately offered to take it from my son if that reality was too painful. He straightened up, trying hard not to react in front of his classmates, and whispered it was OK and walked away from me. I hated what Ryan had done to my child. At that moment, I had to think really hard about the choice to forgive and to remind myself who I wanted to be in all this. Those setbacks happen. They happen when we are busy getting on with life and they are painful. It is just the way it is.

Conclusion: A Sea of Hope

When I think of the breadth of restorative practice I have had the privilege to learn about since beginning this work, I cannot help but think how my story may have changed if some of those supports had been available in my community. What if teachers in Ryan's elementary school had been trained to use restorative opportunities to deal with bullying in the classroom? What if his parents had engaged in family counseling to cope with the breakdown of the marriage? How would Ryan's experience with the police have unfolded had he been diverted into a restorative justice process when he first started causing harm?

I believe the future of restorative practice lies in our educational systems. If we raise children who learn to expect a restorative opportunity to be made available to deal with harm, we will in turn create a generation of young adults who will instinctively build restorative structures within their families, communities, schools, workplaces, and governments. Those structures can rest solidly on the biological foundation formed by ASP.

CHAPTER 6

A Necessary Discovery

Why the Theory is Important

Matthew Casey, William Curry, Anne Burton and Katherine Gribben

Introduction

In Chapter 1, Kelly suggests that restorative interventions work 'because human beings care' and that caring is innate to being human; we agree. In fact, around the world there are any number of marvellous restorative initiatives, but we must face the fact that in some places they just don't appear to make much difference or work any better than other approaches.

For example, an Australian study conducted by Smith and Weatherburn for the New South Wales Bureau of Crime Statistics and Research reported there were 'no significant differences found between conference and court participants in the proportion of re-offending, the seriousness of their re-offending, the time to the first proven re-offence or the number of proven re-offences' (2012, p.1).

What's going on there? Why do some initiatives in restorative practice start well but over time seem to lose traction? Why do people sometimes say, 'Well, it was good but we just didn't have the time.' Or 'Yes, it started well, but then the kids got to know the answers to the restorative questions, and just started to say the things they thought we wanted to hear.' Or why, for example, are we told that restorative practice should not be applied to domestic violence, when in fact our experience is quite the opposite? This chapter explores that conundrum.

Too often, restorative practice is both described and perceived as a process used when things go wrong. Let's look at a current definition with the understanding that in the literature there is quite a range of descriptions. In the main, they refer to a 'process'. For example, we could draw from Marshall's description of restorative justice as 'a process whereby all the parties with a stake in a particular offence come together to resolve collectively how to deal with the aftermath of an offence and its implications for the future' (1999, p.5).

While Braithwaite (2004a, p.28) describes restorative justice as:

> A process where all stakeholders affected by an injustice have an opportunity to discuss how they have been affected by the injustice and to decide what should be done to repair the harm. With crime, restorative justice is about the idea that because crime hurts, justice should heal. It follows that conversations with those who have been hurt and with those who have afflicted the harm must be central to the process.

There are other definitions that explore restorative practice relational aspects, but again many, if not most, are implicit about its theoretical underpinnings. We argue that for restorative practice to evolve and move beyond a niche within generally retributive or oppositional systems it needs to be described in explicit terms.

In some ways the movement is in the early days. As Braithwaite (2004b, p.56) has observed, 'the literature on restorative practice is immature…short on theoretical sophistication, on rigorous or nuanced empirical research'. The result is, however, that both in practice and perception restorative practice is limited in application, in acceptance and in resilience. We argue that it will benefit from:

- a clear definition

- an explicit understanding of why it works, and

- a discourse linking theory to practice.

To begin that conversation it might be useful to describe our journey so far.

Our Story

In 2000, our small group in Goulburn, New South Wales, Australia, was given a grant to develop safety plans for women who were victims of domestic violence. These plans were to be based around restorative interventions involving the victim, the perpetrators and extended families. We saw these interventions as a useful way to hold perpetrators accountable and to address the resulting harm by giving victims and others affected a voice to repair and strengthen relationships, which we thought was pretty standard stuff.

Initially, we thought that we would run a lot of conferences, but we discovered that while the victims and the perpetrators were at times quite keen to be involved, often their extended families lived in other towns and it simply was not possible to get these stakeholders together. We questioned the nature of our interventions if we could not engage stakeholders, and, if we could not, whether our proposed interventions would meet the definitions of restorative justice attributed to Marshall and Braithwaite in the introduction to this chapter. We were also informed by the domestic violence literature that the nature of domestic violence was such that a restorative conference or some version of it was never suitable as the subject matter of such an intervention.

We were stuck, because we knew conferences worked and strongly suspected restorative interventions would work equally well to address domestic violence, but funding and community agencies were at best unsupportive, if not oppositional, to the proposition of using restorative interventions for domestic violence. Importantly, we understood that the issues around domestic abuse and violence were complex and required a nuanced response, and, upon reflection, we too considered that a single restorative conference might be a blunt and limited approach.

Given conferences were often not practical or possible, we pondered how best to provide the benefits of restorative interventions to our clients. We had to work out at a theoretical level what actually happened in a conference, and then explicitly apply the theory so we could replicate these benefits in other settings.

Our clients presented for a range of reasons, but we had noticed some important markers. Surprisingly, many, if not most, of the women who presented around domestic abuse did not necessarily want to end the relationship. What they really wanted was the abuse to end and the relationship to improve.

As discussed above, the complexity of domestic violence discouraged us from holding a single restorative conference. We knew that domestic abusive behaviour impacted not just on the two primary players but the extended family as well, and that an improved outcome would only be possible if we were able to engage everyone affected. This prompted us to engage not just the intimate partners but, whenever possible, family members including children and extended family, and to initially engage them individually and let them tell their story and explore how the domestic abuse had impacted them. We intuitively knew that the principles of restorative interventions would result in improved outcomes and this prompted further research.

It also became apparent across our entire client base that invariably, regardless of their original presenting issues, our clients' important relationships were becoming tenuous, and we could see the benefit of paying attention to engaging the whole family whenever possible to strengthen these relationships.

This seemed to fit with some questions Terry O'Connell[1] often asked: 'When are you likely to feel at your best, emotionally and psychologically? What are the conditions needed for that to happen?' His answer: 'We are at our best when we are in wholesome relationships.' It is our experience that the obverse is also the case: when we are struggling, so are our relationships.

Early on, we had taken notice of O'Connell's advice that the best way to prepare conference participants was to engage them using the conference script. We had been doing this even though we weren't planning to run a conference, and had discovered, particularly in family settings, that the more engagement we did, the less a formal conference was needed. What was going on there?

In simple terms, we were asking some casual but purposeful questions, and clients started to feel more comfortable, and their relationships and general living situations were improving. It sounds a bit simplistic, and at some levels it is, but let's explore it a little more.

---

1   Personal conversations with Terry O'Connell, 1998 to 2003. Terry O'Connell is the director of Real Justice, the Australian affiliate of the International Institute of Restorative Practices. He and Matt Casey continue their collaboration that began in their days as police officers in New South Wales during the 1980s. In 2000, Matt Casey was contracted by Goulburn Family Support Service (GFSS) to work with a government-funded project to develop safety plans for those affected by domestic abuse. From 2001 to 2004, Matt was employed by Real Justice, which funded his early work with GFSS.

We were asking the restorative conference questions, and stakeholders were sharing the negatives about their relationships and rethinking plans and strategies to improve and share more positive experiences and emotions. Sometimes the results were stunning.

CASE STUDY: THE SECRET REVEALED

Bill and Anne sat down with a couple in their late 60s one day. They thought the conversation was to be about supporting the couple through the distress caused by the husband's decline through a chronic, debilitating and ultimately terminal illness. Such was the level of empathy established in simply sharing their story that, in this first meeting, the woman disclosed that her earliest memory was of horrific sexual abuse inflicted by her parents when she was a small girl.

It turned out this was the first time she had ever shared the story with anyone.

The following week when they returned the husband said, 'I don't know what you have done, Bill and Anne, but she has been floating on air all week. In all the time we have been married I have never seen her as happy.'

Explicit Framework

After working initially with O'Connell, we realized that our work was based around a number of key foundations.

Restorative Questions

What is it about asking these questions that was making a difference? For those who had caused harm:

- What happened?

- What were you thinking at the time?

- What have you thought about since?

- Who has been affected by what you did?

- In what way?

- What do you think you need to do to make things right?

For those who had been harmed:

- What did you think when you realized what had happened?

- What impact has this incident had on you and others?

- What has been the hardest thing for you?

- What do you think needs to happen to make things right?

These questions:

- Are non-accusatory but demand an answer.

- Take people from the past, into the present and on to the future.

- Engage people at a cognitive level but also facilitate emotional sharing and awareness regarding both the individual's response and that of others.

  ○ Have you ever noticed that when a person is asked a thinking question, they will often provide a feeling response? For instance, 'What did you think when it happened?' Answer: 'I was shocked; upset; terrified; angry; all of the above.'

  ○ Have you also noticed the understanding that stems from another's disclosure?

Importantly, this emotional engagement provided a somewhat cathartic experience that helped to quickly build a level of trust and empathy, which of itself exerted pressure on people to be accountable for their own behaviour.

We discovered that the restorative conference questions elicited emotional responses and this was different from our previous interventions where emotions were avoided and quickly stifled when they arose.

As one woman said, 'You are the first person that has asked me the right questions.'

CASE STUDY: AN ANGRY MAN AND HIS SON

Another time, Matt was asked by a school to approach a father whose boy had just been suspended for the third time during that school term. 'When you meet him you won't like him,' he was told. 'And when you meet him you will understand why his son's behaviour is so bad.'

Matt arranged the meeting with the boy and his father, a well-built and heavily tattooed man. As soon as Matt arrived, the man started speaking loudly, aggressively and disparagingly about the school and its teachers. Matt listened and when the tirade abated, he asked, 'What did you think when I had to become involved?' Again, the man expressed his rage: the school was always picking on his son; he had been unemployed for months, had just gained employment and was now having to take time off and was worried he might be fired. Matt asked, 'How has this impacted on you and the rest of the family?' The man described how his wife was worried all the time and how this was impacting on the other children. Then Matt asked, 'What is the hardest thing?' The man stopped, was silent for an instant and then broke down in tears. 'He's turning out just like me,' he sobbed, 'and I didn't want that to happen.'

Without going further into a long and difficult case, it is sufficient perhaps to note that the boy was absolutely stunned at his father's emotion and his obvious love. Whilst the outcome, for a range of reasons, was not ideal, the man said later that this was the first time he felt like somebody cared about what it was like for him and his family.

Fair Process

Importantly, the questions engage people in a process that is fair and for everyone, and that is of immense importance. There is at times a misconception that restorative practice is about achieving a state of happiness for all concerned, and forgiveness will naturally flow. Our experience is that this is not the case. In fact, often when restorative practice outcomes are reached and decisions are made that are unfavourable for one or more parties, the evidence is that people, in the main, accept these outcomes. Why? Because the process has been fair.

Kim and Mauborgne (2003) argue that most people will accept an unfavourable outcome as long as the process that reached that conclusion is fair. They further describe the components of fair process as:

- Engagement: giving people the opportunity to tell their story.

- Explanation: explaining what is happening and why.

- Expectation clarity: a clear understanding of the way things will be dealt with as a result of this process and into the future.

This is precisely what restorative practice seeks. The process is often neither easy nor comfortable, and neither should it be.

John Braithwaite (1989) suggests that, of itself, confronting another induces shame; further, that doing so within a continuum of respect and support enables a process of reintegration to occur.

Holding another accountable is difficult and confronting; to do so is to apply pressure around some behaviour or omission that will inevitably interrupt positive affect and induce shame affect. When this is done within a context where the person is clearly valued, support is provided to enable the affect of shame to be effectively tolerated and its intensity reduced. This then provides a pathway for the resumption of the positive affects. In other words, Braithwaite suggests that we need to provide an equal measure of both pressure and support. In our practice, this means listening to each person's story and explicitly sharing the theory of affects (support), whereby shame affect is understood and can be better managed when inappropriate behaviour is challenged (pressure).

Social Discipline Window

Wachtel (1999) has addressed pressure and support in the construction of a Social Discipline Window, which was built from Baumrind's (1989) identification of parenting styles. This suggests that we most help when we work WITH people rather than doing things TO them or FOR them.

Think for a minute about the best school teacher you ever had. What was it about them that enabled you to feel this way? When we ask this question, invariably people talk about someone who was caring, thoughtful, interested in them, used humour, was real, had high expectations but provided a high level of support, nurture and encouragement. It was also someone who set the rules but treated each transgression on its merits, and who was confident enough to apologize if they got it wrong. Most importantly, it was someone who was both firm and fair. People felt this was the environment where they learned best.

Figure 6.1 is our adaptation of Wachtel's (1999) Social Discipline Window. Essentially, the practice of 'the best school teacher ever' is captured in the WITH frame of this window. It supports the notion that people are most helped when they are both supported and pressured.

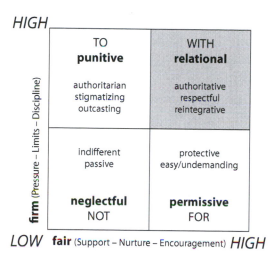

Figure 6.1 The Social Discipline Window
(adapted from Wachtel 1999)

One of the problems we identified in regard to current approaches to domestic abuse is that too often it applies pressure without much support to offenders, and support without any pressure to victims. As a result, neither is really helped, and the problem continues either in this or the next relationship.

We found it useful, particularly when working with victims, to ask two further questions suggested by O'Connell which assist them to take responsibility for their future direction in life:

- What would a difference look like?

- What can you do that will make a difference?

We have found that people who have been victimized often find it difficult to move on. When we think of victims, we think of somebody who needs our help because they were, for example, in a car crash or experienced some other calamity. Victims are often so overwhelmed by their victimhood that it becomes the norm. It requires little effort on their part because other people have either caused the problem or are responsible to make things right. Victimhood results in feelings of hopelessness for the future.

The two questions above gently provide some pressure for people to stop viewing themselves as helpless victims and to begin to take responsibility for their own future. At the same time, these questions provide support by suggesting a belief that they have the capacity to move beyond their current situation and make a difference for themselves. The questions are quite deliberately confronting but within a continuum of respect and support.

So we knew our practice worked, we could explain some of the theoretical underpinnings, and it was clear that the restorative questions engaged people effectively. We were providing fair process and this assisted us to work WITH people rather than doing things TO them or FOR them.

Affect Script Psychology

We now needed to explore why the restorative framework worked.

O'Connell (1998) describes how, during the Wagga Wagga juvenile offenders pilot, David Moore identified affect theory as an explanation for the emotionality contained within the conferencing process, so we began to pay attention to ASP pioneered by Silvan S. Tomkins. In Chapter 1, Vernon Kelly explains ASP – Tomkins's biologically based theory of cognition, emotion and personality.

Tomkins, a philosopher and professor of psychology, explained (1981, p.31):

As a former philosopher and former experimental psychophysicist, I was convinced that personality theory needed to be grounded in a more general theory of the human being (which experimental psychology had addressed, but failed to complete) as well as embedded in a broader sociocultural theory. From the outset, I have supposed the person to be a bio-psycho-social entity at the intersect of both more complex higher social systems and lower biological systems.

His thesis views both cognition and emotion as emanating from the interaction with our inner and outer worlds through what he described as affects. He asserts (1962, pp.169–170):

> The human being is equipped with innate affective responses which bias him to want to remain alive and to resist death, to want to experience novelty and to resist boredom, to want to communicate, to be close to and in contact with others of his species, to communicate, to experience sexual excitement and to resist the experience of head and face lowered in shame.

This introduction to Tomkins fuelled our *interest* affect. It is perhaps useful to give you an idea of how we approached this theory. At the time we had, at best, limited exposure to ASP. As has been said, we were just a 'scruffy-looking group of nonprofessionals', but we saw something in Tomkins's theory which we thought was useful.

Importantly, we reasoned that while all sorts of things might be happening, at its most basic, a restorative conference or any restorative interaction was an opportunity, as per Tomkins's Blueprint (1962, p.329), to mutualize affect and, in doing so, maximize positive affect and minimize negative. We thought this might be the key to being able to replicate the benefits of a conference in another setting.

Acting on this, we started to be very explicit in terms of applying all of the above theory to our practice, and we started to notice some significant benefits for our clients.

Sharing Affect Theory with Our Clients

One of the people who contributed to our journey was John Donald (2004) who assisted in connecting the research, theory and practice. It was John who suggested the benefit of explicitly sharing the theory with our clients, and so we looked for a simple description of affect theory which our clients could absorb in a therapeutic setting and apply in their own lives. We started by simply telling people about Silvan Tomkins, briefly explaining his work and his theory. We tell it something like this:

Tomkins noticed that regardless of where we come from, what race or religion, we all tend to respond similarly. At a really basic level, if we are happy, we smile, and if we are sad, we frown or cry.

From this starting point, he suggests that each one of us is born with nine innate affects. An affect, he argues, is a physical change within our body, including our skin, our muscles and our nervous system, that turns on an emotion. Affects make us conscious that something has changed, and, in fact, we only become conscious that something around or pertaining to us has changed because an affect has occurred. We now know an affect is information about something to pay attention to.

Simply put, an affect is a physical change which produces a feeling within our body, and an emotion is a combination of these two things, along with every memory we have of these two particular things happening.

The really important thing to remember is that affects are physical and that the face is the window that lets us see the affect in others.

There are two positive affects:

- Enjoyment-joy: basically ranging from contentment when we are just comfortable right through to the joy when a baby is born and everything in between; we can see that affect on someone's face, the smile of joy, of recognition, of satisfaction.

- Interest-excitement: this is the affect which makes us pay attention to the world around us – look out the window to see the view, climb a hill to view a landscape, read a book, get attracted to someone, begin a relationship. It moves from mild interest where we might just notice something in passing right up to the wild excitement, for example, when our favourite sporting team wins. Without this affect there wouldn't be much to do – even the drives depend on interest to become urgent. The hunger drive, for example, would be reasonably weak were it not amplified by an interest in food. Again, we can see if someone is interested just by looking at their face.

One neutral affect:

- Surprise-startle: this is like a reset system to blank our mind momentarily and make us aware of a sudden change in our environment. It is really easy to see startle or surprise on another.

Six negative affects:

- Anger-rage

- Distress-anguish

- Fear-terror

- Dissmell: stops us getting something that smells rotten anywhere near our mouth. Involuntarily, our head goes back, our lips protrude and our nose crinkles.

- Disgust: expels anything we have put in our mouth that might have looked all right but tastes or feels awful. Think of how a baby responds the first time it is offered solid food. More importantly, as our species has evolved, disgust and dissmell also start to be about our relationships with others. Think about people who have been in a close relationship, married or close friends, and now they are apart. How do they refer to one another? Have you ever heard a person express disgust at the thought of being touched by a former partner or dismell at the reminder of the perfume or aftershave the other used? Matt once spoke to a little girl about another who had fallen out with the friendship group. 'Oh, we don't like her,' she said with her nose turned up in a sneer of dismell. So if these are the affects of divorce and separation, they are also the affects of racial intolerance. Have you noticed how racist language is almost always couched in terms of disgust or dismell?

- Shame-humiliation: this is the affect that occurs whenever anything partially interferes with our experience of the two positive affects.

Focus on Shame Affect

Think about the physical manifestation of the negative affects. We can tell if someone is angry, upset, disgusted or fearful just by looking at them. Think next about what physically happens when shame affect occurs. Remember, shame affect occurs whenever there is partial interruption to our experience of the positive affects – when we spill a drink, break a cup or embarrass ourselves in some way.

Our face goes red, our head drops, our shoulders slump, and not intentionally. These things happen automatically, don't they? The reason? Shame affect makes our muscles lose tone – hence the head drop and slump of the shoulders. Why does shame affect do this? Well, at one level the affect of shame is taking our attention away from whatever was holding our interest. It is important because it stops us continuing to be interested in impossible or fruitless activities. This is particularly important if our life might depend on conserving energy. Consider this story:

> One day Matt was out walking with his dear old dog, a fine animal descended from a long line of hunters, and he scared up a wallaby. Instantly, the dog experienced intense interest/excitement and started chasing as fast as he could run. The wallaby, of course, immediately experienced fear/terror and hopped away as fast as she could. Initially, the dog might have gained some ground, but quickly the wallaby bounded further away. This partial impediment to the dog's intense interest reduced his muscle tone and he could not run as fast, and as the wallaby got further away, the dog's head dropped, he lost interest, slowed to a walk and returned to exploring the undergrowth.

Shame affect interrupted his interest affect, and this physically impaired his capacity to continue and directly made him abandon the failed chase.

So we know what happens physically. Let's consider how we might respond to the emotion. Shame is always intensely personal; it points to something about us, our strength, dexterity, sexuality, appearance or intelligence in ways that make us uncomfortable.

> Let us picture a golfer swinging at a golf ball. The club makes contact with the ball, but instead of soaring majestically towards

the green, the ball skids off to the right under a tree 15 metres away. The affect shame/humiliation occurs, our golfer's head drops and shoulders slump, the memory of all the times that affect has occurred floods back and creates the emotion of shame.

What would be an appropriate response? Pretty obvious: walk to where the ball is, work out what went wrong with the previous shot, pay attention to the correct technique and hit the ball again. When our golfer does not respond appropriately, what might he do? Swear, curse, throw the club and generally get angry with himself, and often with anyone else who happens to be there. He might try to excuse his poor shot by blaming an external factor, the club, a distracting noise or movement or, in extreme cases, stop playing and walk off the course.

Compass of Shame

Nathanson (1992, p.312) argues that 'for most of us almost any affect feels better than shame' (and that includes our golfer). Hence, we need to develop a set of defensive strategies to convert it into something less toxic, and over our lives we develop a range of responses to suit various situations. When we seek remedial strategies for relief of shame, often our responses revolve around four points of what Nathanson describes as the Compass of Shame. That is: *attack self*, *attack other*, *avoidance* or *withdrawal*. At each point of the compass, we will engage in a range of behaviours linked by the need to escape the punishing emotion of shame. Figure 6.2 shows our adaptation[2] of Nathanson's Compass.

---

2 Early in our practice, the Compass of Shame was adjusted to call *attack other*, *attack others*. And it was moved around to display *attack others* at the top, *attack self* at the bottom and *withdrawal* and *avoidance* at the sides to reflect a kinaesthetic view of the behaviours displayed at each pole of the Compass – for example, *attack others* seen as behaviour over others, *withdraw* and *avoid* moving away, and *attack self* often a down response. This change resonated with our client families.

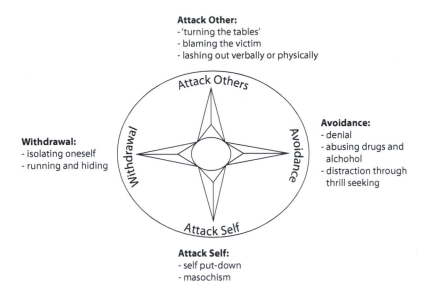

Attack Other:
- 'turning the tables'
- blaming the victim
- lashing out verbally or physically

Avoidance:
- denial
- abusing drugs and alchohol
- distraction through thrill seeking

Withdrawal:
- isolating oneself
- running and hiding

Attack Self:
- self put-down
- masochism

Figure 6.2 Goulburn adaptation of the Compass of Shame (adapted from Nathanson 1992)

Over time, we have also found it useful to describe at the *avoidance* pole: workaholic behaviour, problem gambling and sexual promiscuity; and at the *atack self* pole: self-loathing, self-blame and 'behaving so as to fulfil another's preconception'.

While we might be avoiding feeling bad, when we are 'in the Compass' are we addressing the issue at hand and making things better? The answer is, of course, no. In fact, in all probability we are making things worse.

Tomkins tells us that we have an innate need to feel good about ourselves, and the emotion of shame is the antithesis of feeling good. 'Entering the Compass' is really an efficient but ultimately counterproductive means of dealing with it.

Nathanson argues that when shame affect occurs, and we don't take time to reflect to make things better, we all go into the Compass. It is important to understand that this is a perfectly natural response. The emotion of shame makes us feel bad and we instantly move to one of the defensive strategies we have developed to convert it to something less toxic. At times, this happens so quickly we don't realize what has happened. Have a look at the behaviours and think about when you have seen others and even yourself engaging in such behaviour, to a greater or lesser extent.

What is that about? We argue that our capacity to appropriately manage shame and move out of the Compass is measured by how well we are doing within ourselves. In other words, it is connected to our level of self-worth and emotional security. If I am reasonably OK with my own self-worth and reasonably emotionally secure, I can usually manage shame quite well.

How Does Knowing Theory Help Us?

We have spent our lives developing responses to help us manage shame and, in most instances, this has been done without any explicit insight into what is going on. A lot of people just naturally do it well, most of us do it OK and some just struggle. Just like hitting or kicking a ball, some people are just naturally good at it and most of us can at least manage.

To use the sporting analogy, even really talented players need to understand the fundamentals of how to stand or run, the timing and fundamentals of the swing of the arms or legs. Good coaches help players break down every physical aspect of the game to its most basic movements. The player then has a quite explicit understanding of what is happening; every movement is practised, combinations are understood, sequenced and practised time and again so that the muscle memory is developed and the swing, shot or stroke can be replicated throughout the game. Importantly, when they are not hitting or kicking well, the individual and coach can work out what is going wrong, what the cause is, change the errant action and eradicate it from the player's game.

Armed with an understanding of the nine innate affects and the Compass of Shame, we can make sense and meaning of our own emotions and responses to the inevitable travails, tensions and conflicts of everyday life. Therefore, we started to provide all our clients with, amongst other things, a copy of the Compass. There are now plenty of homes with the Compass stuck up on the refrigerator door, and when things get tense at home, people stand in front of it, work out where they and others are on the Compass, and use the questions to enable everyone to move out of it.

Knowing about affects and the Compass also helps us separate the person from the behaviour. It is important to understand that it is always the behaviour that gets in the way in any relationship, not the person. The dignity and worth of a person is innate and unchanging. Behaviour and actions might be noble and skilful or inappropriate, outrageous, even appalling, but they can be understood with Tomkins's model and Nathanson's Compass of Shame. They can also be changed, modelled, reinforced and replicated to enable us to better respond to the inevitable tensions and conflicts of life and the human condition.

Shame affect points to something about us, how we look, our sexuality, strength, the things we do or how well we do them, but it does not impact on our innate worth as a person. Armed with this knowledge, we are better equipped to move on from the Compass. Consider our golfer again: the fact that he did not hit the ball might tell us many things about his level of skill and dexterity but is no reflection at all on his innate worth or dignity. If he is able to understand this concept, then making the next shot, depending on his level of skill, should not be too difficult. If, however, he remains in the Compass, making the next shot has an extra layer of complexity.

CASE STUDY: A BOY WITH NO WORDS

One time Anne and Matt were dealing with a very sad situation where a little boy had been excluded from school for throwing stones at another boy. He was already on an internal suspension for other behaviour when this happened. At the time, his parents were going through an acrimonious break-up. When the boy arrived with his sobbing mother, Matt initially tried to engage him but quickly realized that the little fellow did not have the words to describe his emotions.

Matt took out the St Luke's Innovative Resource Centre Bear Cards.[3] This is a set of 50 cards with pictures of bears displaying a range of emotions. Matt asked the boy when life had been good

---

3   The Bear Cards are from St Luke's Innovative Resources, which is the publishing arm of St Luke's Anglicare, a leading community service organization based in Bendigo, Australia. Innovative Resources published a recent version of St Luke's Strength Cards 'The Bears' in 2008. They are available as a set of 54 laminated, full-colour cards, 150 × 120mm, in a polypropylene box with a 41-page booklet of text by Russell Deal. For more information, write to St Luke's Innovative Resources, 137 McCrae Street, Bendigo 3550, Australia, or visit www.innovativeresources.org.

and he replied, 'When Mummy and Daddy were together.' Matt asked him if any of the bears showed what he felt like then, and the boy pulled out cards that he described as 'happy and funny'. Then he asked if there were any cards that showed what he felt like before he started throwing stones at the other boy. He pulled out cards he called 'mad' (*attack others*) and 'sad' (*attack self*) and then he produced a card with a bear slumped down and walking away (*withdrawal*). Matt asked what it was and the boy said, 'I don't know but I felt like that.' He then produced another bear standing straight with its head averted (*avoidance*) and said, 'I felt like this too.' Matt and Anne realized the boy had constructed the Compass of Shame.

Some time later they saw another boy who replicated the construction of the Compass of Shame by the first boy. Only this time, once he had pulled out the cards, Anne said, 'Is there a card that shows me how you felt before you felt these things?' and the little fellow quickly said, 'Yes this one, the crumpled one' (shame).

We have replicated this experience of children constructing the Compass of Shame many times and collected comments the children have made. We put their comments about the bears in the figure of the Compass as shown in Figure 6.3.[4]

Figure 6.3 The bears and the Compass of Shame

---

4 The Bear Cards in our Compass are from the edition available in 2001.

Tomkins's Blueprint

As described in Chapter 1, Tomkins suggested that all human behaviour is directed by four rules making up what he called the Central Blueprint:

1. maximize positive affect

2. minimize negative affect

3. minimize the inhibition of affect, and

4. maximize the power to maximize positive affect, minimize negative affect, and minimize the inhibition of affect.

Tomkins argued that anything that enables us to fulfil these rules is good for life. If you reflect on the restorative questions, you will notice they form a template for Tomkins's Blueprint. Notice how they encourage the sharing of negative affect through the acknowledgement of behaviour and its impact. Notice also how they encourage sharing positive affect, creating interest in how things can be made right, what an improved future might look like and how relationships might be forged, repaired and improved. The restorative questions and restorative process facilitate the expression of affects and give power to the sharing of affect.

Having knowledge and a working understanding of affects and the Compass of Shame has given us a framework to understand the fundamentals of our emotional behaviour. Just as a sportsperson needs to understand and practise the fundamentals to be able to regularly hit or kick well, the same applies to our emotional behaviour. Armed with this, we can understand why, for example, we feel the discomfort of shame, and then make a conscious and informed decision to move 'out of the Compass'.

Practice Framework

We had now established the early explicit framework for our practice:

- the restorative questions

- fair process

- the Social Discipline Window

- the theory of affects (ASP)

- the Compass of Shame

- Tomkins's Blueprint for life.

We discovered that once we started sharing our practice framework with our clients, even children and those with intellectual disabilities, they were more able to understand their own and others' behaviours and become more emotionally robust. They were able to respond more appropriately to life's challenges, repair and strengthen relationships, and generally manage a whole lot better.

The Importance of Relationships

It is our argument that the strength of familial and community relationships is the principal predictor of wholesome behaviour. For instance, why is it that most people do the right thing most of the time, and who or what are the influences?

Whenever we ask individuals or groups these questions, and even criminal offenders, the answers are along the lines of family, background, religion, upbringing – 'it makes sense', 'it feels right', 'you just wouldn't do it' or 'it is easier' – and, quite regularly, *punishment never gets a mention.*

When we follow this with the question 'If you did the wrong thing, who is the last person you would want to know?' the answer is both amazing but predictable. Almost invariably it is Mum, Dad and, after that, often Nana. One fellow we met in a traffic offender programme became distressed when he described the impact his conviction for drink-driving would have on his grandmother.

Nathanson (1992, p.251) suggests that 'Shame is the central social regulator which governs our interactions with others.' Shame is used in all societies, communities and families as a means of socializing children, new arrivals and inductees. Braithwaite (1989, p.72) says: 'In fact the family could not develop young consciences in the societal vacuum that would be left without societal practices of shaming.'

The distress our young man felt stemmed from the shame he experienced at the impact his behaviour would have on his grandmother, and his awareness of the tension it would inevitably cause in their relationship. In other words, it was about his conscience.

Let us now consider the importance of relationships by reviewing the following excerpt by Blakester (2006, p.8):

The importance of relationships is generally accepted as a key element in children and adult's level of resiliency when confronted with crises and/or life stresses. For example, a social worker in Sydney had worked with a particular family for over a decade. During this time, the son of the family had become a teenager. One day, the social worker was feeling very low, struggling to find the strength and courage to face another session with the son, knowing just what he had survived over more than 10 years. The following conversation took place:

> **Worker:** Can you tell me, how is it you have survived? What kept you going?

> **Boy:** Every day, when I used to get on the bus to go to school, the bus driver used to ask me: 'How's my little ray of sunshine today?' I knew then that I was someone; that I mattered.

Observations

At the same time the bus driver was fulfilling the required service of taking children from home to school and back again, the driver delivered a relationship (though probably never knowing the difference it made to the boy). The bus driver showed the boy he was valued and valuable. This was the real outcome.

The study from which this case study is drawn was conducted in the western suburbs of Sydney in neighborhoods with high levels of unemployment, social dislocation and crime. It also found that:

While children viewed relationships as the most important priority and goal and, while service providers recognized that relationships are the most important ingredient for wellbeing, they were arguably the most complex outcomes to demonstrate and measure... As a result, service providers' focus was primarily on the delivery of services and needs, which are significantly easier to measure. (Blakester 2006, p.7)

Reflect for a minute on any restorative interaction, or, in fact, any use of the restorative questions. Certainly they enable the disclosure of factual information, but at another level are they not in essence mechanisms to enable the sharing of affect and emotion? Now ask the question: 'Does this process or do these questions enable Tomkins's Central Blueprint for life and Kelly's Blueprint to build relationships?' – to:

- maximize positive affect

- minimize negative affect

- minimize the inhibition of affect, and

- maximize the power to maximize positive affect, minimize negative affect, and minimize the inhibition of affect.

Kelly's (2012) Blueprint for Healthy Relationships

1. Mutualize and maximize positive affect: talk about the good things and make them bigger (e.g. how much we care for one another).

2. Mutualize and minimize negative affect: talk about the bad things and make them smaller (e.g. how disappointed we were at what happened and its impact).

3. Mutualize and minimize the inhibition of affect: deliberately practice sharing things that make us happy, sad, uncomfortable upset, angry, etc. (talking about the thing not the person).

4. Mutualize and maximize the power to carry out 1, 2 and 3: learn about emotion, how to express it, learn how to listen, always focus on the behaviour not the person, understand the importance of sharing strong emotion.

Listen again to the children of western Sydney in Blakester's research who regard relationships as the most important priority and goal, and ask if contemporary service provision results in an explicit forging of strong and wholesome relationships. We suggest that an explicit practice framework enables people to regularly and deliberately do things that produce stronger relationships as an outcome.

A Final Word on Shame: 'A Necessary Discovery'

CASE STUDY: A MAN WITHOUT TOOLS

One day Bill was working with a dad of four children who presented with issues of domestic abuse and poor parenting skills. Working with this family, Bill could see that the man had trouble intuitively relating to others and understanding that others may have a valid perspective on any issue. As we do with all our clients, Bill had taken this man through the nine innate affects and Socratically introduced him to Nathanson's Compass of Shame. This had been followed by a reflection on his habitual behaviour. At the end of a session Bill asked, 'What can you take away from today's session?' The man, reflecting on the whole framework, said his highlights were the identification of his behaviour in the Compass of Shame and the Social Discipline Window that identified his parenting style. He could see that he had been parenting in the TO window, which was about applying pressure and not support. He was sure this knowledge would help him change the way he responded and improve his relationships with his family. He finished by commenting, 'This has been a necessary discovery'.

His partner, who was present through all of this, was quite overwhelmed with his response and his eagerness to put a new approach in place. We knew this man really loved his family; all he lacked was some explicit information on how best to put that love into practice.

Shame is essential in our community and in any restorative interaction. We scold people who have no shame about their behaviour, and Nathanson (1992, p.251) says that 'we cannot feel shame if there is nothing to lose'. We view shame as an essential ingredient for self-awareness and reparation.

Braithwaite (1989, p.72) says:

Shaming is more pregnant with symbolic content than punishment. Punishment is a denial of confidence in the morality of the offender by reducing norm compliance to a crude cost-benefit calculation; shaming can be a reaffirmation of the morality of the offender by expressing personal disappointment that the offender should do something so out of character.

Shaming, then, is both a mechanism for dealing with behaviour and also the gateway to reintegration and repair of tenuous relationships. We operate this mechanism by asking questions that enable people to safely express emotions, often strong ones. When we then explain the theory of affects and use Socratic methods to assist people to construct the Compass of Shame, they are able to understand that the problem is about behaviour and not about the person. People are then able to value themselves safe in the knowledge that behaviour can be challenged and changed without impacting on their own self-worth. This then becomes the gateway to moving from harmful to wholesome behaviours and relationships.

Explicit Affective Practice and the Tools of Life

In this chapter we have both described our journey since the turn of the century and discussed the basic tenets of the clinical counselling and family work practice we have developed. We acknowledge, as others have, that our practice also incorporates additional underpinning theoretical systems; however, the defining difference in our practice is that we have made ASP 'explicit' in terms of our continued learning and sharing of this knowledge as practitioners in peer support, and importantly, with our client families.

We have developed a passionate affiliation with the theory that has potential applications just about anywhere! Our continuing journey using Tomkins's affect lens has enabled us to incorporate ASP in very practical ways we never thought possible.

We have termed our practice 'Explicit Affective Practice' because of its explicit application of the basic tenets which we share with each of our clients. We have termed these practice tenets the *Tools of Life*.[5]

---

5   The *Tools of Life* is a term coined by Bill Curry who remarked that what we had constructed were really tools of life to assist people to live better lives through new understandings. We have found that with the *Tools of Life*, our client families are more able to identify their own and others' affects and behaviours, create a dialogue to repair the harm done to these relationships and develop more peaceful and calmer families.

- the restorative questions

- fair process

- the Social Discipline Window

- the nine innate affects

- the Compass of Shame

- Tomkins's Blueprint for life

- Kelly's Blueprint for relationships.

We have continued to remain active in restorative practice as practitioners and consultants in schools, the community and health sectors, churches, business and government.

Conclusion

We argue that restorative practice is inhibited by definitions that are focused on a process for managing in the aftermath of an 'offence' or 'injustice'. More importantly, the lack of an explicit connection between theory and practice often results in restorative programmes drifting away from an explicit focus on harm and the importance of relationships and community as a predictor of wholesome behaviour. Often, too little attention is paid to the need to hold people accountable in terms of how their behaviour has impacted not just on the victim but on family and significant others.

As a result, restorative practices can often become little more than an alternative means of providing a consequence or penalty, with programmes skewed towards short-term outputs such as predetermined outcome plans, rather than opportunities for long-term sustainable behavioural change. No small wonder, then, the New South Wales Bureau of Crime Statistics research discussed in our introduction indicates that there is often little difference between court and conference outcomes.

At the beginning of this chapter we suggested that, both in practice and perception, restorative practice is limited in application, in acceptance and in resilience, and we argued that it will benefit from:

- a clear definition

- an explicit understanding of why it works, and

- a discourse clearly linking theory to practice.

In this chapter we have attempted to present:

- a theoretical construct firmly based in sociological, community development and a biologically based theory of cognition, emotion and personality to explain why restorative practice works

- a description of our personal and professional journey where this discourse explicitly linked theory and practice.

Our journey has transported us from restorative justice/practices to providing a layperson's interpretation of Tomkins's ASP through our explicit practice framework. It is our observation that this has resulted in happier and increasingly calm and connected individuals and families. Through our story we hope to commence broader discussions and further evolution of restorative practice.

To conclude, we propose the following definition of restorative practice:

Explicitly addressing issues of human emotion, connection and relationships, restorative practice is an amalgam of specifically targeted activities, theoretical and practical constructs to support individual wellbeing and repair harm, through the development of nurturing, robust families and communities.

References

Baumrind, D. (1989) 'Teenagers reap broad benefits from "authoritative" parents.' Presentation of an ongoing study at the 1989 American Psychological Association Annual Meeting, New Orleans. As reported by B. Bower (1989) *Science News 136*, 8, 117–118.

Blakester, A. (2006) 'Practical child abuse and neglect prevention: A community responsibility and professional partnership.' *Child Abuse Prevention Newsletter 14*, 2, 2–10.

Braithwaite, J. (1989) *Crime, Shame and Reintegration*. Cambridge: Cambridge University Press.

Braithwaite, J. (2004a) 'Restorative justice and de-professionalization.' *The Good Society 13*, 1, 28–31.

Braithwaite, J. (2004b) *Restorative Justice: Theories and Worries*. Visiting Experts' Papers, 123rd International Senior Seminar, Resource Material Series No. 63, pp.47–56. Available at www.unafei.or.jp/english/pdf/PDF_rms/no63/ch05.pdf, accessed on 15 February 2013.

Donald, J. (2004) *A Policy Framework for a Knowledge Society: Families and Knowledge*. Victoria, Australia: Deakin University, School of Social and International Studies.

Kelly, V.C. (2012) *The Art of Intimacy and the Hidden Challenge of Shame*. Rockland, ME: Maine Authors Publishing.

Kim, W.C. and Mauborgne, R. (2003) 'Fair process: managing in the knowledge economy.' *Harvard Business Review*, January.

Marshall, T. (1999) *Restorative Justice: An Overview*. London: Home Office Research Development and Statistics Directorate. Available at www.restorativejustice.org/articlesdb/articles/83, accessed on 25 April 2013.

Nathanson, D.L. (1992) *Shame and Pride: Affect, Sex, and the Birth of the Self*. New York, NY: W.W. Norton.

O'Connell, T. (1998) *From Wagga Wagga to Minnesota*. Available at www.iirp.edu/article_detail.php?article_id=NDg5, accessed on 25 April 2013.

Smith, N. and Weatherburn, D. (2012) 'Youth Justice Conferences versus Children's Court: A comparison of re-offending.' NSW Bureau of Crime Statistics and Research. *Contemporary Issues in Crime and Justice 160*, 2.

Tomkins, S. (1962) *Affect Imagery Consciousness. Volume I: The Positive Affects*. New York, NY: Springer.

Tomkins, S. (1981) 'The quest for primary motives: Biography and autobiography of an idea.' *Journal of Personality and Social Psychology 41*, 2, 306–329. Reprinted in V.E. Demos (ed.) (1995) *Exploring Affect*. Cambridge: Cambridge University Press.

Wachtel, T. (1999) 'Restorative Justice in Everyday Life: Beyond the formal ritual.' Paper presented at the Reshaping Australian Institutions Conference: Restorative Justice and Civil Society, 16–18 February. Canberra: Australian National University. Available at www.iirp.edu/article_detail.php?article_id=NTAz, accessed on 25 April 2013.

Part 3

The Theory in Action in Organizational Settings

CHAPTER 7

Keep Calm and Carry On

From Fear to Fun over Two Years in a British Youth Arts Organization[1]

Siân Williams

Introduction

This chapter tells the story of change over two years in a British youth arts organization where I was employed as the person responsible for the pastoral care of its young people. The changes happened over time as a result of putting restorative practice (RP) at the heart of how staff worked with young people within the organization.

RP had a transformative effect on how staff and young people communicated and on how the whole organization 'felt' to its young people, staff and those coming into contact with it. Working restoratively provided a structure that held people accountable for the harm they caused, but at the same time kept them connected to the community of the arts organization. By using this approach, the amount of harm caused to others reduced over time. The organization became a friendlier and more trusting environment, where more artistic risks were taken and a lot more fun was had by both young people and staff alike.

In affect script psychology (ASP) terms, becoming restorative meant that the organization's relational scripts changed, shifting the focus over time from emotions and behaviours stimulated by negative affects to those stimulated by positive ones. Changing the scripts

---

1 This chapter is dedicated to the memory of Tine Dewilde, whose joy and excitement about life were inspirational.

also supported the development of the four Central Blueprint rules referred to by Vernon Kelly in Chapter 1:

- maximize positive affect

- minimize negative affect

- minimize the inhibition of affect, and

- maximize the power to minimize negative affect, maximize positive affect and minimize the inhibition of affect.

This chapter aims to explore some of the links between restorative practice in an informal educational setting and ASP by:

- summarizing the status quo at the beginning of my time with the organization

- outlining how we worked restoratively within the organization

- reflecting on the effects of our RP on the organization's collective scripts and emotions.

As with all change, this process was messy! I have written about the trends towards the positive in this chapter, but there were, of course, many irritations and mistakes made along the way.

Setting the Context
The Organization

To maintain the anonymity of those involved in this story, I have withheld the name of the organization. In brief, the organization selects more than 150 young people aged 13–19 from all over the UK, through a two-stage audition process, to take part in residential arts courses of two weeks during school holidays. Each of the three annual residentials ends with performances in well-known venues across the UK.

The mix of young people within the organization is unusual: roughly one-third from state schools, one-third from private schools (including some of the most expensive schools in the UK) and one-third from specialist, private, arts-focused boarding schools. This ratio in no way reflects a typical cross-section of UK society in which only between 6 and 7 per cent of young people are educated outside the state sector (Hensher 2012). The mix of young people also means that during residentials the organization works with and cares for more than 100 of them who go from school to the residential venue and then, after going home for a couple of nights post-performance, straight back to school.

The organization grows about 200 percent on courses, adding to its small core staff team a large group of freelancers comprised of professional tutors and a support team responsible for the care and wellbeing of the young people, as well as the logistics of eating, sleeping and moving them safely around the country. I led this latter team during my two years with the organization.

When I joined, the organization had been through three years of rapid change following a period of 60 or so years of total stability. The organization had been running along very traditional lines with a complex hierarchy that the new director had upset simply by being appointed. When I arrived, her vision for bringing the organization up to date was part-way through, and she was keen to start developing a more democratic community that empowered the young people and gave them more ownership of the organization.

My Background

I had spent ten years working in inner London secondary schools and another eight in an inner London local authority, where I specialized in supporting schools to develop RP. I rarely worked with children from families with much money, and many of my previous students had a fairly low level of emotional literacy. They found it hard to manage their feelings; this unpredictability led to frequent emotional outbursts and meant that boundaries needed to be very clear and regular reminders about expectations were needed.

The young people within the arts organization were very different from those I was used to. The majority of my new set of young people were super-bright, highly articulate, knew how to handle adults in authority and had a high level of emotional literacy. In theory, this should have made working with them easier, but from the very beginning I found it much more challenging. These young people were more skilled in covering up their real feelings. An external veneer of politeness often — at least to start with — masked the emotional issues normally found in a large group of young people.

In the Beginning: My First Residential

I came to the organization late in the academic year with about three weeks to go before the final residential. I had been made redundant four months previously, so was happy to be working. But I also came with a certain amount of apprehension — the feeling that most people out of work for a while get about whether they can actually converse sensibly with colleagues about anything that isn't applying for jobs, gardening or that evening's dinner. In short and in ASP terms, a fear/shame script, although my interest was high. In addition, I was nervous about meeting such a large group of young people, the likes of whom I had never worked with. I was also aware that I was walking into the job of someone who had been there on the previous residential a few months earlier. The young people did not know my predecessor was not coming back or why she had left, and they had no idea who I was.

On the plus side, several of the support team of ten I worked with were efficient, friendly, hard-working and experienced — including my deputy, who was invaluable and showed me the ropes with patience and humour.

On this first course, many young people treated me with suspicion. I found them all outwardly polite, but many of them were difficult to read and gave nothing away emotionally. I spent the course learning the routines of the job and names, observing how the young people interacted with each other and with the support team, and how the staff worked within this team.

Relationships

The young people's relationships were predominantly cliquey. Most hung around with their friends from boarding school or similar types of schools; there was one group of socially dominant young men who even had hoodies delivered to the residential with 'Alpha 1' to 'Alpha 8' printed on the back. Established staff reported a number of conversations with young people who felt inferior to others, saying they weren't good enough at what they were doing compared with other people. The group who regarded themselves as elite and wore the hoodies fed into these feelings of inferiority.

The cliquey and guarded young people's relationships seemed to exist on an inferiority–superiority axis that exemplified Kelly's (2012) triangle model of the co-occurrence of shame, jealousy and competitiveness, as represented in Figure 7.1.

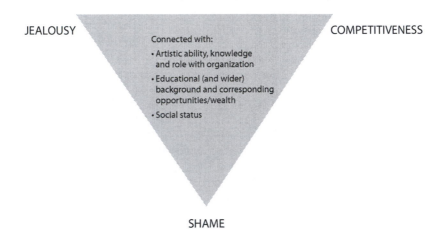

JEALOUSY   COMPETITIVENESS

Connected with:

- Artistic ability, knowledge and role with organization
- Educational (and wider) background and corresponding opportunities/wealth
- Social status

SHAME

Figure 7.1 Shame–jealousy–competitiveness in relationships

Between young people and staff, there was ultimate respect for the professional tutors but less for the support team and core staff. This disparity showed through punctuality, a difference in general attitude (that polite contempt that many teenagers do so well) and through language used in the post-course feedback forms. Some of the feelings hidden by young people on the course came out in force through these forms in full *attack other* Compass of Shame mode. In ASP terms, whilst there were notable expressions of interest and enjoyment in this feedback, a lot of negative affect was articulated, most notably anger, dissmell and disgust.

Within the support team were staff members working within all four corners of the Social Discipline Window discussed in Chapter 2. It is reproduced here, in Figure 7.2.

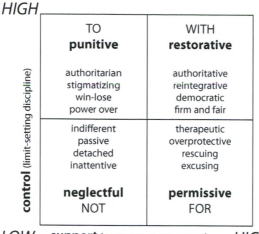

HIGH

	TO **punitive**	WITH **restorative**
	authoritarian stigmatizing win-lose power over	authoritative reintegrative democratic firm and fair
	indifferent passive detached inattentive	therapeutic overprotective rescuing excusing
	neglectful NOT	**permissive** FOR

control (limit-setting discipline)

LOW   **support** (encouragement, nuture)   HIGH

Figure 7.2 The Social Discipline Window
(adapted from Wachtel 1999; Coloroso 2003; Thorsborne and Blood 2013)

There was a distinct mismatch between:

- about half the staff who were keen to problem-solve WITH the young people and empower them to generally take more ownership

- those who flipped between doing everything FOR the young people, then getting angry with them when things didn't work out, becoming punitive (doing TO)

- those who really didn't care either way (NOT), were sometimes disrespectful to the young people but wanted them punished when they were disrespectful in return (doing TO).

In summary, whilst there were many individual relationships characterized in ASP terms by interest and enjoyment, what I initially saw and experienced in terms of collective scripts and relationships – between groups of young people and between a significant number of young people and staff – was dominated by negative affect and emotions, as shown in Table 7.1.

TABLE 7.1 Initial feelings in young people and staff

Feelings experienced or noticed – First residential	Affect/s
Apprehension and nervousness (me; young people of each other and of me)	Fear; distress; shame
Suspicion (young people of me)	Fear; dissmell; shame
Competition, jealousy and inferiority (young people)	Shame
Outrage (some young people; some staff)	Anger; fear; disgust; shame
Upset (me in *attack self* mode after reading feedback forms)	Distress; shame

It was almost as if, organizationally, the emotional connections based on our most primitive social scripts referred to by Vernon Kelly in Chapter 1 had developed some sort of fault. Most young people and staff concentrated just on getting themselves and their small group of trusted friends or colleagues through each long day. Whilst these small groups were interested in and enjoyed each other, and were able to support each other through difficult times, these emotional connections were limited to within these rather insular groups. Across the organization, the social scripts could not function because – to use an electrical analogy – it was like a series of small, isolated, weak circuits rather than a single powerful one that both supported friendship and collegiate groups and connected them. Emotionally, there was no common bond linking us all together. So, in affect terms, our collective capacity to support each other and experience mutual interest and enjoyment was at best severely restricted and at worst (when tested by additional stress) non-existent. This lack of capacity for maximizing positive affect at a basic level meant that negative affect could easily dominate relationships across the organization because it was usually left unresolved. Affective resonance – the reason feelings are contagious – created a prevailing organizational mood that was one of worry, suspicion and distrust.

Making the Change

If these residentials were going to be bearable (the possibility of them being enjoyable was not even in my mind at this point), changes needed to be made by me, by the support team and by the young people. The following section explores how we made these changes, at the core of which was RP.

Developing Restorative Practice
WHY RESTORATIVE PRACTICE?

Working restoratively in its broadest sense – and particularly within its values of participation, respect, honesty, accountability and empowerment – fitted with the director's vision of increasing the young people's ownership of the organization and their decision-making role within it. She wanted them to match increased ownership with a corresponding sense of responsibility for each other as a community and for the organization as a whole. The director felt some young people lacked a sense of responsibility towards the organization; she felt they had an air of individual entitlement, as opposed to collective ownership and responsibility. She had communicated her vision to staff and young people but did not have the practical experience to make the changes she wanted. My work with schools had taught me that making this cultural shift was hard work but attainable over time. I turned to a restorative model for schools (Blood 2004) with which I was familiar and adapted it for our purposes (Figure 7.3).

Reaffirming Relationships

This is where the bulk of our work needed to happen. Change in these situations involves everyone and therefore has the greatest overall impact on everyone within an organization. What follows is a summary of the changes we made over two years in this area.

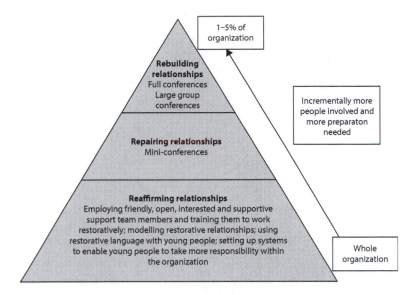

Figure 7.3 A model for whole organization restorative relationships

DEVELOPING THE TEAM

I knew from working with school staff that restorative change starts with the behaviour of staff. My first task, then, was to recruit some new staff for the support team to add to existing staff we wanted to keep. We wanted a team that would take a genuine interest in the young people, enjoy working with them, be able to maintain professional boundaries calmly and know how to problem-solve. In other words, we wanted a team who would be happy to work in the top right-hand quadrant of the Social Discipline Window – 'working WITH'. Once we had recruited some suitable staff, we trained the team in restorative basics so that we would have a consistent approach to managing relationships and solving minor problems. Over the two years I was in post and beyond, this team remained mostly stable and became the hub from which we were able to shift the culture of relationships.

MODELLING RESTORATIVE RELATIONSHIPS

To counteract the prevailing negativity, we set out to model being approachable, friendly, interested, caring and unendingly positive, as well as remaining calm under pressure. In particular, we made a point of asking individuals about their day when we saw them at bedtime, either alone or in small friendship groups; soon we were getting some interesting insights into how the young people were feeling about both themselves and the organization.

Over the course of my first year, these open conversations became the norm with the majority of young people and were a key part of improving communication. They allowed us to really get to know the young people; to pay attention to those who were struggling and put the right support in place quickly but subtly; to reinforce the values we wanted to work within; and to give the director good advice when making organizational decisions.

We also made a point of modelling the relationships we wanted the young people to have. We aimed for ours to be characterized by good humour and warmth (thankfully, this came naturally – I have never laughed so much with workmates) whilst staying focused on the task in hand. Whilst we got some strange looks, especially from the 'Alpha hoody' group who would never join in with our humour, being seen to get on well and have fun seemed to allow an increasing number of the young people to do the same – with each other and with us too. By giving permission for others to outwardly show interest and enjoyment, a more positive affective resonance started to work its magic on the organization, which slowly (and shakily) began to shed its prevailingly negative mood.

USING RESTORATIVE LANGUAGE: GROWING COOPERATION AND COLLABORATION

Using restorative questions was also a key part of our strategy for change. We focused on the six key restorative questions, as follows:

- What happened?

- What were you thinking when…happened?

- What have you thought since?

- Who has been affected, and how?

- What needs to happen to fix things?

- How can we make sure this doesn't happen again in the future?

One aim was to use restorative language to empower young people to take ownership of minor problems – for example, missing laundry/possessions and forgotten pieces of equipment. During the first course, I was struck by the 'learned helplessness' of some young people that had seemingly grown from a previous staff culture of doing everything for the young people. We used restorative language to shift this culture by using the question 'What needs to happen to fix this?' when a young person came to us with a minor issue, which allowed them to come up with their own solution. The staff member could then gauge whether they needed some support (looks of blind panic were a frequent give-away) or could resolve the situation on their own. This question shifted the focus of conversations from 'Can you do this *for* me?' to 'Can you do this *with* me?' or 'Can *we* do this *together*?' It also increased the contact the young people had with people working in our various venues, which meant they gained more of an awareness of their wider community, as well as the considerable effort these people put in to looking after them.

Working through small problems like this made it more usual for us to then use restorative language for bigger issues. For example, as time went on our relationships improved with the more senior young people within the organization who had some responsibility for and influence with others with whom they worked closely. Using restorative language, we were able to discuss – confidentially – young people within their part of the organization who needed some support. We planned and monitored ways to support these young people together, which had some success for the young people (ingrained scripts are hard to change!) and strengthened the idea of staff and young people collaborating to resolve issues together.

This sense of togetherness – one cooperative community – was helpful with our mass logistical arrangements, particularly so for the support team, who were the only team that stayed with the young people throughout the residential and cross-country travel for performances. This travel often meant late night 'get-outs' from performance venues and even later night 'get-ins' at accommodation venues when everyone was completely exhausted. My early experience of this was of many young people and some staff being entirely focused on their individual needs (I have clear memories of staff carrying sandwich crates being mobbed, and staff mysteriously disappearing when we arrived somewhere to be found with their feet up nursing a cup of tea an hour later) rather than thinking of us as one community with collective needs.

By the end of my second year, we found that even 3 a.m. 'get-ins' were pretty good-tempered and calm. Again, the key to this change was the word 'need', a key principle of RP. We were able to let young people know that we understood their needs, but that to get things sorted out for everyone as quickly as possible, we needed a bit of time to get things organized. Then everybody's needs would be met, and we could all get some sleep/food/peace and quiet. This change signified an organizational script change from 'I' to 'We'.

SETTING UP SYSTEMS TO PROMOTE RESPONSIBILITY AND OWNERSHIP

YOUNG PEOPLE'S VOICE

Whilst there was a representative group of older young people who had a say in the artistic side of the organization, we also felt that we needed a way of giving young people a meaningful voice in the way residentials were run.

During my first year, we set up this group and together we instigated some 'quick win' changes – for example, to bedtime and break-time arrangements. We also organized some problem-solving training for them. During this session, they decided to explore the lack of mixing that went on between young people (I was so surprised at this that I nearly fell off my chair at this point, then had to contain my excitement that they had raised this issue independently). What came out of their discussion was interesting and helpful, but more fascinating was the delegation that arrived at the staff area afterwards to carry it on. This comprised a small group of state school-educated young men who spelled out just how challenging they found the residentials coming from a background with more limited facilities and opportunities compared with many of their peers. It was the first honest, in-depth discussion we had with a group of young people, and the mutual interest, understanding and enjoyment it sparked was our initial breakthrough in terms of the relationships between the staff/young people. We were able to capitalize on this breakthrough later in the year by implementing some of this group's ideas –

another response to the 'what needs to happen' question – which others received well.

The skills and scope of this group grew naturally, and during my second year we focused on a problem we knew was happening, but mostly 'under the radar': low-level verbal bullying. We worked with the group to explore the nature of this bullying in more detail and get their opinion on how widespread it was. Their discussion produced what quickly became a question used whenever something jokey might escalate into something hurtful: 'Is it bullying or banter?'

This phrase was a totally unexpected outcome but one that went a long way to raise awareness of bullying and to prevent it. The phrase enabled young people to communicate in a non-threatening way, within an accepted structure, that they didn't like what other people were doing. The fact that it was often said as part of the 'banter' helped diffuse any tension, and, at the same time, it held people accountable in a very simple way. The group went on to work on the outline and content of a new anti-bullying policy, but it was this catchphrase that had the most impact.

Buddies

During my second year, we added an additional role of responsibility for young people. When we asked them what it was being like being new in the organization, they all agreed that one of the worst things was what they called 'the walk of shame' after you had collected your first meal from the canteen and headed out into the seating area wondering where to sit. They found this moment excruciatingly uncomfortable. They also talked about not knowing where to go and when, and the difficulty they had generally settling in quickly and making friends – all of which caused an impediment to positive affect and, therefore, a shame reaction. Consequently, the less confident young people would typically simply *withdraw*, both physically and mentally, and/or wear the 'deer in headlights' look of fixed anxiety and distress. One young man voiced his distress indirectly when he asked a member of the support team, 'How long does it take to make friends here?'

Having asked the young people the now normal 'What do we need to do to fix this?' question, we decided to introduce a team of *buddies* who would take responsibility for new members, making sure they addressed the issues mentioned above and that no one had to do 'the walk of shame' alone. We called this team to the residential early and ran a training session for them. For the majority of new young people, and for the buddies, this was a successful scheme and new members commented positively on it. As a team, we noticed a reduction in the number of new members who found it difficult to settle in and we were therefore able to focus more support on those young people who were in need. It also supported our aim of empowering young people to problem-solve for themselves where possible.

EVALUATION

During my second year, we also rethought the feedback forms and changed their name to 'evaluations' to mark the shift. We wanted them to focus much more on the residentials as a learning experience for individuals and the group as a whole – again reinforcing a sense of community. We still allowed room for young people to tell us about things they did not like, but made this part of a 'sandwich' where we asked for high points, low points and 'eureka' moments. This helped both staff and young people see the negatives in a more balanced context.

We also experimented with giving the young people more ownership over when they completed evaluations, rather than fill them in en masse at the end of a residential. We had noticed during my first year that there were some young people telling others what to write, and some forms contained identical sentences. Whilst increased flexibility resulted in a lower return rate, what we received was more reflective and constructive.

Repairing Relationships

To repair relationships that had suffered some harm, we used more mainstream educational restorative practice. We ran mini restorative conferences as necessary, preparing and meeting with smaller groups to deal with less serious issues that didn't need involvement from parents or venue staff. They were invariably needed to resolve fallings-out due to negative emotions caused by comments made face to face, behind the back or on social media. The hurt feelings that resulted usually involved shame, coupled with distress and anger, and they created power shifts that needed rebalancing. As with all restorative processes, those who facilitated allowed space for:

- everyone to understand each other's version of what had happened

- negative thoughts/feelings to be aired

- the extent of each person's harm to be explored

- apologies to be made or bridges to be built

- a plan to be developed that meant everyone felt more positive about the future – not necessarily finishing up as friends, but definitely with an easier relationship based on increased understanding of each other's feelings and needs.

By the end of my two years, young people were asking for these conversations (one memorably with 'or I'm going to go back in there and punch him' tagged on the end).

We used the same process to work through damaged relationships between staff and young people. The two most significant of these mini-conferences we held were between the director and two influential individuals, who had been members of the organization throughout its changes and were openly negative about them. Their attitude – which was causing ripples across the young people in the organization – made the director angry, and the relationship between her and the young people was breaking down. The outcome of each of these conferences was positive and had a calming effect across the young people in the organization. It was especially important these two young people saw that, as the facilitator, I was absolutely neutral throughout these meetings. By sticking to the role and the process (and calling the director to account a couple of times when her anger spilled over) they could see it was fair, and that it really was a space where they could air what they genuinely felt. The increased understanding that came out of their willingness to share was crucial to breaking what was fast becoming a deadlock.

Rebuilding Relationships

Whilst major incidents were rare within the organization, we used full restorative conferences three times during my two years there. All of these incidents took place during the first year. The first, during my first residential, provoked an interesting reaction from some of the young people, and is worth exploring a little.

A young man of 16 set up a porn film on his laptop in his room late at night, making sure the sound was loud enough for the whole corridor to hear. He waited until the member of staff responsible for the corridor came to say goodnight and then switched the film on, with the intention of embarrassing the member of staff in front of his peers. Given that it is illegal in the UK to possess porn under the age of 18, and that he had downloaded a number of similar films at home, we decided to involve his parents and asked them to attend a restorative meeting. The young man in question was remorseful and we were able to repair relations between him and the organization quite effectively. The most significant need and emotion that emerged from the conference was centred on him rebuilding trust with his parents, for which the family made a plan.

The conference itself was what might be expected from a restorative process. What was more interesting was the reaction of outrage of other young people not at the conference – particularly again the 'Alpha hoody group' – but towards the fact it was happening. I had explained how I would work during an introductory talk on the first night of the course, but this was the first 'outing' for the restorative process within the organization. The outrage was picked up by other members of the support team and later expressed on the course feedback forms (as they were then) but never directly to me. It centred on:

- that I hadn't just told the young man off and let the matter drop

- that I dared to involve the young man's parents in the meeting.

Both of these reactions clearly triggered shame in the 'hoody' group, as their scripts for problem-solving, as well as what they perceived to be a problem, were turned upside down.

We carried on as normal, keeping the process confidential as is usual with restorative meetings, but with a sense of underlying hostility from a significant minority of the young people (eventually expressed post-course on feedback forms). As it became more common for us to run conferences, this sense of hostility slowly diminished, and by the third conference in the last residential of my first year, it had lost its bite.

Progress and Affect

Year 1

At the end of Year 1, there was still a core of negativity that affected the whole organization. However, as a team, we felt the balance was starting to tip towards the positive. Young people told us privately that they were fed up with the negativity of this core group, but they were too intimidated (with the exception of one young woman who was then subjected to a barrage of sexist comments) to tell them. I too had found this core group tough going and was glad the majority of these young people were leaving. Despite this group, I felt I had grown into my role. I had learned to be more subtle, less 'teachery' and more trusting; in turn, many young people started to trust me and the rest of the team. The majority of us were genuinely starting to enjoy each other's company and working together through what could be a punishing, highly distressing schedule. Year 1 emotions, then, might be summed up as illustrated in Figure 7.4.

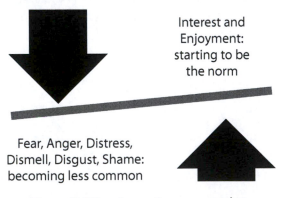

Interest and Enjoyment: starting to be the norm

Fear, Anger, Distress, Dismell, Disgust, Shame: becoming less common

Figure 7.4 Year 1 emotions summed up

I can also see some connection between our progress by the end of Year 1 and the first two rules of the Central Blueprint mentioned in Chapter 1:

- *Rule 1: Maximize positive affect.* We deliberately set out to do this as a team, and had good success during Year 1 with this strategy. On reflection, I am sure that there was also some affective resonance at work here that helped grow positivity over the year.

- *Rule 2: Minimize negative affect.* Working restoratively gave a space for negativity but always within a context of supporting people to move towards something more positive. This structure meant that negativity no longer dominated in the way it had previously.

Year 2

The hard work of Year 1 meant that Year 2 was a lot more pleasant for everyone. The support team was stable, restorative processes and structures were established, relationships between the team and the young people were mostly very good, and the whole mood of residentials was calmer and lighter. Venue staff commented on how much friendlier and more polite the young people were during this year than previous years. Whilst there was still the odd rumble of dissatisfaction with organizational changes, improved relationships meant these were aired more openly and did not have the same destabilizing effect as when they had been an undercurrent.

The 'Is it bullying or banter?' catchphrase from the work on the anti-bullying policy gave young people the means and confidence to start telling each other about behaviour they didn't like. Those who really enjoyed what the organization was doing also had the confidence to be more open about this and show their interest and excitement. In doing both of these things, they illustrated Rule 3 of the Central Blueprint: *Minimize the inhibition of affect.*

Problems during this year were connected with relationships rather than serious misconduct, and the young people knew there were people and a structure that would help. There was even one example, shown by the young man who asked for a restorative conversation with two colleagues (or he would hit one of them), of Rule 4: *Maximize the power to maximize positive affect, minimize negative affect, and minimize the inhibition of affect.* By taking the initiative and asking for a conversation, this young man was maximizing his power to do something positive in order not to do something negative, but his strength of feeling was clear if nothing was done – there was no inhibition there!

In summary, by the end of Year 2, the prevailing emotions of the organization were positive; in ASP terms, there were more stimuli provoking positive affects, which turned into positive emotions and, over time, positive scripts. As in any organization, there were negative feelings and scripts, but these were now in more or less the right proportion. There was less collective anger, distress and fear about artistic changes that were happening, and the more the young people relaxed, the more they found they became interested in, and enjoyed, at least some of the new ways of being that the organization was promoting. The amount of competition, insecurity and related shame, whilst not completely gone (performers are renowned for it), had lessened, allowing space for more trusting relationships that allowed young people and staff to be genuinely interested in each other and to enjoy each other's company.

This enjoyment showed itself in abundance on the last course. I had decided to leave the organization and wanted to make sure I said a proper goodbye to the young people en masse. During this goodbye, something funny happened which sent a staff member into fits of laughter. He set other people off, and before long 180 of us were laughing together. This is a lasting and very happy memory of my time with these young people and staff, and a great illustration of how far I, the team and the young people had come in our respect and regard for each other. Slowly, we had moved from a disconnected group of cliques to one large herd: a connected community.

Conclusion

I have no doubt that working restoratively was the key to moving our relationships from those rocked by negative affect to those made strong by positive affect. Figure 7.5 is an attempt to pull together how I think this process worked for us.

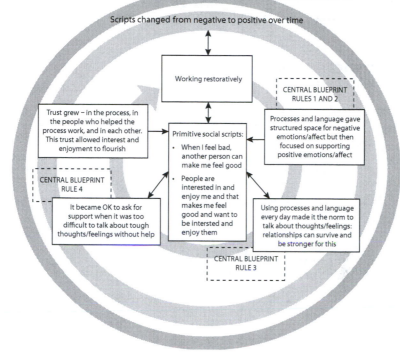

Figure 7.5 How the restorative process worked in the organization

I had experienced RP working successfully elsewhere and knew how to adapt it for the organization. What ASP added was a theoretical framework that explained the organization's collective negativity, helped me analyze what was happening and make a plan to tip the balance towards the positive. It also helped me keep my sanity and hope when things seemed frustratingly stuck in the negative. Happily, it also made me more aware of the interest and enjoyment that was abundant by the time I left.

My successor is someone who was in the support team during this time, and who was a major proponent in our efforts to be outwardly positive and demonstrate how to have fun throughout this period of change. Whilst I am sure he has put his own stamp on the role, I know that the changes to the culture of the organization made in the two years I was there have lasted, and that interest and enjoyment still prevail. This leaves me with a real sense of satisfaction that we achieved something important, which now has a chance of lasting and being further embedded within the organization's culture.

References

Blood, P. (2004) 'A Whole School Model of Restorative Practices: An Integrated Approach.' In B. Morrison (2007) *Restoring Safe School Communities: A Whole School Approach to Bullying, Violence and Alienation.* Sydney: Federation Press.

Coloroso, B. (2003) *The Bully, the Bullied and the Bystander: From Preschool to High School – How Parents and Teachers Can Help Break the Cycle.* New York, NY: HarperCollins.

Hensher, P. (2012) *Rejecting Oxbridge isn't clever – it's a mistake.* Available at www.independent.co.uk/voices/commentators/philip-hensher/philip-hensher-rejecting-oxbridge-isnt-clever--its-a-mistake-6292041.html, accessed on 7 May 2013.

Kelly, V.C. (2012) *The Art of Intimacy and the Hidden Challenge of Shame.* Rockland, ME: Maine Authors Publishing.

Thorsborne, M. and Blood, P. (2013) *Implementing Restorative Practices in Schools: A Practical Guide to Transforming School Communities.* London: Jessica Kingsley Publishers.

Wachtel, T. (1999) 'Restorative Justice in Everyday Life: Beyond the Formal Ritual.' Paper presented at the Reshaping Australian Institutions Conference: Restorative Justice and Civil Society, 16–18 February. Canberra: Australian National University. Available at www.iirp.edu/article_detail.php?article_id=NTAz, accessed on 9 December 2013.

CHAPTER 8

Drama Queens

Margaret Thorsborne

In the following case study, I explore the nature of relationship breakdown in a school faculty with unresolved conflict escalating over a period of time and poorly managed. I pay particular attention to the behaviours of those members of staff who were most closely involved and describe the affect and scripts that motivated those behaviours as individuals became more shamed and distressed by increasing hostilities. I also describe the process (a workplace conference – WPC) we[1] used to resolve some of the issues and to minimize the emotional pain all faculty members were suffering; how in this process this group came to decisions about how to go forward; and how this process obeyed the Central Blueprint described by Vernon Kelly in Chapter 1, by:

- minimizing the inhibition of affect (i.e. giving people involved a chance to talk about what had been happening and how it was impacting on them)

- minimizing negative affect (both in the conference itself by giving people the chance to *unload* safely with each other, and also to create a plan to govern future behaviours in the faculty)

---

1   This process was done with two facilitators. I led the process but the interviews and follow-up were shared with Sharon Borrows, a close colleague, whose expertise lay in executive coaching and leadership development. Sharon died suddenly in November 2013, and this chapter is now dedicated to her memory and the legacy of her contributions to the complex task of managing organizational change. She had a firm grasp of restorative principles and it was extremely useful to have her perceptions of the broader structural and management issues in the faculty that either created or exacerbated the relationship breakdown between the two drama teachers. Her work has had a profound influence on the way I think about transforming workplace conflict. I will miss her by my side in this work.

- maximizing positive affect (this happens if the two previous jobs have been done effectively, and people become very interested in creating a plan for the future after they are relieved of the burden of negative affects such as shame, distress and disgust, and that this hard emotional work had been done).

CASE STUDY: DRAMA QUEENS
Scenario

The case study involves a high school performing arts faculty beset with high-level conflict between two drama teachers that had persisted for a period of at least three years. It had started, as is often the case, with small issues that remained unresolved, largely caused by unhelpful structural issues (poor induction processes for a start), which then placed great pressure on the relationship between these two teachers, even before it had time to develop. The negative feelings gradually escalated to the point where the faculty staff became divided into two major teams that lined up behind each teacher, who themselves were deeply distressed by the situation.

The faculty had a poor reputation because of the conflict and was regarded by other faculties as a 'nest of vipers'. One long-standing member of staff commented that the performing arts faculty was the face of the school because performances were public, and this raised the level of distress from the pressure that all faculty members were under. So what was already distressing was made infinitely worse by the ongoing conflict.

In terms of the Central Blueprint, there had been little in the way of processes in place to create positive relationships of goodwill and trust with the induction of a new staff member (that is, to maximize positive affect); when things went belly-up between the drama teachers, little was done within the faculty that was helpful to minimize the negative, and a mediation that was attempted by the school principal failed in this regard as well. Finally, there was little done in terms of any of these processes to minimize the inhibition of affect (i.e. to share and understand each other's perspectives, experiences and feelings) until we were engaged to help.

The major players (names have been changed)

Drama teachers: Annie and Colleen (new)

Friend of Annie: Jenny (Annie and Jenny shared a flat and were good friends)

Head of faculty: Frances

School principal: Jack

Five other staff: Ben, Maria, Sally, Sam and Val

School counsellor: Maryanne

The case was taken up after a call from the principal, Jack, who knew of the restorative work that we had been doing in workplaces and, in particular, schools. Once we had met with him, it seemed that it would help if we utilized a restorative process called workplace conferencing, but that decision would not be confirmed until after we had completed interviews with the key parties (11 in all).

The interviews revealed the following:

- A history of unresolved issues, each not really so serious, but they added insult to injury as they layered one on top of the other with the harm done deepening with each incident. There appeared to be no mechanisms for resolving conflict.

- The head of faculty was regarded fondly by all the staff, but was conflict-avoidant. She had no understanding of the difference between management and leadership, and no skills or understanding about line management.

- There had been an attempt by the principal to mediate, but it failed and served to drive a greater wedge between the women and others – intensifying the harm.

- Issues around workload, planning and rehearsals in theatrical productions, class allocations and timetabling, and roles and responsibilities added pressure.

- Each of the women had gone to a particular staff member for support and advice but because these colleagues had no real conflict coaching skills, they ended up being 'recruited' and so began a division of the faculty into Annie's team and Colleen's team.

- Distress levels were very high – to the point that we believed the situation was becoming a health and safety issue.

The Interviews

To better understand how things got to be so difficult, I have included the substance of the interviews with the key players. Their relationships and realities were so intertwined that it is somewhat difficult to separate them, so I have bundled some together.

ANNIE AND COLLEEN

Annie, whose training was through an education degree with a major in drama, had arrived at the school a year before Colleen. Annie, no longer *new* (by one year), was given the responsibility of mentoring Colleen when she arrived, to help her settle in and figure out how things worked. Annie, however, had been poorly mentored herself when she arrived, and had no understanding of what should have happened to settle Colleen in (to maximize interest and enjoyment, and minimize the shame and distress that go with being new). She simply did what she had seen modelled. Colleen felt 'let down' and 'undervalued' as a result of being left to find out things on her own. She had a picture in her head about what her first days and weeks would be like – her anticipation and expectations were high and her disappointment was correspondingly high – and so here was the first impediment to her interest and enjoyment and the trigger for shame and the emergence of shame-managing behaviours.

Colleen's path into teaching was built on industry training and experience (actual theatre), and her views of how to teach and assess drama were very different from Annie's; over time this became one of the issues that was problematic. She had very high expectations of herself and of her students (in our view, unrealistic on both counts).

It was clear that very little in the way of *getting to know each other* processes were in place. These might have, if done well, allowed each of the women who had to work so closely together to get to know a little more about what was important to each of them, and it might have been possible to harness their differences for creative purposes, rather than becoming further impediments to their working relationship.

When it came time to design assessment items, Colleen would (according to Annie) alter the in-class tasks and assignment sheets, 'making them more complex'. From interviews with other staff, it seemed that Colleen was a perfectionist (a script developed perhaps to manage her shame) who made huge demands on students and herself. Imperfections in performance that emerged were taken personally by her, motivating some of her more unhelpful shame-driven behaviours (more on that later). In my opinion, this would have been a case where the head of faculty, Frances, could have stepped in and sorted the issues, but this didn't happen.

Colleen reported that about three weeks into her employment in the faculty she attempted to share some of her resources with Annie. She assumes in hindsight that Annie might have felt she was showing her 'how much better she was' because she noticed that Annie *withdrew* (a Compass of Shame response) from that moment. Colleen suspected that, from then on, her attempts to share were interpreted as wanting to show Annie up (an *attack other* by Colleen) and were, therefore, again shaming for Annie. Colleen reported that Annie then no longer shared resources or information or cooperated with her (other staff reported Annie's behaviour as passive aggressive – with my view that it was a combination of *withdrawal* and subtle *attack other*). Because Annie shared accommodation with Jenny, Colleen also believed that the pair of them colluded in matters affecting her. She noticed 'looks' that passed between them in the staffroom and they stopped talking when she walked in. This made her feel isolated, excluded and alienated – all words used to describe the feelings when shame is triggered. Colleen reported that she cried every day coming to school and in the afternoons after school (her distress was unremitting), and that she believes she had a mild 'breakdown'. She also began to doubt her own competence (*attack self* Compass of Shame thinking). Colleen was reluctant to talk the matters over with her head of faculty, Frances, because she was 'too nice, and doesn't like confrontation' (more about that later).

As the next year unfolded, more issues emerged. Colleen believed that she was being assigned the lion's share of the workload by Annie (more out-of-class work for upcoming performances), and she was getting the 'dregs' of classes, while Annie continued to teach more senior and preferred classes. Annie had reported that she thought Colleen had a sense of entitlement – that she would automatically be given senior classes without having done the hard yards. This is an often unspoken rule in class allocation in high schools – new staff members are given younger students and more difficult classes, while more experienced staff deserve the 'cream' – an odd rule really, given the need for new staff to be supported! Other observers in the faculty commented that they thought it was Annie who had the sense of entitlement because she had always seen to it that she retained the more advanced students. These issues surfaced every time there was a change in timetable – mostly yearly, but sometimes a semester event. Again, the absence of clear guidance by Frances, the faculty head, added to the pressure on relationships. Both Annie and Colleen thought the other was manipulating Frances around decisions that affected both of them.

Annie had no memory of the early incidents that Colleen reported, but was clear that, by the beginning of the second year of her employment, Colleen had issues with her. She also reported that Colleen's 'true colours' were emerging. She was beginning to behave badly – that is, venting loudly in the staffroom, being very negative about everything, physically standing over Annie when complaining, veiled 'digs' at Annie and door slamming when she left the room clearly angry about something. These behaviours were obviously shame-related (*attack other*) and triggered by some impediment or other. It was also clear from interviews with others that Colleen was quite vulnerable and becoming over-sensitized – hyper-vigilant – to anything that could possibly be a criticism of her. It seemed to us that Colleen's perceptions of what was happening were very skewed by her view that collusion was afoot.

Annie described another incident that demonstrated these same patterns on the evening of a major performance by students. Colleen was very stressed (distressed, and thus neurologically predisposed to quick bursts of anger – see Chapter 1). Colleen yelled at Annie in front of students, who were also yelled at. Some students were so concerned about the abusive incident that they approached Annie later to check to see that she was coping. Other reports from students in Colleen's classes included her yelling and screaming at students, calling their performances 'shit' and that they made her 'want to vomit' (*attack other*, distress, disgust). Annie reported these incidents to the head of faculty, Frances, who spoke to Colleen about them (publicly), and, unsurprisingly, Colleen erupted (*attack other*).

As a result of Colleen's behaviours, Annie felt that she was not respected by Colleen. This triggered shame for Annie, and she responded by withdrawing and, according to Colleen, undermining her decisions about almost anything (the subtle form of *attack other*). Colleen described Annie as being cold and withdrawn. Other staff reported on this coldness and also about a 'look on her face' when confronted with anything difficult – a smile that would emerge. My guess was that it was a smile to mask the shame she felt in that moment.

Annie sought help from the departmental employee assistance scheme (EAS) to cope with the difficulties, and became a little more assertive rather than withdrawing, although this new assertiveness was seen as condescending by Colleen, who at this stage was beyond seeing any change in Annie's behaviour as positive. Annie reported now that she simply did not care to try any more – there was little to be gained by attempting to reignite interest and even smaller chance that the relationship with Colleen would be a source of enjoyment or, at the very least, professional satisfaction.

Annie reported that she now hated coming to work with the tension in the staffroom. When she asked what she thought needed to happen to improve the climate, she suggested that the coalitions had to split (in other words, the group that supported Colleen) because they were so negative. She also talked about her distress (my language, not hers) and that she simply wanted to be able to relax at work. She felt that the issues had now had an irreversible impact on her promotional opportunities, and they had poisoned every aspect of her life (disgust). When she walked in to the staffroom each day, she was not sure what reception she would get – attacked, ignored, passive aggression (with veiled barbs directed at her).

In Chapter 1, Kelly proposed a triangle to demonstrate the connections between jealousy, competitiveness and shame. It seems to me that this was indeed the case between two young drama teachers with different backgrounds and ideologies – one who had been at the school long enough to establish routines, productions and classes to her own satisfaction, and the other new, earnestly trying to establish herself and her credentials. With no processes to develop a positive relationship and no effective processes in place to intervene early, it became a recipe for disaster!

FRANCES

The head of faculty was a key person in what unfolded over time. She was regarded by all her staff as a very nice person, keen to keep people happy and to placate them if there was an issue (conflict-avoidant). They had great respect for her hard work and her technical skills in the curriculum and around performances put on by faculty staff and students. She was out of her depth, however, when faced with the increasing hostilities between the two young women. Her conflict avoidance meant she was inclined to minimize the conflict instead of transforming it (avoidance behaviour on the Compass of Shame). Eventually, when she could no longer stay in denial, she found the whole situation deeply disturbing and became, as one faculty member commented, an 'emotional wreck'. In the language of ASP, her behaviours and symptoms could be described as ongoing shame caused by an increasing sense of incompetence as hostilities escalated and the distress experienced when something had gone wrong and stayed wrong.

SAM

Sam described the atmosphere as a 'fog' in the staffroom. Volcanic moments when Colleen let fly were very embarrassing for him. He felt that the problems had been left too long and he worried that it was too late for any real resolution and healing. He commented that some of the behaviour he saw was very immature and that some of it made him physically sick. Sam experienced shame, distress and disgust.

MARIA

Maria didn't like the way Colleen had been treated by Annie and Jenny, and tried to comfort Colleen in the afternoons when she was crying after school. Colleen's anguish triggered her nurturing behaviours and she felt she had to support her because no one else would. She was, therefore, Colleen's support during the mediation and found the process awful (more about that later) and now believed that she was forever linked to Colleen because of her role in the mediation. She believed that Annie's failure to accept responsibility for anything that had happened to this point meant that she had 'got away with a lot' and never had to apologize.

BEN

Ben was relatively new to the staff and had noticed when he took up his position how tense the climate in staffroom was. He described the air as 'thick' and initially thought it was about him – that he had done something (an *attack self* response). He also said that there was a 'big fat elephant in the room' that no one was talking about.

VAL

Val described the situation as tense, uncomfortable, awkward and that she wanted the ground to open up and for her to disappear – a clear sign that shame had been triggered.

JENNY

Jenny was Annie's flatmate and had tried on many occasions to facilitate conversations around issues between Colleen and Annie, but had been effectively silenced by Colleen's nastiness, feeling very 'stung' by it. She reported that Colleen's *attack other* behaviours really had a huge impact on everyone who ended up withdrawing and no longer wanting to speak up for fear of being diminished.

The Mediation

I want to comment here about what we understand happened in this process because it drove such a wedge between the parties and escalated the relationship damage.

Because the increasingly hostile behaviours were becoming such an issue, the principal, Jack, who had some mediation training, facilitated a process in an attempt to resolve the issues. It has to be said that Jack was a deeply relational leader of the school, who cared very much that people were so upset. He was committed to positive relationships and this was a core value in the school. He had spent many hours in conversations with the key people in this situation in an attempt to support them and to help them reach solutions. This individual work was appreciated, but because his efforts up to this point didn't bring these people *together*, there was no opportunity for them to talk about how their behaviours were impacting on each other.

Colleen attended the mediation, supported by Maria. Annie was supported by Jenny. Frances, the faculty head, was also present. It was agreed that people in support roles would have no voice in the process. In preparation for the process, both women had been sent a list of four questions and were to come with their answers ready for dialogue. While the substance of those questions was never revealed to us in our interviews, what transpired was that Colleen's understanding of one of the questions differed greatly from Annie's, so right from the start the process was doomed. Annie came prepared with screeds of notes; Colleen did not.

They got no further than question 1, and Colleen's support person, Maria, out of sheer frustration, but breaking the golden rule of an observer to never become involved, said, 'Oh, for God's sake, can't you two get along?' Annie immediately shut down (withdrew, as was her usual pattern). She and Jenny left the room, and Frances followed to check on them and convince them to return to the mediation. Maria apologized for her gaff, but the process became overwhelming for Colleen (Annie had listed her behaviours that were problematic, and she tried to refute them) and she terminated her participation and left with Maria.

Post-mediation (which everyone agreed had not turned out well), Frances, as head of faculty, worked with the two women to develop a contract for them to act in a professional manner towards each other. This actually held for a while, until another crisis moment when high emotions spilt over under the added pressure of a particular performance – the event where Colleen abused Annie in front of students.

It was clear to us in our interviews that people had wanted to talk about these issues for a long time, but there had been no safe vehicle to do so. It seems to me that we are naturally wired to mutualize our affect with each other and to want to get along (Chapter 1). It was also agreed that the WPC process would be the right vehicle to allow everyone that chance to talk through the issues safely. There was no assumption that every relationship that had soured could be healed in the space of a few hours, but here was a chance to talk about that 'big fat elephant in the room', reach some shared understandings about what harm had been done and see what the group could do to improve the situation. In other words, the process would deliver on the Central Blueprint.

The Workplace Conference

We invited the whole faculty to the WPC, along with the principal and the school counsellor who had been offering occasional support to staff and would have the same role in the future. Provision was made at our request to take the process and people off campus, and an appropriate venue was chosen, catering organized and relief for classes provided (the cost for the venue, teacher relief and consultant fees was considerable and demonstrated the senior management team's commitment to improving the situation). We knew it would take the whole day to deal with the issues.

The room was arranged with chairs in a circle (free of a table). Beforehand, we had developed a seating plan with key people on either side of me and their supporters close by. The rest of the faculty was arranged according to the polarization that had occurred, and the principal and head of faculty sat together and between the two cliques. This arrangement allowed full access to all expressions of affect: what could be seen on people's faces, how they sat in their chairs, how they were connecting with each other (or not!), and the level of eye contact or heads hung as shame was triggered.

The air was tense when people arrived and were led to their chairs. They had been carefully briefed before the meeting (conference) about seating, about the process and how they might be feeling now, during and by the end. It's useful, I think, at this point to recount my introduction at the beginning of the meeting. It went something like this:

Good morning, everyone. Thanks for agreeing to participate in this process today when the whole situation has not been easy for any of you. Before we start, can we sort some ground rules about what's to happen here today?

Here are some basic things I think are really important that we need to agree:

- Confidentiality about our discussions – to prevent gossip (which has been a problem for the faculty) and so that we can all feel safe. If there is something we think others should know about, then we can decide that as part of our agreement.

- Our dialogue today is to remain respectful – no character assassinations – and I will call it if I become aware that it is happening; again, we need to feel as safe as possible.

- We are not here to decide who is to blame for what has transpired, or to decide if anyone is good or bad.

(I checked with the group if these points had merit and whether or not they wanted to add to this list – yes to the first, and no to the second.) I continued:

The purpose of our coming together today is to kick-start a change for the faculty, so today is not the end, it is the beginning. The last couple of years have become increasingly distressing and all of you here have been affected to a greater or lesser degree.

Before we make any decisions about how to improve the situation in the faculty, we will talk about how each of you has experienced what has been happening, and how that has affected you – in other words, what harm has been done. If we can understand that, then we can turn our thoughts to how to move on.

You will be expected, however, as the day progresses, to take responsibility for the impact your behaviour may have had on others. This means that each of us will need to listen very carefully to what others might say about that, and try to be as honest as possible with yourself and with the group.

Whatever the plan we develop, we will follow up with you after the conference.

For those readers familiar with the scripted conference approach, the introduction was a version of that: rules of engagement, what the purpose was and wasn't, and, for this particular group who were mired in the mindset of 'it's all someone else's fault', an exhortation to attempt to view the situation through someone else's experience – in other words, to develop *empathy* for others.

At this point, participants were tense, steeling themselves for a difficult few hours, not wanting to look at each other across the circle (avoiding eye contact – shame), but, despite that, interested! And I have to remark at this point that, as an experienced facilitator, I was deeply interested as well!

We began by asking each person in turn two things (recorded on butcher's paper and posted up for the day on the whiteboard): what outcomes did they seek for the process today, and what outcomes did they want for the faculty? This served two purposes. First, it was something we could come back to at the close of the meeting to see if we had kicked some goals; and, second, but more importantly, it helped to ease them into speaking – that is, to ease them into:

- minimizing the inhibition of affect (i.e. giving people involved a chance to talk about what had been happening and how it was impacting them).

Once we'd relaxed a little with this 'easy' work, I began with Jack, the principal, and asked him to explain why we were here and why he had employed us to help. We had previously coached him to talk about the school vision and values – and he did this perfectly by linking the process to school values.

The next part of the process was to employ a circle technique (a slight departure from the scripted conference), giving each person in turn, around the circle, an opportunity to answer the following questions:

What is it like to be in the staffroom now? What has changed for you over time?

This, from an ASP perspective, followed the Central Blueprint:

- minimizing negative affect (both in the conference itself by giving people the chance to *unload* safely with each other).

From a facilitation point of view, it was important to gradually develop this sense of safety for being emotionally honest because of the more detailed work that would come next. It worked. Each person began to open up and describe their distress and shame (although, for the latter, not using that term) and fear of more

191

shame. A few shed tears. People began to realize that harm had affected everyone – no one was untouched by the issues. We were on the way to a shared understanding.

For the next part of the process (the conference proper), I began by saying something like:

> It's hard to know where to start because there have been so many incidents, so we will now focus on some of the defining moments which seem to have been lightning rods for the conflict in the faculty.

Where there has been a history developed over a long period of time, it is important to go back to the beginning when it all started to go wrong. This gives everyone access to the information and an opportunity to view behaviours of others through a lens of understanding and empathy, even though they might not agree with the behaviour itself.

In our preparation for the process we decided that the following events needed to be unpacked:

- Colleen's arrival and arrangements for mentoring

- allocation of classes

- Colleen's public abuse of Annie at a school performance

- the mediation

- an upcoming musical that was putting stress on already distressed relationships.

This would involve those most directly involved in each incident, with an occasional question to others less involved if we knew they had been affected as a bystander. This would give the main players an understanding about how their own behaviour had affected a wider community of people. So often when we are in the middle of a conflict, we become so self-absorbed (either blaming self or blaming others, withdrawing – all Compass of Shame thinking) that we end up thinking and feeling that it's all about the self. We have to *defrost* this thinking.

The questions used in this part of the process are typical restorative script, appreciative enquiry, curious questions:

- What happened?

- What did you think at that point?

- What were you thinking when you did that?

- What were your expectations?

- In what ways were they not met?

- How did this breach your values?

- What impact did that have on you? On others?

- What's changed for you?

- How has this changed your relationship with…?

- What was the point at which things came off the rails? How did that affect everyone?

- What did you see happening to others?

- What was the worst of it?

- Is there anything you would like to say about that?

Occasionally I asked the principal and the counsellor:

- What are you thinking when you are listening to this?

These questions again allow both minimizing the inhibition of affect (i.e. giving people involved a chance to talk about what had been happening and how it was impacting on them) and minimizing negative affect (i.e. by talking about the impact and being understood by others).

As you can imagine, this was a long process. Many, many tears were shed. No one remained unaffected by the emotional outpourings, mostly of distress and shame, that had at last found a way to be expressed. There were acknowledgements made, and these were helpful in building bridges. Morning tea and lunch punctuated the timeline and its stories of harm. These breaks were tense. People did not yet feel reconnected. Our job was to check how individuals were coping – reassuring them that we could get through the day – and what issues still needed attention.

At lunch, I had to speak with Colleen who, when she was telling her story at one point, had such a look of contempt (lip curled – dissmell and anger) on her face and was using sarcasm (*attack other*) that I could see it was hard for people to warm to her. She had previously told us in interviews that she 'gets angry

> and aggressive and doesn't fight well'. We were now seeing an
> echo of that as she spoke. She took the feedback well and settled
> after lunch into a much more conciliatory approach. Her facial
> expression changed and so did her tone of voice.

I am reminded of Kelly's advice:[2]

> Shame reduction by shame induction – because exposure (of
> shame) is mandatory to resurface shame hidden beneath Compass
> of Shame defenses.

It was only then that the people assembled were able to connect with
each other, once they understood the behaviour of 'other' and their
own behaviour, in terms of the way each of them managed their
disconnectedness – in other words, their shame.

(I remember a post-conference workshop for another group of
professionals in another industry who had endured an extremely
toxic workplace. I had showed them some basics about shame and
the Compass of Shame family of behaviours, and asked them to
think about what had happened to them in their workplace. One
woman, who had been named by others as extremely difficult, sent
me a text later in the day, telling me that I had described exactly
what she had felt and done – 'You were talking about me,' said the
text. The information about shame had a profound impact on her
understanding of what had happened to her and to others, and she
became easier to live with.)

> Finally, the group was in a position to begin deciding what could
> be done to improve the issues that were problematic. I asked each
> in turn, 'What needs to happen now to improve things for the
> faculty?' and their suggestions were recorded on the whiteboard
> so they could see the plan developing. Despite their emotional
> exhaustion at this point, the minute we began this part of the
> process we could see that interest had been triggered. People sat
> more upright in their chairs. They were more united and animated
> now, committed to improving outcomes for the group as a whole
> and preparing to change the unhelpful scripts the faculty had
> developed around problem-solving, decision-making and how
> they treated each other. Siân Williams, in Chapter 7, describes a

---

2   Workshop presented at the inaugural Restorative Practices International conference at
    Twin Waters, Australia, October, 2007 on ASP and its connection to restorative practice.

similar change of script for the organization where she worked. This change of script was on a smaller scale, of course.

They together decided on strategies (I have written these here in general terms):

1. Improving communication to minimize the likelihood of misunderstandings.

2. Consultation in decision-making around the calendar of events, class allocation, etc., and careful planning to minimize the stress of these events.

3. Helping each other instead of withdrawing and undermining.

4. Deliberate attempts to better understand what is happening in people's lives outside of school – ask more questions, but to be genuine about it.

5. Professional and respectful behaviours when issues arise, particularly in the presence of students.

6. Using the *script* questions to begin the problem-solving process instead of blaming and criticizing.

7. Re-structuring of faculty and departmental meetings so they are more effective and promote dialogue.

The strategies they developed were absolutely following the Central Blueprint:

1. maximizing positive affect

2. minimizing negative affect

3. minimizing the inhibition of affect, and

4. maximizing the power to maximize positive affect, minimize negative affect, and minimize the inhibition of affect.

As Kelly states in Chapter 1, 'Wellbeing results from a life lived with numbers 1–3 as balanced as circumstances permit. When that is the case, number 4 progressively generates more and more advanced skills to carry out 1–3.'

The group was also asked at the end of this planning whether or not they had been able to deliver on the outcomes for the process they had hoped for at the beginning of the day. The consensus was that it had, although the longer-term outcomes for the faculty as a whole would still be to come, and would be the proof of whether the scripts that governed the identity and behaviour had changed permanently.

Follow-up was arranged. My colleague Sharon would meet with key and most vulnerable individuals (Colleen, Annie, Frances) to monitor and support their wellbeing. The three of them had taken considerable knocks to self-worth and feelings of competence (immersion in shame and distress) over time, and their recovery was not instant nor was it achieved by the end of the meeting.

People left the conference totally exhausted, a couple of them with serious headaches, and they were advised to take the next day off to recover. One of them took advantage of the offer. Everyone needed time to reflect and settle.

Reports from the senior leadership team in the wake of the conference indicated that issues and hostilities had indeed settled, and all of them were striving to comply with the plan. Sharon met again with the group for a meeting after school and they continued to plan to embed the changes they had decided on. Over the summer holidays, a member of Colleen's family suffered some serious health issues, and she decided to move interstate to be closer to them.

Conclusion

We realize that there is a great deal of work needed to build social capital in workplaces – the stuff of goodwill, of cooperation and trust. This extends to a better understanding of effective management and leadership so that structural and cultural issues that cause conflict can be eliminated or at least minimized.

A firm understanding of the Central Blueprint would seem to be needed by leaders and managers to improve their understanding of emotional motivation. Resources need to be allocated to positive, relational work, so that crises of the proportions we met on this occasion could be prevented in the first place. We continue to understand the value of the restorative approach to problem-solving because it suits the way we are, as human beings, wired. And it is not sufficient that this kind of work is done to improve relationships and learning in classrooms. The adults in the school community need this approach for their own wellbeing so that they can deliver the best possible educational outcomes – cognitive and emotional – for young people.

Part 4

The Theory in Action in Education

CHAPTER 9

Affect and Emotion in a Restorative School

Graeme George

> There is no trust more sacred than the one the world holds with children. There is no duty more important than ensuring that their rights are respected, that their welfare is protected, that their lives are free from fear and want and that they can grow up in peace.
>
> *Kofi Annan (2000)*

Introduction

Most teachers working with young people in schools have some familiarity with educational psychology – that is, they would recognize the names Piaget, Kohlberg, Vygotsky and, perhaps, Skinner. Those who have pursued higher studies would have considered behaviourist, cognitivist, developmental and constructivist theories, among others, at some stage in their careers. They may have found some application of these theories to particular aspects of their work as teachers, in the design and evaluation of curriculum, in the design of assessment tasks, and perhaps in their understanding of the cognitive development of their students.

Many would be unfamiliar, however, with affect script psychology (ASP). Those who have some acquaintance with it may have been introduced to Nathanson's (1992) Compass of Shame through their involvement with restorative practices in the school setting. For most of us, this is how we first became introduced to Silvan Tomkins's work. But as powerful as the Compass of Shame is, there is much more to Tomkins's theory than that. Put simply, it's about understanding ourselves, our motivations and our relationships with others. What could be more important for a teacher than these understandings?

Very little of educational psychology has direct application in understanding who we are as people, and how we interact and form relationships with others, including our students. Again, little of traditional (or modern) educational psychology addresses the fact that a school is a complex human society in which each of its members lives an emotional, flesh-and-blood life.

Teaching is *emotional labour*. It is not just cognitive work. It is not just instruction, and students are not just machines to be topped up with knowledge. Teaching is *moral work* that is attempted by fallible and very human people as a service to other fallible and human people still developing fully into the adults that they will become. Teachers have hopes, dreams, fears and disappointments, and so do their students. They are emotional beings. Teachers who are able to understand themselves, their colleagues and their students can help ensure that the mini-society that is their classroom, and their society which is their school, will flourish. ASP provides teachers with a theoretical framework for developing these understandings.

In this chapter, I outline how the insights of ASP can have direct application to the moral, emotional work of teachers in schools, both in the area of behaviour management with restorative practices and in learning and teaching in the classroom. I assume the reader has read the first two chapters and gained some familiarity with the basics of ASP.

At the heart of ASP, and key to the functioning of an effective school, is Tomkins's Central Blueprint for Motivation, in which we are believed to be happiest and healthiest when we are achieving the following, in a balanced way:

1. maximizing positive affect

2. minimizing negative affect

3. maximizing the expression of affect (or minimizing its inhibition)

4. maximizing the power and ability to achieve 1–3 (after Kelly 2009).

This Central Blueprint in many ways describes one of the key aims of school communities, not surprisingly because schools wish to have balanced, healthy, happy students (and teachers).

In affect terms, we would all hope that the predominant affects being triggered in the school environment were interest-excitement in the learning process, as well as enjoyment-joy at being together with others of like mind and at achieving success either as students or teachers. Of course, students and teachers in a school cannot escape the human condition in order to be totally 'free from fear and want', and so negative affect inevitably arises no matter how diligently teachers and administrators work to prevent it. The high concentration of people in a school building or campus will predictably give rise to conflict from time to time, perhaps as distress-anguish bubbles over into anger-rage, or when shame-humiliation is triggered. The diversity of any school population can be a source of disgust or dissmell in the form of (conscious or unconscious) prejudice or discrimination. It would be the hope of all adults who work in schools that students never experience fear-terror while in their school, but the 'surprise quiz' or the sudden realization of an incomplete homework assignment will inevitably trigger this affect at some level in students at times.

Of the nine innate affects, shame-humiliation was perhaps the last to evolve. Shame-humiliation is triggered by any impediment that occurs to disrupt our ongoing enjoyment of the positive affects, interest-excitement or enjoyment-joy. While we may experience scenes involving this affect as initiating the emotions of frustration, disappointment, rejection, loneliness, or feeling ashamed, embarrassed or mortified, the basic affect shame-humiliation simply serves to shine a spotlight on an impediment to the former pleasant enjoyment of the positive affect. Nathanson (1992) identifies that, since the positive affects of interest-excitement and enjoyment-joy are often experienced through our communion with other people, the shame-humiliation affect is often experienced as an interruption to this pleasant communion or connection with others. It is, therefore, a particularly social affect, and this makes it of great interest to those who work in schools.

I now begin to examine how schools can better follow the Central Blueprint by attempting to bring into alignment with ASP some recent psychological theory and research from just a little outside the area.

The Self-Reflective Emotions: Differentiating Shame from Guilt

Shame and guilt are two members of a larger family of *self-conscious* emotions, so-called because they rely on the individual's ability to reflect on and evaluate the self by reference to a set of internal or societal standards. In much of the psychological literature the two terms are used almost interchangeably and are included in the group of 'moral emotions' as they are presumed to inhibit undesirable behaviours and encourage positive, altruistic, pro-social behaviours. In this way, 'shame, guilt, embarrassment and pride function as an emotional moral barometer, providing immediate and salient feedback on our social and moral acceptability' (Tangney, Steuwig and Mashek 2007, p.346).

ASP tells us that, at the biological level, we all share the same nine innate affects. The affect shame-humiliation, for example, produces the same stimulus-affect-response (SAR) scene in every individual for whom there has been some impediment to interest or enjoyment. The same physiological response of a lack of muscle tone in the neck and shoulders, a slumping forward of the head with an aversion of the eyes to the side or downward – and perhaps a blush – can be felt by all for whom this affect has been triggered. (Note that a frequent problem caused by the loss of eye contact is that it can be misinterpreted by those in authority as meaning the person experiencing shame is either being disrespectful or not listening.) Finally, all people in the very moment of shame affect are in a state of 'cognitive shock' – an issue that is explored later in connection with the learning process itself.

Once we become aware – conscious – that shame affect has been triggered, memories of similar scenes are drawn upon, which in themselves amplify the conscious negative feelings produced by the affect that has been triggered. We refer to this feedback loop, in which our biography has come to amplify and enlarge the initial physiological and affective response, as an emotional state. This emotional state is the end result of a vast array of memories of previously triggered shame affect. It is this emotional state that then determines which scripts will be played out in response. These *emotional states* of shame and guilt, both of which result from the affect shame-humiliation are our focus in this first section.

Perhaps the most useful, and commonly accepted, distinction between the emotions of shame and guilt was proposed by Helen Block Lewis (1971) and developed and extended through empirical studies by Tangney (Tangney 1990, 1994; Tangney and Dearing 2002; Tangney *et al.* 2007; Tangney and Tracy 2011). In Lewis's view, both emotional states result from evaluation against a set of standards, either personal or social, but the object of the evaluation differs in the two cases. It is proposed that a person is more likely to feel the emotional state of shame when they evaluate *the whole self* against a particular standard, but they would be more likely to experience the emotional state of guilt when they are able to evaluate *their behaviour* against the standard. For both, the initial trigger prompting this evaluation is the impediment to ongoing positive affect that has caused the shame affect SAR scene. It is their biography – the sum of all their previous experiences – that then determines the object of their evaluation, and hence which of the two emotional states results.

Put simply, when people feel shame they feel badly about themselves, whereas when they feel guilt they feel badly about a specific behaviour. Empirical research supports that this differential emphasis on the self ('*I* did that horrible thing') versus a specific behaviour ('I did that *horrible thing*') results in very different emotional experiences and very different patterns of subsequent behaviour (Tangney *et al.* 2007).

Of the two emotional states, shame is the more painful of the two, since in shame the entire core self is at stake, and hence shame is often associated with a sense of shrinking or of *being small*, as well as feelings of worthlessness and powerlessness. Guilt, on the other hand, is less painful because the object of concern or condemnation is just a specific behaviour and not the entire self. Consequently, people experiencing guilt are not challenged to defend the self but rather are drawn to reflect on their specific behaviour and are more able to consider its consequences, especially for others.

Tangney and Dearing (2002) report that guilt has been found to be associated with motivation towards reparative actions including confessions, apologies and undoing the consequences of the behaviour. In contrast, shame is associated with attempts to deny, hide or escape the shame-inducing situation – that is, to avoid dealing with the cause of the shame by recourse to what we would recognize as being the sets of scripts described by Nathanson's Compass of Shame and as outlined by Vernon Kelly in Chapter 1.

The four sets of scripts described in the Compass of Shame are maladaptive because they don't enable or require us to examine and address what the spotlight of shame has highlighted about us or our behaviour. They are common responses to the experience of shame simply because, as Tangney (1994) has identified, acknowledging fault with and addressing some defect of the self is a daunting task. The self is who we are, and it is all we have. The Compass of Shame responses enable us to ignore whatever it is that we would rather not admit is part of our self by denying or by-passing the painful shame emotion.

It is important to note here that it would in fact be possible, if not likely, for a person to feel both shame *and* guilt over a particular transgression. Even in those situations in which a person predominantly evaluates *their behaviour* against the standards and finds it wanting (a guilt-like response), it is still likely that they will feel less than good about *themselves* (a shame-like response) (Kelly 2012, personal communication). In this way it is difficult, from an ASP viewpoint, to imagine the 'shame-free guilt' to which Tangney refers. Certainly, the guilt-like response has only been initiated as a result of a scene involving the triggering of shame affect. To not have some level of shame-like response coassembled with the guilt-like response would appear unlikely.

Additionally, experience in restorative processes attempting to address the harm which results from wrongdoing shows that, within a particular individual, shame-like responses and guilt-like responses can appear to emerge at different times in response to the same incident or behaviour. As I suggest later, perhaps both responses can serve useful and healthy purposes in a social context at the appropriate moment and at an appropriate intensity. We shall also see how a restorative approach to dealing with wrongdoing and conflict can be used to encourage the transition from a shame-like response towards a more guilt-like response.

While putting forward fairly compelling evidence to consider shame as a largely undesirable emotional response, Tangney and Tracy (2011) agree with Nathanson (1992) that, in some specific situations, shame's painful focus on the self may in fact be helpful in order for the individual to be sufficiently motivated to examine some aspect of the self that would best be corrected. In these cases, the challenge would be to engage in the reflection necessary to perhaps revise one's fundamental values and priorities in the desired direction, without being diverted by defensive or denial reactions such as the scripts at the four poles of the Compass of Shame (Nathanson 1992). The supportive yet challenging environment created through the use of restorative practices in schools, as explored later, would assist people to make these necessary yet painful adjustments.

Similarly, Tangney and Tracy (2011) admit that guilt can also become a maladaptive response to transgressions or failure when an exaggerated or distorted sense of responsibility develops, when guilt becomes fused with shame, or when the individual is unable to find a successful path toward redemption. Most students of ASP would identify guilt as the coassembling of shame affect with fear – especially the fear of damaging the relationship with a significant other. Guilt, in this view, would be maladaptive if the fear is predominantly amplified in the emotional state, hence preventing the other-centred focus often associated with the guilt response. This would be particularly likely in a school with a highly punitive discipline regime. Such an environment could amplify the fear affect experienced by the student swamping the more positive, other-centred motivations associated with a guilt response. A more restorative school climate, on the other hand, encourages the student to first consider the consequences of their behaviours for others rather than to dwell on the consequences for themselves.

Group Shame and Guilt

While the distinctions between shame and guilt in response to personal transgressions have been explored here, Tangney *et al.* (2007) also report that other researchers have been investigating the capacity of individuals in groups to experience vicarious guilt or shame as the result of some transgression or failing of a member of the group. In their work, parallels between individual and vicarious shame and guilt have been found.

Group-based shame has been found to be most likely to result when the nature of the shared identity is threatened by one member's behaviour, leading to challenges around maintaining the positive group identity. If the impediment to ongoing interest or enjoyment is triggered by some characteristic central to the identity of the group itself, this is more likely to lead to a sense of vicarious shame. For a group of students whose shared identity is built largely around being the 'sports stars', for example, then one of their members being defeated in some competition of physical strength can lead to a shame-like response since the nature of their shared identity is threatened. For this group, *attack other* scripts are a possible way of reasserting their threatened identity.

Group-based guilt, on the other hand, appears to be more dependent upon the interdependence one feels with the perpetrator (Tangney *et al.* 2007) – a sense of indirect responsibility for the behaviour of the individual. Such group-based guilt is more likely when the nature of the failing or transgression is unrelated to the shared identity of the group. In these cases, the behaviour can be condemned – or at least recognised as unacceptable – without the group identity being threatened. For example, if a group of students whose shared identity relates solely to their being musicians of a particular type contains a member who begins engaging in bullying behaviour of students outside the group, it is unlikely that this behaviour would be felt as threatening the identity of the group itself. Instead, it is likely perhaps that those group members closest to the 'perpetrator' may feel vicarious guilt and may act to stop or limit the bullying behaviour in their friend.

As with personal experiences of guilt, group-based guilt has been found to have a greater association with empathy and a motivation to repair and make amends. The link between shame and anger in the personal case also holds for vicarious shame, reinforcing the negative nature of shame. While there is some suggestion from the research that group-based shame could encourage a motivation to improve the image of the group in a more proactive fashion than is found for personal shame (Tangney *et al.* 2007), it could also easily be imagined to lead to denying or by-passing the shame similar in this group sense to that of the scripts described by the Compass of Shame in the personal case. Consideration of the behaviour of some groups in schools, and in wider society, would allow a ready identification of the playing out of dominant scripts such as *withdrawal, attack self, avoidance* and *attack other.*

Identification of some undesirable group behaviours in schools as being Compass of Shame responses can be useful if it allows teachers to address the cause(s) of the shared shame affect, rather than simply to respond to the group behaviour itself. Responding to the behaviour in these cases, without looking at possible shame affect triggers, would be treating the symptoms without going to the source of the problem. In most schools there are, from time to time, ongoing conflicts between groups or cliques of students. In most cases, these conflicts can be traced to group shame affect triggering an *attack other* set of scripts. Simply responding to the conflict itself without giving attention perhaps to the lack of understanding and empathy between the two groups, or to whatever else has been triggering shame affect, will likely ensure that the conflict will rise again at some point, no matter how effectively it is suppressed for the moment. A restorative approach to conflict, as described later, is one way of effectively getting to and dealing with the root cause of the conflict.

Affect Script Psychology in Restorative Practices in Schools

Promoting Moral Development in the School Setting

The positive moral development of students would appear to depend upon three factors or approaches (after Tangney and Dearing 2002), namely:

1. the development and adoption of appropriate moral standards

2. the development of moral reasoning skills

3. the development of the capacity for appropriate and healthy moral emotions.

Of these, the first two are probably most commonly addressed in schools through specific programmes that could broadly be labelled character education, or social-emotional learning. Some of these specific programmes have been described and evaluated by a number of researchers (see Benninga *et al.* 2006; Berkowitz 2006; Berkowitz and Bier 2006; Cann 2002; McGrath 2007) and will not be explored here. (See also the Collaborative for Academic, Social and Emotional Learning [CASEL] at www.casel.org for extensive materials on social/emotional learning programmes in schools.)

In schools that employ such specific programmes aimed at development in this moral realm, it is worth considering that the success or otherwise of these programmes is most likely influenced or mediated by, if not dependent directly upon, other issues outside the specific programme such as the school culture or climate, the school's disciplinary style, the pedagogy employed in classrooms, and the quality of the relationships between students as well as between students and teachers. After all, students spend the majority of their time in school outside any formal character education programme. This suggests that even in schools where character education programmes form an explicit part of the curriculum, attention needs to be given to the totality of the experience of schooling for the students in order to best support the developmental aims of the programmes.

It could be argued that it is in fact the total experience of schooling (what some have referred to as the 'informal' or 'hidden' curriculum of the school) that could be more influential in all aspects of moral development of students, but particularly important in the third dimension, the development of the capacity for healthy moral emotions. Certainly, some researchers have connected various aspects of this broader conception of the curriculum of a school, in particular the predominant disciplinary style of the institution, with the development of shame management styles in students, and consequent implications for anti-social behaviours such as bullying (Morrison 2005).

Strategies from the literature to assist young people to develop guilt-proneness over shame-proneness tend to converge both with common sense and with the restorative approach to discipline and relationship building, as well as with what was promoted by Baumrind (1971, cited in Berkowitz and Grych 1998) as authoritative parenting. The common thread through all of these is the understanding that distinguishing between approval/disapproval of the self versus the behaviour is central to healthy development.

Consideration of the sequence of development of the infant into the child and on to the adolescent provides an important challenge to this separation of the self from the behaviour. It is widely accepted that the infant first identifies the sense of self around the second year of life. From that point forward, the child has not only a sense of the self but also a vital relationship with the primary caregivers. As Kelly (2011) has eloquently described, from its earliest moments after birth the infant learns that people are the source of relief of negative affect (when they feed or change the baby) and that they can also be sources of positive affect (e.g. in play). This realization is a key learning that contributes to the development of attachment scripts between the infant and the primary caregivers.

It would also be in this period, however, that the inevitable impediments to that ongoing positive affect provided by the caregiver first begin to build scenes that will result in later script formation around shame affect. During this early formative stage, the infant is not yet able to separate his 'behaviour' from his 'self'. When we say, 'Alec, that's a naughty thing you did', Alec often takes away the message 'You're a bad boy' – conveyed as much through tone of voice, gesture and posture as by the words used. That is, the negative affect prompted by the reprimand prompts a shame response in which the infant is not yet able to separate the behaviour from the self. In this way, shame-proneness could be considered a default position for the human condition (Tangney 2011, personal communication), and those young people who later develop a predominantly guilt-prone approach to life's difficulties have made a successful transition from these early shame-based scripts to a more adaptive set of responses.

Even though research from longitudinal studies suggest that the tendencies or dispositions, either guilt-proneness or shame-proneness as well as the corresponding forms of the positive emotion of pride, may be well established by middle childhood and that these dispositions, once formed, are remarkably stable over time at least through until late adolescence and early adulthood (Tangney and Dearing 2002), there is evidence that the dispositions are still susceptible to change, even well into adulthood (Tangney 2011, personal communication).

The weight of the empirical evidence in favour of guilt-proneness over shame-proneness leads Tangney and Dearing (2002, p.146) to conclude that these are 'individual differences that *matter*' in the light of their far-reaching implications for the individuals and the communities to which they belong. They are therefore individual differences that matter to those responsible for working with and educating young people.

If parenting styles have an influence on the development of guilt-proneness (Berkowitz and Grych 1998), then so does the socialization process of schooling and, in particular, the disciplinary style of the school. How the school community responds to conflict and wrongdoing is known to be influential in determining the shame management style of its students (Morrison 2005), and it could be suggested that this could also either encourage or discourage a move within its individual students from shame-proneness towards guilt-proneness. A punitive institutional style of discipline has been shown to be associated with management styles that centre on enhancing shame, encouraging recourse to the Compass of Shame scripts. A more restorative style of discipline, where the focus is first upon repairing the harm that has resulted from conflict or wrongdoing, is more likely to promote guilt-like responses in student offenders, encouraging the development of guilt-like, other-centred scripts. When the student offender's energy is not consumed defending his *self* from condemnation, he is likely to be more open to repairing the harm his behaviour has caused for others.

Separating the Self from the Behaviour

The importance of separating the selfhood of the person from his/her behaviour has long been an emphasis in the practice of restorative justice where behaviour is confronted with disapproval within a continuum of respect and support (Braithwaite 1989). This aim to separate the approbation of the behaviour from the potential condemnation of the offender himself finds expression in the adage that *the problem is the problem; the person is not the problem.*

The aim in any restorative process, according to Braithwaite, should be *reintegrative* shaming in which the offender experiences disapproval of his behaviour, but within the loving support and personal acceptance of his community of care. In the light of later work on shame and guilt as discussed above, perhaps this notion of reintegrative shaming could be better constructed as a process of encouraging the offender to move from a predominantly shame-like response towards a more guilt-like response. The community of care draws upon the affect interest that already exists in the relationship with the offender, and encourages him to take interest in making things right in the wake of poor behaviour. Such reintegrative shaming (or encouraging the emotional shift from shame to guilt) is proposed to encourage the offender to move from an egocentric focus towards a more empathic, other-centred response to those he has harmed. The modelling of the offender's community of care extending empathy towards the victim of the wrongdoing encourages the offender to move towards a more guilt-like response, focused on the needs of those who have been harmed, rather than turning inwards on the self in defensive responses.

Proactively Building Community in the School

One of the key aims of any school is the building of a sense of community among its students, and between students and the adults in the school. For such cooperative relationships to best develop, according to Tyler and Blader (2000), individuals need to feel a high level of pride in membership of the group and a high level of respect within the group. A high level of pride in being a member of the group means that the student feels that 'It's good to be a student here!' whereas a high level of respect is felt when the student believes that he 'has a place here at the school'. Other authors have used different pairs of descriptors for these key needs and the pair that most appeals is *belonging* and *significance*. For students to feel part of the school community, they must feel that they belong (i.e. they are *interested* in being part of the group), and that they are significant (i.e. they feel that others are *interested* in them being part of the group).

After Kelly (2011), this is the basis of the relationships that form between students, and between students and teachers, when they become *interested* in others being *interested* in them.

That these twin needs are central to the students' sense of wellbeing and attachment to the group is borne out by the results of the investigation into the school massacres in the US after the Columbine tragedy (Moore *et al.* 2003). In studying the characteristics of the student shooters across a number of cases, the only significant common characteristic that could successfully be identified was a level of 'social marginality' – that is, the students' needs for belonging to the group and significance within the group were not being met, with tragic consequences.

Schools build this sense of belonging and significance for students through encouraging and enabling students to meet the requirements of the Central Blueprint. Kelly (2011) has reframed the Central Blueprint in relationship terms that could be paraphrased as follows:

1. We should come together to share and maximize positive feelings.

2. We should come together to share and minimize negative feelings.

3. We should come together to express our feelings in order to maximize our ability to do 1 and 2.

4. We should encourage and share the ability and power to do the above three things.

Following this Blueprint helps create among students a sense of belonging and significance – by maximizing the positive affect that binds people together in shared interest, and minimizing the negative affect that isolates or separates them. All the usual ways in which schools build community – for example, through team activities, sport and extra-curricular activities, parades, assemblies, rallies – are really attempts at encouraging a sense of belonging and significance through application of this Central Blueprint. As anyone working in schools with young people would be aware, if the school itself does not, through its activities and structures but mostly through its relationships, successfully encourage this belonging and significance among its students, the students will do it for themselves within sub-culture (or counter-culture) cliques that may or may not be conducive to school-wide harmony and cooperation. Either in ways that we might describe as pro-social or anti-social, students in schools are going to find ways of meeting their needs under the Central Blueprint. Obviously, it pays to encourage them to meet these needs in positive, pro-social ways, both for the sake of the school climate and for the students' own development.

Affect Script Psychology in Teaching and Learning in Schools

While this discussion has focused on the power of understanding affect in terms of the processes used in restorative practices in schools, it has not addressed the insights that ASP enables for teachers working with young people outside these (more or less) informal processes.

A significant benefit of understanding affect in working with young people is being able to understand what would otherwise be interpreted as volitional, intentional misbehaviour instead of actions motivated by particular affects. This is true of ourselves and our colleagues, as well as the students. Such insight can often prevent misinterpretation and miscommunication, and can assist us in designing more effective strategies to lead students in our schools in their learning and development. Being aware of how affect drives our motivations, and being able to correctly identify and interpret these affect drivers, can enable teachers to de-escalate potential problems with student behaviour by seeing through the 'acting out' towards more fundamental factors that might be triggering shame, fear, distress or anger in students. To paraphrase Kelly (2011), if you don't understand what motivates you, then how can you understand who you are, and what you do?

All Attention is Affect

According to Tomkins's Central Blueprint discussed earlier, in the classroom, teacher and students alike are motivated to maximize positive affect and to minimize negative affect. Anything that acts as an impediment to our ongoing enjoyment of these positive affects will trigger shame affect, and in a classroom situation there can be many such impediments to ongoing positive affect. In such a public situation, we are not usually encouraged to minimize the inhibition of affect (the third requirement of the Blueprint) due to the socialization we have experienced prior to coming to that point. With affect expression suppressed and shame affect regularly triggered, it is likely that our negative emotions will become evident from time to time in other ways – for example, as frustration or annoyance on the part of the teacher, or by off-task and even disruptive behaviour by students. Off-task or bored students might very well find their own way to maximize their positive affect and minimize their negative affect in ways that the teacher would prefer not to happen in class!

The socialization that causes us – and our students – to suppress the unbridled expression of affect in public (such as in the classroom) is, on some levels, essential to our successful functioning in these situations. The affective resonance that could occur in a classroom of 25 people would play havoc with the purposes of the lesson. Even with such suppressed affect, every teacher knows the contagious nature of affect in a classroom – for example, in the last lesson on a warm summer afternoon.

Thus, ASP can give us some insights into the learning process by considering the affects at play in the complex social situation of the classroom. It is particularly important to consider the potential for shame affect and subsequent shame emotion to interfere with classroom goals, given the very public nature of everything that happens in a class. Things that might, in one-on-one situations, only elicit a minor shame reaction can be magnified seemingly exponentially by the feeling that it might be being observed and judged by 24 peers – or, in the case of the teacher, by a room full of students not always sensitive to the frailties of their teacher.

First, it is important to recognize that all ordinary attention – that is, the attention of students to the work in the class that the teacher expects – has its source in affect. Recall that no stimulus makes it through to consciousness without an affect spotlight first being triggered and a scene established. While in the classroom situation it would be hoped that this attention would be the result of the triggering of positive affect, it is also true that negative affect gets our attention. Hearing footsteps behind you when walking alone in the dark at night certainly gets your fearful attention, as would the announcement of a surprise quiz at the start of a lesson.

That all attention is driven by affect is not intuitively obvious to us. Attention is such a commonplace thing in our lives. As Kelly (2011) identifies, much of the time interest is not a very intense experience so we don't necessarily become aware of it. We do not notice that we are interested. We just are. If we were not, then the object of our attention – whether it's reading a book, or doing some gardening, or watching a movie – wouldn't keep our focus. As Nathanson points out in the Prolog to Silvan Tomkins's *Affect Imagery Consciousness* (2008, p.xviii): 'Each of the nine innate affects is equally responsible for the attitude we call "attention" and the universal sense that attention requires some form of effort or work leads us to claim that we "pay" attention to a stimulus.'

Further, he identifies that when we – or our students – have difficulty with paying attention, it always involves the affect system. Either the stimulus is insufficiently novel or significant to gain our interest or some other stimulus is triggering another affect distracting us away from the task as, for example, if we are hungry or thirsty and hence in distress (Nathanson 1992).

Affect in Simple Learning

In a productive, positive classroom in which students and their teacher are engaged in simple acts of learning, the repeating sequence of interest and enjoyment affects is somewhat similar to that of a parent and child playing a game of peek-a-boo. The affect interest is triggered in response to some novel stimulus, resulting in a pleasant increase in central nervous system activity. In the game, this is the result of the engagement of the child by the parent, and by the parent covering her face so she can't be seen by the child. In the classroom, while working with simple lower-level learning tasks, this interest is the result of the teacher introducing something new, either by direct instruction or by some indirect pedagogy. The interest affect for students in the classroom would also be sourced from the positive relationship between the teachers and the students. Students are naturally interested in their teacher being interested in them. This is the basis of the teacher–student relationship, and why classes can be very difficult when that relationship has never been nurtured, or has deteriorated for some reason.

The enjoyment affect, which is triggered in response to a decrease in central nervous system activity, is brought about in the game by the parent removing her hands to reveal her face once again to the child. In the classroom, enjoyment is triggered when the students realize that they understand, and can therefore assimilate into their pre-existing knowledge framework, the new piece of information. This ongoing sequence of positive affect can be depicted in terms of central nervous system activity cycles, as in Figure 9.1.

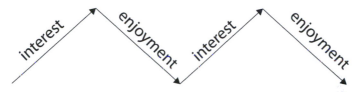

Figure 9.1 A recurring sequence of interest followed by enjoyment

Of course, any impediment to this ongoing cycle of positive affect will trigger shame affect.

In simple learning tasks, this shame affect can be quickly overcome by the teacher explaining the new point in a slightly different way, or reframing what it is that is being learnt, in order to recapture the student's interest and, hence, attention. Often, the most effective way to reframe what the student is thinking erroneously is for the teacher to acknowledge that the error is understandable and to ask questions that bring the student back to the more correct interpretation. Acknowledging that the error is reasonable extends empathy to the student, relieving the pain of the shame affect. Asking questions enables the student to reconsider his position from a new angle. It also rekindles interest through the interest shown by the teacher.

This empathic response requires the teacher, though, to first notice that shame affect has been triggered in one or more of the students, often by correctly interpreting whatever behaviour the shame affect may have initiated. Since the affective response is usually in proportion to the intensity of the shame affect triggered, it is unusual for these minor glitches in the learning process to escalate beyond a quizzical look or some minor off-task behaviour. That is unless, for a particular student, this has become a regular pattern of impediments presenting themselves and interrupting the learning process. I consider such cases of chronic learning shame later.

While it is important for the teacher to recognize that the shame affect in the student indicates that he has probably not understood a particular point the teacher was making so that the teacher can then take steps to overcome the impediment for the student, it is also important to recognize that the child's lack of understanding can also trigger shame affect in the teacher. The child's failure to understand something is an impediment to the flow of the lesson, and hence an interruption to the positive affect the teacher was enjoying a moment ago. If the teacher is not aware of this, he could himself be drawn subconsciously to one of the four sets of scripts from the Compass of Shame, and respond in an inappropriate manner – perhaps with frustration, annoyance or sarcasm, for example, as *attack other* scripts. Any of these inappropriate responses could initiate a shame spiral (as described below) since they would act as an impediment to the interest the student has in the teacher being interested in him. Such a negative or shaming response threatens the positive relationship that exists between student and teacher because it adds to the shame affect already triggered by the student's lack of understanding.

Affect in Complex Learning

In the case of more meaningful or more complex learning tasks, the potential for shame affect on the part of the student and/or the teacher is much more significant, and shame affect may in fact play a pivotal role in the learning process itself. More complex learning tasks in this description could include, for example, the difficult process of learning to read in the case of very young children, beginning to work with algebra in middle school classes, or studying and integrating complex concepts in physics or history at the senior level. In each case, the stakes can be high because of the complexity of the task for the student and also because of the importance of mastering the material or the skill for later learning. In each case, the experience of failure along the way is almost inevitable. Indeed, recent research in learning seems to suggest that, for deep or complex learning to occur, failure (or confusion, impasse or disequilibrium) may be a necessary part of the learning process without which the higher-level thinking that is required would not be prompted (Graesser *et al.* 2005; VanLehn *et al.* 2003).

In such complex learning, the fact that shame affect is triggered is simply an indication that something is not yet understood. As information for the student, this is vital input to the learning process, if the student and the teacher can correctly interpret the message before it becomes a Compass of Shame response. In this view, the triggering of the shame affect is not necessarily negative. It simply identifies that there is something the student needs to understand better, and this is exactly what the students and the teacher are there in the classroom to achieve. In this way the triggering of shame affect, the focus of Nathanson's spotlight of shame, is identifying what has to be understood more clearly in order for the student to make progress in his learning.

In a complex learning situation, the sequence begins as for the simple case above. The students experience interest in novel work and in a positive relationship with a teacher that brings predominantly positive affect. When an impediment intervenes in the ongoing positive affect – that is, when there is some aspect of the new work that the student cannot grasp – the affect shame-humiliation is triggered. The spotlight of shame identifies that a certain part of the new work does not yet make sense to the student. The student falls headlong into the physiological shame response. In that moment, there is cognitive shock[1] and the student can't think clearly. He is unable to bring to bear the cognitive processing that might actually serve to unblock the impediment. The fact that he is potentially being observed by his peers can also serve to magnify the negative affect.

In that moment of confusion, of cognitive shock, the student may attribute the block to one of two causes. He may attribute the impediment to not thinking clearly enough or deeply enough (i.e. to some behaviour on his part). This is a 'guilt-like' response to shame affect. Alternatively, he may attribute the block to some deficiency in the self that will make it impossible ever to grasp this concept. This is a 'shame-like' response to the same affect.

---

1   See Nathanson (1992, pp.142ff.) for more about the phenomenon of 'cognitive shock'.

The predominantly guilt-prone student is likely to attribute the current confusion to some temporary lack in listening or attention, or ability to see clearly what the teacher is saying. This student retains the interest in knowing what he now knows he doesn't know, and maintains the belief that he will be able to know it by refocusing his efforts, and perhaps asking a question. The ongoing interest for this student is enough to push through the shame affect and, once he has sufficiently regained his composure, redouble his efforts to understand. If successful in pushing through the shame affect, the resulting understanding leads to the positive affect of enjoyment as the new information is able to be assimilated within the student's existing knowledge, and the student's equilibrium is restored. The student has worked around the confusion by applying cognitive skills essential to the deep or complex learning that is being acquired.

The confusion – the shame spotlight – has in fact assisted this student's learning by prompting higher-order thinking about the subject. This notion has prompted David Boulton to refer to shame as a 'learning lamp', since without it the student can't readily identify what it is that needs to be learned (Nathanson and Boulton 2003). Other authors have quite rightly identified that being required to 'reflect, problem solve and deliberate in an effortful manner in order to restore cognitive equilibrium' actually results in deeper understanding of complex material than would otherwise be achieved (D'Mello and Calvo 2011, p.262). For these students, then, shame affect is being put to the service of the learning sought.

In contrast to the guilt-prone student, the predominantly shame-prone student would perhaps be more likely to make a more global evaluation of failure involving the entire self, prompting recourse to Compass of Shame scripts in order to lessen the resulting negative feeling. This may be especially true if the student has regular experience of this situation without having the learning strategies to overcome the shame affect and return to successful, interested learning. For such students, eventually fear and anticipatory shame will prevent them from even attempting any work that they find challenging. If their prior experience of such work has been regularly and consistently coloured by shame affect, confusion, cognitive shock and negative emotions, it is clearly not in their interests to invest themselves in learning tasks of this type. It would contradict the Central Blueprint's aims of maximizing positive affect and minimizing negative affect. For them, anticipatory shame would be likely to result in some of the Compass of Shame responses as outlined below, well before the learning challenge is even presented.

Compass of Shame in the Classroom

Teachers will recognize the following Compass of Shame scripts as they present in classrooms.

WITHDRAWAL

The student who withdraws in the face of shame prompted by difficulties with learning shuts down. He's there physically but not involved in learning activities. He is the student who 'doesn't care about school' and who passively avoids investing himself in tasks. He'll forget his books, or his pens, or his laptop. He won't have his homework done. In fact, he'll proudly assert that he 'doesn't ever do any work'. Not investing himself in the tasks expected of him protects him from the shame he expects to feel when he can't succeed at them. At the extreme end of this behaviour is the student in school-refusal for whom the experience of school is unremitting negative affect.

ATTACK SELF

The *attack self* response can be seen in the student who regularly puts himself down, because he gets into it before others do it for him. He's the 'I'm hopeless at maths' student, or the 'I'm just dumb' student who has this excuse for not trying. At the extreme end, he is the student engaged in self-harm in various forms.

AVOIDANCE

Avoidance scripts are evident in those students who build their persona around some other pursuit, such as the 'jocks' who see themselves only as athletes rather than students, the class clowns who are everyone's greatest friend. When these avoidance strategies won't dull the pain, these students are likely to engage in risk-taking behaviours, perhaps involving drugs or alcohol.

ATTACK OTHER

Students who deal with the pain of shame via *attack other* scripts tend to be most vocal in the classroom. By putting down other students, by ridiculing those who are trying to learn, these students regain a sense of power instead of the helplessness they feel in the shame emotion. 'This is stupid!' is an *attack other* response to a task at which they believe they will not succeed. 'He is/you are stupid!' is a more aggressive form of *attack other*. Sometimes the attack is directed at the teacher, but often at other students. Bullying or other physical aggression can be the end result of unresolved shame over learning.

Shame Spirals

A teacher who doesn't identify the student's Compass of Shame response for what it is – namely, an indication that the student has reached an impasse in his learning – is likely to experience shame affect of his own. Because we are rational beings, we tend to attribute willfulness and reason to people's behaviour even when affect is most likely to be the primary cause of that behaviour. A teacher faced with shame-bypassing behaviour on the part of students can easily misinterpret that behaviour as intentional, rational acting-out when in fact it is mostly unconscious behaviour on the part of the student. With this misinterpretation, the teacher is likely to respond to the student's shame response with his own shame response, triggered by the impediment to his own ongoing positive affect – his interest in being an effective teacher. This can then draw on past scripts the teacher has learned to lessen his own shame. On a bad day, this will result in a shame spiral where Compass of Shame scripts in both the teacher and student feed off each other and increase each other's triggering of negative affect. A predominantly shame-prone teacher with students who are also predominantly shame-prone, both unaware of how affect is driving their behaviour, is a recipe for extended shame spirals in which very little would be learned, other than how to successfully 'press the buttons' of all concerned.

This would seem to be a particular risk with beginning teachers. In the first years of teaching, the demands on teachers' attention can be overwhelming, especially in the light of their underlying need to demonstrate competence in what is, for them, the very public forum of their first classroom. Not only do they feel the eyes of their students upon them, but those of the school administrators, faculty heads and colleagues, as well as those of the parents of their new charges. In an attempt to appear competent and in control, and trying to cognitively process the demands of the teaching content and other administrative needs, beginning teachers are often simply unable to effectively read affect-driven behavioural issues. The more experienced teachers in the school, usually unaware of the language of affect and shame, are often unable to assist the new teacher other than to try to verbalize for them understandings that are implicit (and often sub-conscious) in their own more successful practice. It's not surprising that significant numbers of beginning teachers decide to pursue another career after the experience of their first year or two of teaching.

Even 30 years on, recalling my own shame spirals in my first few years of teaching still brings a shudder of negative affect. With the benefit of hindsight and some understanding of ASP, I can see it for what it was – namely, an inexperienced teacher being drawn into negative self-evaluations by students who felt much more at home in their room than I did. At the time, though, each lesson seemed like an emotional nightmare from which only the sound of that much-longed-for bell could wake us.

Getting Back on Track

The only real path to prevent – or break out of – such shame spirals is through awareness of the affect at play and an understanding of the behaviours that enable the student to bypass their shame. The antidote to shame is empathy, and the teacher aware of shame affect can look beyond the behaviour to the root cause, often a cause that the teacher knows only too well through his own experiences of encountering confusion in his own learning, and in teaching.

By empathizing with the confusion that the student is experiencing, the teacher lessens the pain of the negative affect. The student is then better able to think clearly, and the interest shown by the teacher in the student's learning sparks interest affect in him also. The task is then to rekindle interest in the subject by guiding the student's thinking, sharing with him recovery strategies that the teacher has successfully used in similar situations. By modelling such strategies – often by asking questions as much as by direct example – the teacher encourages the student towards the higher-order thinking required for understanding. This coaching in cognitive strategies is often described as an *apprenticeship model* of pedagogy, in which the teacher (the *expert* or *master*) inducts the student (the *apprentice* or *novice*) into the cognitive processes employed in the particular subject context in question. The modelling of cognitive strategies that work to overcome confusion is a key part of this master/novice relationship.

By taking this empathic route, the teacher strengthens the relationship between himself and the student through the interest shown, and helps the student to develop his own set of coping strategies to get themselves back on track.

The sequence of complex learning through the shame spotlight can be summarized diagrammatically, as in Figure 9.2.

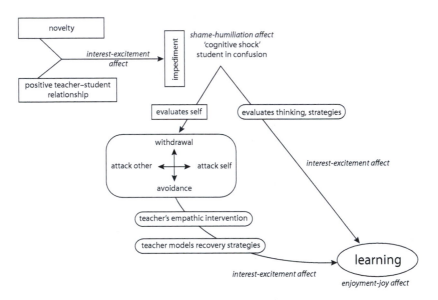

Figure 9.2 The process of complex learning

Indeed, the byproduct of shame in this situation is learning, and the path through shame is empathy, 'colluding' with the student against the confusion that exists.

Chronic Learning Shame

Of course, all teachers encounter some students for whom learning experiences have been a regular source of unresolved negative affect. These students present as effectively 'learning-disabled' since their anticipatory shame affect acts to prevent their investment in learning activities as alluded to above. For them, it makes sense to avoid the shame they expect to accompany any learning experience by recourse, before the fact, to one of the sets of scripts on the Compass of Shame.

For these students, the nature of scripts themselves and the way in which the mind builds scripts serves to magnify the negative affect beyond what might be expected. Initially, when first encountering negative affect associated with a lack of success in learning, these scenes are organized in the mind as negative learning experiences and associated with emotional responses of frustration and hopelessness. At this stage, the scenes are associated by content – that is, they are all negative experiences in the classroom. Over time, though, these negative learning experience scenes become associated with all other scenes in which the student has felt frustration and hopelessness, such as on the playing field, in personal relationships, or a thousand other pursuits. The negative emotion that wells up when the challenge of a new learning experience accesses this black pool of conflated scenes can be overwhelming for the student.

For many students 'learning-disabled' by shame, scripts at the *attack self* and *withdrawal* poles of the Compass are effective ways of reducing personal negative affect in a manner that is seen as 'socially acceptable' within the classroom environment. These students are very much in danger of simply being overlooked in a busy classroom.

Even once identified, overcoming these entrenched scripts in such students proves very difficult for any teacher. Making the tasks easier in the hope of providing opportunities for the student to achieve success is a reasonably common tactic in attempting to deal with cases of chronic learning shame, but, depending on the nature of the scripts operating for the student, this can sometimes only increase the feelings of helplessness as the student realizes that the teacher has lowered his expectations of him. His sense of isolation from the rest of his class is only confirmed by the teacher presenting him with different work or with lowered demands.

Perhaps the best way forward is to take the path of empathy as outlined above, and, while building a relationship based on mutual trust, slowly rebuild the student's capacity for learning through guided thinking and modelling of recovery strategies. Sharing the teacher's own strategies for dealing with cognitive shame achieves both ends: the mutual trust in the relationship is nurtured through this empathic sharing, and the student begins to see that particular strategies can indeed help them approach more difficult material. The interest affect prompted by the interaction within a patient teacher–student relationship can be supplemented by growing interest in learning ways of overcoming the obstacles previously thought insurmountable. The strategies described in the next section are also valuable in working with students with chronic learning shame.

Building Resilience Towards Shame in Learning

The learning process – particularly when it involves complex or deep learning – can never be free of shame affect. Learning inevitably involves failure, and failure inevitably triggers shame affect. Indeed, as stated above, it may be that such shame affect triggered by impediments to understanding is required for students to be prompted to undertake the higher-order thinking necessary to complex learning. To not encounter such impasses in learning might result in a less profound understanding than that which is otherwise available to the student. It would seem from the above that the key to successful learning may lie in the students' initial response to the confusion wrought by the shame affect. The scripts that the students have formed over time to deal with the negative affect of shame-humiliation would seem critical at this point.

MINDSETS

Ways in which teachers can encourage the development of more positive responses to the inevitable triggering of shame affect, and assist students to develop scripts involving greater resilience in responding to challenge, can be found in the work of Stanford University psychologist Carol Dweck (2012). Put simply, Dweck's work can be understood as another example of the need to separate evaluation of the self from evaluation of behaviour in encouraging script formation.

Dweck (2012) describes two mindsets that students bring to their learning, as follows. In a *fixed* mindset, a student believes that her capabilities are fixed since they are an integral part of the self, and the self by its nature is constant. By contrast, a student with a *growth* mindset believes that her capabilities can be developed through effort and application – that is, through her behaviours. These mindsets can be understood fundamentally in terms of the scripts that students use in response to challenge in learning – especially when shame affect has been triggered. Fixed-mindset students have developed shame-prone scripts which encourage them to evaluate *themselves*, while students with a growth mindset predominantly follow guilt-prone scripts which call for an evaluation of their *behaviour*.

Dweck's research demonstrates that holding a particular mindset has significant implications, especially for academic success in school. Those students who bring a growth mindset to their study demonstrate significantly greater improvement in their learning over time and develop their capacities and their resilience further in the face of academic challenge, compared with those holding a fixed mindset. Similarly, students with a growth mindset in regard to social attributes have been shown to be more resilient psychologically when encountering the social challenges of transitions between schools (Yeager and Dweck 2012).

The differential outcomes from the two mindsets can be understood if one considers the behaviours that are reasonable within each mindset when faced with a learning or social challenge. Those with a fixed mindset who believe that their ability is part of their self, and hence unchangeable, are more likely to rely upon more rigid Compass of Shame defences in the case of receiving negative achievement feedback. For a student with a fixed mindset, failing at a task is evidence that the self is faulty, which is something to be avoided at all costs. With a growth mindset, on the other hand, a student assesses failure at a task as an indication that she needs to work and study harder, and perhaps use different strategies.

An interesting aspect of Dweck's work (especially for classroom teachers) is that she demonstrates that it is possible to *teach* students to change from fixed mindsets (shame-proneness) to growth mindsets (guilt-proneness) through a programme of instruction about the brain's plasticity and by encouraging them to consider their abilities malleable and, therefore, open to improvement through specific study strategies (Yeager and Dweck 2012). Through repetition of this instruction, and the teacher modelling the study strategies himself, the students in her studies have been encouraged and enabled to re-script themselves towards the more positive growth mindset. This is remarkable given the implicit and very widespread belief in academic circles that intelligence or ability is indeed fixed for individuals. This shame-promoting belief underpins much of the philosophy and practice of educational systems worldwide and is an unchallenged assumption in many classrooms.

Dweck demonstrates the power of teachers modelling their own positive responses and strategies when shame affect is triggered in their own learning as a means of assisting students to rescript themselves from shame-proneness and default reliance upon the Compass of Shame responses.

Editorial Note

ASP predicts such an outcome. Shame is triggered innately in all people by impediments to positive affect. If one removes the impediment, shame is reduced or eliminated and positive feelings return. The teacher who shares his affect openly with students is creating positive emotional connections with students by not hiding behind a Compass of Shame script and creating impediment. Furthermore, positive emotional connections increase the amount of interest-excitement and enjoyment-joy in people. The greater the positive affect in someone, the easier it is for that person to overcome and manage shame. For example, in Tomkins (2008) Nathanson wrote of eye movement desensitization and reprocessing (EMDR) therapy – commonly used for reducing the harm of trauma – that:

> *The EMDR protocol 'tricks' the mind by transforming old scenes previously amplified by the negative affect shame-humiliation to what are essentially new scenes when amplified by the positive affect of interest-excitement. Since the patients' scripts had been formed by the steady accretion of new scenes to an established sequence, as each painful scene was revisited therapeutically in the ambience of the positive affect interest-excitement, the established*

pathological script was sequentially disassembled and rendered ineffective. I suspect that script theory will become an increasingly valuable system for the explication of much that is now obscure. (pp.xxii–xxiii)

The power that teachers have to increase or decrease shame-proneness is magnified by the amount of time students spend in school from childhood through adolescence. Restoratively oriented schools are a powerful antidote against the development of shame scripts.

The Critical Importance of Language

The language employed in restorative processes has long been held to be important, in particular the avoidance of globalizing language which serves to diminish the entirety of the person to a single label. The separation of the evaluation of the person's *behaviour* from the evaluation of the *self* has long been another critical aspect of restorative practices. What we have seen here is that this separation can be critical in the teaching and learning process as well as in managing behaviour.

The more negative outcomes demonstrated for the shame-prone student or for the student with the fixed mindset all point to the need to extend this separation into our academic language as well. Teachers need to do this in order to encourage the development of healthy, positive scripts that students can use to deal with the inevitable shame affect triggered as part of the learning process.

This is important in giving students either positive or negative feedback. It is important in giving feedback in the classroom, on the sports field and in every other area of student life. In all cases, feedback that praises or criticizes specific behaviours helps to reduce the likelihood of the student making an undesirable global assessment of the self, either positive or negative. The student will be more likely to see difficulties as being related to changeable behaviours that are within her control. Such praise or criticism of specific behaviours increases the chance that the student will approach future difficulty and challenge with resilience and as an opportunity to grow and to learn, rather than as simply confirmation of her belief that her ability is fixed and beyond her control.

Conclusion

A school in which a restorative practices philosophy guides the development of the total experience of schooling for its students is likely to be one in which students learn to form guilt-prone scripts rather than shame-prone ones. It would be a school in which teachers and students are encouraged to follow the Central Blueprint and to build a community characterized by empathy. It would be a school in which harm would be addressed in authentic ways which respect people while confronting unacceptable behaviours and challenging wrongdoers to make amends. It would also be a school in which students would be enabled to develop the social-emotional resilience to deal successfully with the many psycho-social challenges of adolescence.

A classroom in which effort is recognized and celebrated, and where an authentic relationship exists between the students and the teacher built on mutual trust, is likely to be a classroom in which the demands of the Central Blueprint are being promoted. It would be a classroom in which the benefits of confusion and disequilibrium (learning shame) are explored and shared, and it is likely to be a classroom in which guilt-prone scripts can be developed, where students believe that effort can improve ability, and where students learn resilience against the negative side of learning shame. It would be a classroom in which learning shame is valued as an aid to greater understanding of ourselves, each other and the subject under study through the firm conviction among teacher and students that ability can be improved and developed through effort.

The affect shame-humiliation evolved presumably for just such a purpose: to provide essential information for our survival and growth. Without an understanding of affect and shame, however, the triggering of the affect shame-humiliation inevitably leads to negative emotions and recourse to destructive, maladaptive behavioural scripts.

An understanding of ASP enables teachers and other school personnel to restore this affect to its rightful, adaptive role as an aid to the process of learning, both in the classroom and for life.

References

Annan, K.A. (2000) *The State of the World's Children*, UNICEF. Available at www.unicef.org/sowc00/foreword.htm, accessed on 10 November 2011.

Benninga, J.S., Berkowitz, M.W., Kuehn, P. and Smith, K. (2006) *Character and Academics: What Good Schools Do.* Available at http://charactered.epsb.ca/documents_for_website/CharacterandAcademics.pdf, accessed on 3 November 2011.

Berkowitz, M.W. (2006) *Character Education as Prevention.* Available at www.tanglewood.net/projects/teachertraining/Book_of_Readings/Berkowitz.pdf, accessed on 28 November 2011.

Berkowitz, M.W. and Bier, M.C. (2006) *What Works in Character Education.* Available at www.characterandcitizenship.org/component/content/article/2-uncategorised/42-what-works-in-character-education, accessed on 3 November 2011.

Berkowitz, M.W. and Grych, J.H. (1998) 'Fostering goodness: teaching parents to facilitate children's moral development.' *Journal of Moral Education 27*, 3, 371–391.

Braithwaite, J. (1989) *Crime, Shame and Reintegration.* Cambridge: Cambridge University Press.

Cann, K. (2002) 'Do Schools have a Role to Play in Crime Prevention? Use of the Protective Behaviours Program in Schools as a Primary Prevention Strategy.' Paper presented at the Role of Schools in Crime Prevention Conference, Melbourne.

D'Mello, S.K. and Calvo, R.A. (2011) 'Significant Accomplishments, New Challenges, and New Perspectives.' In S.K., D'Mello and R.A. Calvo (eds) *New Perspectives on Affect and Learning Technologies.* New York: Springer.

Dweck, C.S. (2012) *Mindset.* London: Constable & Robinson.

Graesser, A.C., Lu, S., Olde, B.A., Cooper-Pye, E. and Whitten, S. (2005) 'Question asking and eye tracking during cognitive disequilibrium: Comprehending illustrated texts on devices when the devices break down.' *Memory and Cognition 33*, 7, 1235–1247.

Kelly, V. (2009) *A Primer of Affect Psychology.* Available at www.tomkins.org/uploads/Primer_of_Affect_Psychology.pdf, accessed on 26 October 2011.

Kelly, V. (2011) *Affect and Emotion in Restorative Practice.* Available at www.rpiassn.org/practice-areas/affect-and-emotion-in-restorative-practice, accessed on 26 October 2011.

Lewis, H.B. (1971) *Shame and Guilt in Neurosis.* New York, NY: International Universities Press.

McGrath, H. (2007) *Making Australian Schools Safer.* Canberra: Australian Government.

Moore, M., Petrie, C.V., Braga, A.A. and McLaughlin, B.L. (eds) (2003) *Deadly Lessons: Understanding Lethal School Violence: Case Studies of School Violence Committee.* Washington, DC: National Academies Press.

Morrison, B.E. (2005) 'Restorative Justice in Schools.' In E. Elliott and R. Gordon (eds) *New Directions in Restorative Justice: Issues, Practice, Evaluation.* Cullompton: Willan Publishing.

Nathanson, D.L. (1992) *Shame and Pride: Affect, Sex, and the Birth of the Self.* New York, NY: W.W. Norton.

Nathanson, D.L. and Boulton, D. (1993) *The Role of Affect in Learning to Read: How Shame Exacerbates Reading Difficulties.* Available at www.childrenofthecode.org/interviews/nathanson.htm, accessed on 26 October 2011.

Tangney, J.P. (1990) 'Assessing individual differences in proneness to shame and guilt: Development of the self-conscious affect and attribution inventory.' *Journal of Personality and Social Psychology 59*, 1, 102–111.

Tangney, J.P. (1994) 'The Mixed Legacy of the Superego: Adaptive and Maladaptive Aspects of Shame and Guilt.' In J. Masling and R. Bornstein (eds) *Empirical Perspectives on Object Relations Theory.* Washington, DC: American Psychological Society.

Tangney, J.P. and Dearing, R.L. (2002) *Shame and Guilt.* New York, NY: Guilford Press.

Tangney, J.P. and Tracy, J. (2011) 'Self-Conscious Emotions.' In M.R. Leary and J.P. Tangney (eds) *Handbook of Self and Identity.* New York, NY: Guilford Press.

Tangney, J.P., Steuwig, J. and Mashek, D.J. (2007) 'Moral emotions and moral behaviour.' *Annual Review of Psychology 58,* 345–372.

Tomkins S. (2008) *Affect Imagery Consciousness: The Complete Edition.* New York, NY: Springer.

Tyler, T. and Blader, S. (2000) *Cooperation in Groups: Procedural Justice, Social Identity, and Behavioral Engagement.* Philadelphia, PA: Psychology Press.

VanLehn, K., Siler, S.A., Murray, C., Yamauchi, T. and Baggett, W.B. (2003) 'Why do only some events cause learning during human tutoring?' *Cognition and Instruction 21,* 3, 209–249.

Yeager, D.S. and Dweck, C.S. (2012) 'Mindsets that promote resilience: When students believe that personal characteristics can be developed.' *Educational Psychologist 47,* 4, 1–13.

CHAPTER 10

They Suck, School Sucks, I Suck

The Secret Emotional Life of a Child with a Brain That Learns Differently

Bill Hansberry[1]

Introduction

In this chapter I want to put the interaction between affect, learning disabilities and impaired executive brain functions under the spotlight. I hope to paint for you a big picture of the challenges that many young children affected by these conditions face at school. Most of all, I hope to highlight the devastating toll that conditions such as attention deficit hyperactivity disorder (ADHD), learning difficulties and the resulting shame have on these kids' social connections in the school environment.

Make no mistake, wherever there's a human difficulty, there's negative affect attached to it. For those of us working day in and day out in close emotional proximity to distressed children, it's an understandable emotional response for us to switch off to the depth of suffering that many kids endure. This ability to tune out to the emotions of others is sometimes referred to as *emotional detachment* and can guard against the constant threat of burnout.

We who work with children in institutionalized settings, such as schools, have also all inherited a centuries-old paradigm that tries to distinguish *emotion* and *learning* as unrelated entities. With this

---

1 This chapter was written in consultation with Jane Langley. I'd like to acknowledge Jane's contribution to my and others' thinking in the area of restorative practices. Jane's work has inspired us to think differently and creatively about adapting our work to cater for early years children – kids whose delayed functioning has made it hard for them to engage with traditional restorative script language – and, of course, husbands! Thanks for your help with this chapter, Jane.

paradigm comes a flawed belief system that dictates that for humans to be rational, analytical and logical learners, emotion must be pushed aside and ignored. Affect script psychology (ASP) challenges this old but popular paradigm and shows us that our emotions are the only gateway to attention. In other words, we simply cannot be aware of anything until it triggers one of our nine innate affects. This is how our brain sorts through the millions of bytes of information that our senses register every second, and makes decisions about which piece of this otherwise overwhelming sensory bombardment is important for us to pay attention to, so we can survive, even thrive, in any given moment. This naturally leads us to the conclusion that learning is only possible inside emotion. Maureen Gaffney (2011, p.44) makes this point well by saying: 'Emotions are your instant decisions about what is important, so they affect every aspect of your existence. They determine what you pay attention to; how you think; the meaning you put on events; and even what you remember.'

Lucky kids start school with a brain that can, most of the time, process information in the way it is delivered in mainstream schools. These lucky kids typically have secure attachments to their caregivers and are free from traumatic early life experiences. These young people spend much of the school day experiencing the affects of *interest* and *enjoyment*. This makes learning a mostly manageable task for them. As a result of their capacity to regulate their emotions (within normal limits), these children are pleasant to be around. They trigger positive affect in the adults and children who share classrooms and playgrounds with them, making them good company enough of the time for them to be accepted and warmly regarded by those around them.

This chapter is about our not-so-lucky kids whose slower development, learning challenges and sometimes even traumatic backgrounds wreak havoc with how their brains develop, process information and manage emotion. For many of these kids, their unpredictable functioning and fast feelings take a truly disastrous toll on their interactions with peers and teachers. As a result, the negative affects of shame, anger, fear and distress are constant companions as these kids battle circumstances and conditions that continually rob them of their capacity to think first, calm themselves, problem-solve and make good decisions based on their past experiences.

You are about to be introduced to one of these kids. His name is Bradley. Bradley is fictional, but, as you read, you will discover that you already know him and that you've met him many times before. Bradley's story highlights the powerful window that ASP gives us to the inner world of kids who function just like Bradley. It is my hope that, at the end of this chapter, you will see the Bradleys in your life in a different way – a way that empowers you to see the desperate longing to connect with others that lurks not too far underneath the awful behaviours that demand our attention and cause so much upset.

CASE STUDY: BRADLEY

Bradley: Part 1

Lydia is on playground duty when Dana, a student in her grade two class, reports that she has been kicked in the leg by an angry Bradley, a grade two student from the classroom next door. A wave of irritation comes over Lydia. Until now, it's been a peaceful playground duty. Lydia allows her negative affect to pass and takes a deep breath. Some days it's hard to act restoratively, she thinks to herself! Deep in Lydia's brain, her *caudate nucleus*[2] screams, 'That kid deserves a long stay in detention!' but Lydia has been teaching kids with tricky behaviours for far too long to give into instinctive 'tit for tat' responses. She knows that Bradley's volatile behaviours have everything to do with how he handles feelings of shame and rejection by peers and his worries about being left alone with no one to play with. Bradley's challenges will not be fixed by emotionally detached behavioural modification techniques. Bradley has a problem of connection.

Lydia listens while Dana tells her what just happened with Bradley, gently prompting at times with 'and then…' and 'what happened next?' and tactfully allowing appropriate wait time for responses to be given. Dana is distressed, confused and feeling shame. She needs to reduce her distress by telling her story. She needs be listened to: no interjections, no interruptions or fast answers – all of those things that are tempting for busy and distressed teachers, faced with many issues at once. When Dana has finished, Lydia pauses for a few important seconds – she's

---

2   Decisions to exact revenge have been shown to show a rush of activity in the *caudate nucleus* – the area of the brain known to process rewards (Jaffe 2011).

learned how pausing can save so much time down the track. Lydia then employs her second restorative strategy. She simply asks Dana, 'What do you think will help?'

Dana thinks for a few seconds and then says that she wants Bradley to know that she doesn't want to be his friend if he's going to 'go psycho' and kick her when she suggests that the two of them play with other kids. She shares that sometimes she likes to play with a bigger group of kids but that makes Bradley angry because he wants to keep her all to himself, as if he owns her. Dana says that she just wants to talk to Bradley about what happened and that she wants him to say sorry for kicking her. 'Sorry! Is that it?' Lydia's inner punisher screams sardonically. 'I don't want Bradley to get into trouble and I know he has trouble with his anger,' Dana adds anxiously. Dana knows what every kid with a scrap of social intelligence knows: Bradley getting sent to detention or being suspended won't make anything better for her, or for Bradley.

Understanding Dana's wishes, Lydia's intention is to first get Dana and Bradley together to talk about what happened, how they both feel about things and what will happen next. Lydia has run hundreds of small group restorative conferences like this over the years; the vast majority have been successful. Some haven't exactly gone to plan, but every conference has taught Lydia something valuable about how her students process their world. Conferences have helped her understand and build relationships between the kids she's worked with.

Lydia values restorative approaches because they make people think deeply about the reasons they do what they do. For kids like Bradley who get it wrong – often – restorative conferences allow them to reconnect with others. Importantly, restorative chats give other children incredible insight into the thinking and feelings of kids who 'do it tough', so they can better understand why things have happened. The understanding that evolves from these processes helps kids see the scared and worried person beneath the hard-to-deal-with behaviours, making these behaviours less scary. With these understandings, empathy is allowed to do its work. Kids like Bradley need understanding peers around them who see the good human being beneath their very public outbursts. Restorative approaches alter brain states, through many processes. One of these systems releases oxytocin – a hormone that settles threat (defensive) responses – allowing neural activity to spread from the reptilian and limbic regions to the neocortex, where perspective taking and cognitive empathy reside.[3] When these higher brain areas are activated, kids can wade through 'yucky feelings' so they can name issues and articulate their needs. These neural circuits simply can't be accessed when kids feel humiliated, threatened, anxious or angry.

Despite Lydia's steadfast faith in restorative approaches and her experience, she considers the approaching interaction with some apprehension. Lydia knows Bradley quite well. He is often at the time-out desk in her classroom when he needs space from an incident in his class or others need space from him. Bradley's yard behaviour is often the hot topic of staffroom discussions. This isn't the first time that young Bradley has lost his cool and struck out angrily.

Lydia looks at Dana, smiling hopefully and sighs. 'Well, shall we go and find him, then?' 'He's at the far edge of the oval,' Dana says. 'That's where he always goes when he gets his knickers in a knot.' Lydia imagines the Compass of Shame. Bradley has shorn himself from the herd and withdrawn to a place where students don't go. It's one of his only defences from the terrible thoughts and feelings that flood his mind when things go wrong for him.

THE SHAME THAT COMES FROM A BRAIN THAT CAN'T THINK BEFORE REACTING OR PLAN AHEAD

Bradley lives with ADHD. This means that he has little ability to put his brakes on. As a result, Bradley lives a life of constant regret, wondering why he can't make better decisions when somebody says something that hurts his feelings or when somebody does something he doesn't understand in a game. Sometimes Bradley hates his own brain – he calls it a 'stupid brain'. He wonders if he's just a bad person, one of the ways Bradley *attacks self* when he feels diminished and flawed.

After he calms down following problems, Bradley can always explain to teachers what he 'should have done, or should have said' instead of swearing, pushing, hitting somebody or refusing to follow the instructions of an adult. Bradley's been told over and over that he needs to 'think before he does things' by teachers who just don't understand enough about executive functioning problems in the brain. Some teachers just think he's plain evil!

---

3   See Lewis, Amini and Lannon 2000 for an explanation of these concepts in greater depth.

They wonder what kind of kid does the wrong thing over and over, when they know what they are doing is wrong.

The result for Bradley is that he feels like the naughty kid who hits, swears and loses his temper too often. The self-disgust that accompanies the desperate feeling that he can't change is almost unbearable, but somehow comfortable at the same time, like a pullover that fits well. Bradley's tricky behaviours are beginning to define who he is: the naughty kid who hits and curses people. Bradley thinks he's the kid no teacher wants to teach and no one wants to play with. His relationships with peers and teachers suffer terribly. He's rarely invited to play games because kids find him unpredictable. Bradley can't recall being invited to a birthday party of someone in his class but he knows that he's often been the one not invited. It hurts him deeply every time.

The double-hit for Bradley is that this sense of social rejection further diminishes his ability to regulate his emotions (Baumeister, Twenge and Nuss 2002). While feeling rejected, he is less able to use the higher, problem-solving parts of his brain to think through his anxious moments and to consider carefully a range of possible responses to problems and their likely outcomes. The shame triggered by the sense of rejection causes Bradley's brain to go into cognitive shock, a temporary condition where he can't think clearly and make well-thought-out decisions (Nathanson 1992). Cognitive shock is experienced by all of us in the first moments after the affect shame is triggered.

Bradley: Part 2

Lydia and Dana walk toward Bradley for a chat. He's taken himself to an out-of-bounds corner of the schoolyard. He is kneeling, angrily hacking at the ground with a stick. As Lydia approaches, she takes in the picture that is Bradley. Dirty tears stain his cheeks. His shoulders are tensed, his head bowed, his forehead furrowed. This is a child deep in the affects of shame and distress. Lydia feels her own jaw clench and her weight move to the balls of her feet. She's taken notice of her own emotions – something good communicators do. Lydia is feeling angry – her brain and body have resonated with Bradley's emotional state, because affect is contagious. She's experiencing emotional empathy. This is the same experience that urges people to soothe a crying baby or cross the street to avoid an arguing couple on a sidewalk. Lydia's experience with and understanding of ASP is the reason she pays attention to her own response as she observes Bradley. Because Lydia understands her own emotional response to Bradley, she can keep it under control and help him instead of escalating the situation.

Bradley is muttering angrily to himself. Lydia hears him say, 'I hate myself, and I want to blow this fucking school up.' These are distressing words from a seven-year-old. They carry such threat. Bradley's self-talk is swinging wildly between *attack self* and *attack other*. Bradley looks up and sees Lydia and Dana approaching. He springs up, throws his digging stick to the ground and begins to walk further into the out-of-bounds area, toward the fence, his shoulders hunched, fists clenched at his sides, head down. Bradley is currently in flight from shame. This is, in essence, *withdrawal* – hiding from others.

SHAME-AWARE BEHAVIOUR MANAGEMENT

Lydia knows she has to choose her words carefully. They will either intensify Bradley's feelings of shame or let him see her and Dana as people who will help him to feel better. 'Hey, Buddy. Dana would love a chat with you about what happened.' Bradley calls back in an angry voice, 'I only talk with friends, not people who I hate… Suspend me. I don't care what you do!'

'Well, that didn't go to plan,' Lydia whispers to Dana. Dana smirks, shrugs and rolls her eyes. Trying to force Bradley into a restorative chat in his current mood will only deepen his distress and make things worse, not better, for Dana. Lydia can't guarantee that she'll be able to keep her own emotions in check with Bradley throwing off so much anger. Lydia turns to Dana and says, 'Hey Dana, do you think it's best to let him cool off before we have a chat?' 'Yeah, he'll just lose it if we try to do it now.' Dana's right. She's watched lots of teachers get caught up in unwinnable power struggles with Bradley when they've tried to make him talk or acquiesce when he's distressed. In these moments, Bradley has ended up suspended because he's lashed out at teachers, sworn or turned furniture upside down.

Lydia calls out to Bradley, 'Bradley, we can see you are upset about what happened and we don't like seeing you upset. We'll find you for a chat later.' Bradley isn't a flight risk at the moment. He *has* fled from the school grounds in the past, but only when teachers have carelessly pursued him, demanding instant compliance. Lydia adds, 'For now, we need you to come back in bounds so we know you're OK… Thanks, Bradley.' With that, Lydia and Dana turn and walk away from Bradley, leaving him to calm down and giving him space to comply. Lydia hears Bradley's toxic mutterings. She ignores the abusive words. She knows that Bradley is on his last and frequent stop of the Compass of Shame – *attack other*. She also knows that this is his only defence against how he is feeling. Once upon a time, Lydia would have spun around and spat, 'What did you just say?' But she's learned that nothing good ever comes of this approach.

Lydia decides that if Bradley doesn't engage in a conversation with her and Dana later on today, she might refer him to detention, although that won't help matters. She will try to get Bradley and Dana together for a chat again later in the day. If that can't happen, she'll ask Greg, the school counsellor, if he's able to take the issue. Lydia is quietly determined to have the restorative conference, one way or another, for Bradley's sake as well as Dana's.

Bradley: Part 3

Bradley struggles at school. He lives with diagnosed ADHD and, despite being on stimulant medication, a disorganized home life makes it difficult to settle him into a steady dosage regimen.

Editorial Note: ADHD through the Lens of Affect Script Psychology

To better understand the behavioural profiles of adults and children diagnosed with ADHD, it is critical to understand the biology of human motivation. ADHD is, of course, not a singular disorder but an entire spectrum of disorders involving inherited differences from so-called 'normal' in certain areas of the central nervous system. It is a permanent condition as opposed to various other diseases of the brain that get worse over time. ADHD has a characteristic but somewhat variable set of symptoms including hyperactivity, distractibility and often intense excitability.

Since all behaviour is motivated by affect, it is easy to understand ADHD as a disorder of the affect system. ADHD involves a malfunction in the amplification component of the affect system, causing the affects to be overly intense when triggered. For example, something that would excite any child causes children with ADHD to become so excited that their bodies respond with highly excited, uncontrollable hyperactive behaviours. When anger is triggered, it becomes unmanageable rage, fear becomes unmanageable terror, and shame becomes unmanageable humiliation. Furthermore, distractibility caused by this condition is an impediment to positive affect and thus a trigger for the innate affect shame, making shame a prominent feature of these kids' experiential world from early in life. Many children with ADHD are forced to develop powerful Compass of Shame scripts from an early stage, scripts that become the source of the difficult-to-manage behaviours arising from attack other, attack self, withdrawal and avoidance defences against shame.

Bradley acts out during lessons, particularly when he is required to read or produce written work. He spends about three out of five lessons a week in time-out in the deputy principal's office because his behaviour is so terribly disruptive. There's a very good chance that Bradley's low literacy levels are connected to an undiagnosed learning disability, quite possibly dyslexia, because Bradley appears to have otherwise normal intelligence for his age. Bradley cannot remember a set of verbal instructions due to his auditory sequential memory weakness, so he often forgets what teachers ask the class to do. This is regularly mistaken by teachers as wilful defiance.

Bradley has significant difficulty making and keeping friends. He often starts heated arguments about whose friend is whose and regularly complains to teachers and peers (anyone who will listen) that other kids are stealing his friends from him. He is caught in the shame–jealousy–competitiveness triangle described by Kelly in Chapter 1. Bradley likes to hang around with only one or two other children most of the time as he feels terribly vulnerable and anxious in larger groups. When he does find himself in larger groups, Bradley has difficulty because he can't control what happens. He is quick to feel shame and then becomes over-excited or angry and unable to keep up with games like tag or ball sports. Bradley simply doesn't notice social cues that let other kids know when to move, when to laugh, when to keep quiet and when to say something friendly. Because of this, Bradley is quickly left behind, left out or ostracized because his mistimed words and movements, and poor social judgement come across to others as odd, insensitive or downright hurtful.

This social vulnerability causes Bradley to spin out of control with a range of unhelpful behaviours. Withdrawing and sulking, pretending to be hurt or showing off by trying to be the 'tough guy' in the group, playing too roughly or making cutting remarks to try to sound clever. Bradley's clunky behaviours frustrate and offend other kids, and when they ignore him or move away from him, Bradley becomes anxious and distressed. He resorts to name calling, threatening violence toward those he sees as a threat to his friendships, and threatening his friends that he'll bash them if they play with somebody else. Alternatively, out of desperation, Bradley may promise gifts to coerce friends to stay with him.

During the short-lived moments when Bradley feels connected and secure with one or two other students, he has all the outward appearances of a well-adjusted seven-year-old – delightful and cooperative in the yard and classroom, despite troubles with learning. It's as if he develops a sort of temporary resilience that otherwise evades him. However, when Bradley feels that peers are withdrawing from him or that he's being excluded from a group, a dark cloud descends over him and his behaviour deteriorates remarkably. He becomes aggressive toward other students and sullen and uncooperative with adults. He acts out in a range of ways in the classroom, mostly attention-seeking behaviour (making noises, clowning, wandering, or even outright aggression, like belching in other students' faces). All of these are desperate attempts to be noticed and included, but are defences against his shame. These behaviours invariably land Bradley in time-out, or out of the classroom. This compounds his feelings of exclusion and shame, and escalates his demanding attention-seeking behaviours.

BRADLEY'S TEACHER

Bradley's teacher, Shane, is inexperienced. Like many young teachers, overwhelmed by curriculum demands and standards, he has little room left to think about classroom culture or social skilling programmes. He doesn't know about using circles to build cohesiveness in his class, and he's had no training in conflict resolution or restorative approaches. Shane is so challenged by Bradley's aggressive and disruptive behaviour that the underlying reasons for Bradley's actions evade his awareness. Shane feels that his only option is to deal with Bradley's behaviour in increasingly severe ways, including keeping Bradley in during break times more and more, and sitting Bradley away from others in the classroom. To Shane's despair, Bradley's behaviour is just getting worse.

Shane is at the point where all he feels he can do is try to keep other students safe from Bradley's outbursts in the classroom and yard – damage control. Shane is also under pressure from a group of parents who have made Bradley's challenging behaviour the topic of ongoing carpark discussion. These parents have formed an anti-Bradley movement out of concerns for their children's safety.

BRADLEY'S HOME LIFE

Bradley lives at home with his mother, Suzie, stepfather, Rick, and three other younger children. Suzie does her best to give Bradley as much time as she can but she is kept very busy with Bradley's siblings (six, three and six months old). Rick tries hard with Bradley but gets frustrated with Bradley's behaviour at home and at school. Rick struggles to say anything encouraging to Bradley. Suzie and Rick are deeply concerned and ashamed about Bradley's behaviour but they are mostly supportive of Shane and the leadership staff at the school. Suzie and Rick feel they are failing as parents in the eyes of the school. They are worried because lately Bradley has been crying himself to sleep, complaining that he has no friends and that he wants to kill himself.

BRADLEY'S RESPONSES TO THE AFFECT SHAME-HUMILIATION

In Chapter 1, Vernon Kelly described the nine innate affects, the evolved function of the affect system and its primary role in human motivation.[4] For review, the affects are listed in Table 10.1.

TABLE 10.1 The nine innate affects

Positive affects	Negative affects
Interest-excitement	Distress-anguish
Enjoyment-joy	Fear-terror
	Anger-rage
Neutral affect	Shame-humiliation
Surprise-startle	Disgust
	Dissmell

---

4   See also Kelly 2012 for more about the biology of motivation and the affect system.

Bradley lives with almost constant impediments to his ability to feel *interested* in schoolwork or to *enjoy* his learning and his interactions with other children and adults at school. The result is that Bradley's school experience is tainted by constant negative emotional states. This is exhausting for Bradley and those around him. Bradley is painfully aware of his inability to concentrate on his schoolwork, to remember what he is supposed to be working on and to plan and complete tasks.

Bradley's mind is bombarded by loud and intrusive thoughts that make it next to impossible for him to follow a train of thought from beginning to end. Added to this is the social cost of his poor impulse control: getting too angry or too excited too quickly, and not being able to take hold of himself before reacting to situations. Bradley also has an undiagnosed learning difficulty that makes it almost impossible for him to experience even more than a fleeting moment of genuine interest or enjoyment when he is attempting academic tasks.

Bradley's affect system spends much of the time directing his attention to those things that stop him from feeling interest and enjoyment. Every time Bradley tries to read,[5] spell, or do mathematical tasks, unrewarded efforts trigger feelings ranging from mild embarrassment through to humiliation (all aspects of the innate affect shame-humiliation).

When an exasperated teacher directs Bradley back to his seat because he has lost focus and wandered from his desk, when Bradley unwittingly irritates classmates with a failure to respond in a socially appropriate way, or reacts poorly with hurtful words or actions, the affect shame is triggered. This affect demands that Bradley pay attention to what just happened so he can take action to rescue or restore social bonds with peers and teachers. The sad thing for Bradley is that the ability to take action to repair the relational harm is out of reach.

Even though the innate affect shame's job (evolved function) is to provide all of us with the information that something has interrupted our interest or enjoyment, it feels awful. This is how shame affect works in humans. While shame's first moments are confusing and disorienting for all of us, this is doubly true for Bradley whose affect system is hypersensitive to everything and therefore reacts with too much intensity. He can't think straight.

---

5   See Nathanson (2003) for an in-depth discussion of the effect of shame on learning to read.

In a blink of an eye, his conscious memory floods with scenes and feelings from his past – other times he felt just as awful as he does now. Nanoseconds after that, an inner search takes place where Bradley searches desperately for evidence that he is an OK person who is loved and accepted by others. 'Am I a good boy whom people like?' If the answer to these questions is 'yes', Bradley, and other humans, old or young, are able to take on board the information that shame affect wants them to pay attention to. They can then take action to restore connections.

Unfortunately for Bradley, the answer to these questions is often 'no'. As long as Bradley feels disliked and excluded by peers and adults in his school, no amount of punishment or behavioural intervention will help; in fact, these approaches will further isolate him and accelerate his behavioural decline. Nathanson (1992) tells us that people who don't believe they are loved, or lack the ability to love themselves, cannot do anything helpful with the information shame affect is trying to get them to consider. When humans start from a baseline of feeling unloved and unlovable, moments of shame are simply too much to deal with. In these moments, Bradley's only defence against a complete collapse in his self-esteem is to use mental scripts (sets of unconscious instructions of what to say and do) from the four poles on the Compass of Shame.

THE FOUR POLES OF THE COMPASS OF SHAME

Without the capacity to love himself, the affect shame sends Bradley spiralling into behaviours that come together to be classified under the four poles of the Compass of Shame, as depicted in Figure 10.1.

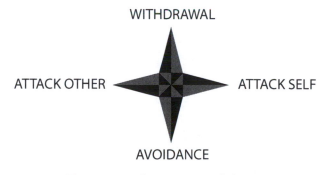

Figure 10.1 The Compass of Shame

- To *withdraw* from social contact – hide away and reduce the chance that he will be held in contempt by even more kids or teachers. 'I'm running away and hiding now so I can't do or say anything else that will make people hate me even more. I won't feel any more shame for the time being. I can't stand to feel disliked or rejected at the moment so I will beat them to it and cut myself off.' Bradley uses the back of the school sporting field for this – a place that is out of bounds to students, a place he knows he will be alone for a while. As a younger child, underneath tables and cupboards were places that Bradley would withdraw to.

- To *attack himself*, to accept diminished status as a lesser human being – as someone who controls how much shame he feels by putting himself down: 'I have a stupid brain, I hate myself.' Bradley may allow others to put him down by acting the class clown, or offering gifts in exchange for friendship, hoping to still be accepted, even pitied by others, because of his faults and shortcomings. Bradley gives others permission to treat him badly in exchange for remaining connected. 'You can call me stupid, I'll even act stupid for you, I deserve your contempt – just let me stay connected to you.'

- To *avoid* information that shame wants him to deal with by using bravado, being the tough guy, being the clown or openly challenging teachers to discipline him: 'Suspend me. I don't care what you do.' Bradley wears these masks to hide a deeply ashamed self from the eyes of others. Bradley is attempting to appear proud as the class clown, the show-off or the tough guy: 'Whatever you do, don't see the real me because I am vulnerable, scared, flawed and shameful.' Bradley's misbehaviour hasn't gained him social status with peers. When Bradley is older, and these strategies don't work as well, he will be at risk of turning to alcohol and other drugs to chemically avoid his feelings of shame.

- To *attack other* in an attempt to feel as worthy or superior to others through efforts to make them feel just as shameful as he does. Bradley's escalating violent behaviour, threats and physical responses to moments of social disconnection (when Dana suggests they play with other kids) turns the tables on others as Bradley cheats at the game of self-esteem. *Attack other* behaviour is Bradley's last line of defence against the awful thoughts and feelings that are triggered when he struggles with his concentration, his learning or his relationships with others. Bradley's comments about blowing the school up and his quiet abuse of Lydia and Dana are all desperate attempts to defend his self-esteem against shame. As Bradley grows, he will be vulnerable to instigating bullying behaviours and, at the same time, may also be the recipient of bullying when he uses scripts from the *attack self* pole of the Compass of Shame.

HOW BRADLEY RESPONDS TO MOMENTS OF SHAME

The innate affect shame is triggered when there's any impediment to the affects of interest or enjoyment. Feelings of shame further switch off the positive feelings of interest and enjoyment and direct our attention to whatever it was that interrupted the positive affects that were 'switched on' just a moment ago. Think about the types of events that would interrupt the affects of enjoyment or interest for Bradley – a teacher scowling at him, being left out of a game, experiencing difficulty with his schoolwork, being teased, seeing a friend walk away. The list is endless, and these experiences are commonplace for Bradley. What's more, because Bradley has come to expect that these things will happen to him often, the very thought of these events also triggers shame. This is a reason Bradley's moods swing so wildly and others find him unpredictable.

WHAT'S THE PURPOSE OF SHAME AFFECT?

Why has such an affect evolved in humans? Simple: to make us think about what just happened so we can evaluate our actions and make necessary adjustments. Shame affect has evolved to also be a *social* affect, an alarm bell that goes off when the information we receive from our environment indicates a loss of social connection. Our primitive brain is hardwired to know that our survival depends on our ability to stay socially connected to other humans. So it's no wonder that a system has evolved to warn us when something puts our social connections to others at risk and motivates us to take action.

Because Bradley doesn't feel loved, and lacks the ability to love himself, he can't do anything helpful when the affect shame is triggered. Table 10.2 categorizes the behaviours (scripts) Bradley called on in the incident with Dana. It also categorizes the scripts Bradley calls on to defend against feelings of shame in other situations when he feels abandoned or challenged.

TABLE 10.2 Bradley's Compass of Shame behavioural scripts

	Withdrawal responses	Attack self responses	Avoidance responses	Attack other responses
Bradley's behaviours following him kicking Dana	Taking himself away to the out-of-bounds area Walking away when approached by Dana and Lydia	Saying he hates himself Inviting suspension	Saying 'I don't care...' Being sullen and defiant when approached	Kicking Dana Putting Dana down Saying he wants to blow the stupid school up Angry words toward Lydia
Bradley's history	Sulking Running and hiding Inviting suspension	Inviting scorn by being defiant with adults Referring to his brain as 'stupid' Negative self-talk when friends want to play with others Inviting suspension	Clowning behaviour Attention-seeking Being sullen and defiant with his teacher	Name calling Threatening others when he thinks he is losing friends Being sullen and defiant with his teacher

A PLAN FOR BRADLEY BASED ON CONNECTEDNESS

By now, you've probably concluded that increasing the severity and number of punishments for Bradley is not the answer. Bradley needs teachers and peers to take the risk of getting personally involved with him. Approaches based on human connection are his only way out of reducing the tricky behaviours that plague his interactions with others and trigger layer upon layer of shame. Bradley is quickly giving up on the idea that he can ever be a 'good boy'.

Previous attempts to modify Bradley's behaviour through remoteness and isolation have made his behaviour worse. Put simply, relational and restorative approaches are the only thing that will make the difference for Bradley. A behaviour learning plan for Bradley will be a mixture of good management as well as good teaching.

We have outlined below five ideas that we have seen make a wonderful difference for kids just like Bradley. Are they quick and easy? No. Many of these ideas will only be effective within a restorative school culture that's conducive to them. These ideas cannot be bolted on because they require a restorative mindset. Only schools that go hard and deep with restorative practices will be able to implement and sustain these approaches. Without the right culture, these ideas will fail.

Restorative Approaches to Difficult Children

1. Restorative Conferencing as a First Approach (Not a Last Resort)

When Bradley is involved in incidents of harm or upset with other students, restorative conferencing should always be the preferred approach. Nothing else will deliver the same outcomes in terms of protecting and restoring Bradley's relationships with peers. Some schools make the dreadful mistake of only conferencing lower-tariff incidents with the more socially competent children, reserving the punitive approaches for kids like Bradley. The underlying belief for this practice is that punishment is the most effective response to the trickiest incidents and the trickiest kids. These schools simply don't get it.

Any restorative approach for young children and many children with learning difficulties must be explicit. We already know that restorative approaches are much more explicit than punitive processes. Children simply understand and retain more when engaged in restorative approaches. Being explicit in our practice becomes even more important when working with young or developmentally delayed students.

The best possible outcomes for Bradley will come from Lydia concentrating on *just one social rule or value* in her restorative conference with Bradley and Dana. This is what Lydia was mindful of when she took the time to find out what happened from Dana. It is also the focus she will be mindful of when she follows up with Bradley to check his perception of the incident. When Lydia brings Bradley and Dana together for a restorative conference, this one rule will be repeated to Bradley.

Below is a modified example of the early years small group conference script written in consultation with Jane Langley (Hansberry 2009, pp.72–74). Dana and Bradley's names have been incorporated into this script to show the language Lydia will use in the conference with Dana and Bradley. Early years restorative questions differ from other restorative scripts in one main way. Notice in particular the sixth step where Lydia says respectfully to Bradley:

> 'At school it's not OK to kick people when you are worried or upset with them. Next time I want you to take a deep breath and go and get a drink before you do anything else.'

This is the one explicit social rule/value built into the script that sets it apart from the scripts we use with older students and adults. The remainder of the script is Socratic – made up of a brief lead-in by the teacher (facilitator) and then questions to Dana and Bradley.

RESTORATIVE PRACTICE EARLY YEARS SMALL GROUP SCRIPT
When it's clear who's made the mistake and who's been hurt
Calm yourself, settle students and acknowledge feelings.

Teacher begins with: Big 3: Be respectful, Be honest, Take turns to speak: If you can't do this, I will have to deal with this differently.

1. *Ask Bradley:* What happened?

2. *Ask Dana:* What happened from your side?

3. *Ask Bradley:* When you kicked Dana was that a good choice or a bad choice?

4. *Ask Dana:* How did you feel when Bradley kicked you?

5. *Ask Bradley* (to check understanding)*:* How did Dana feel when you kicked her?

6. *Tell Bradley* (calmly and non-judgementally)*:* At school it's not OK to kick people when you are worried or upset with them. Next time I want you to take a deep breath and go and get a drink before you do anything else.

7. *Ask Bradley:* What do I want you to do to keep yourself and others safe next time?

8. *Ask Dana:* What could Bradley do to make things better?

9. *Say to Bradley:* To make this better, Dana would like you to…? Can you do that or would you like me to help?

The agreed outcomes of conferences for more serious incidents involving Bradley can be formally recorded as a 'conference agreement'. These types of agreements typically outline:

- what has been agreed by everyone will happen to repair the harm

- any commitments made by Bradley about using strategies to better manage himself

- support that will be put in place by the school to help Bradley better manage himself

- possible responses and further support if Bradley fails to live up to the agreements.

Recorded agreements must be reviewed in follow-up meetings between students involved in an incident. Managing conference agreements is an important step in signalling that the school takes conferencing seriously and is interested in managing relationships as well as behaviour. Bringing students together to review conference agreements creates moments of positive affect when students share interest in the fact that the school is interested enough in their relationship with each other to hold a review meeting. Agreement review meetings are often enjoyable moments for students and teachers. This shared positive affect strengthens relationships. Hansberry (2009) further elaborates on these considerations.

2. Explicit Teaching about Feelings

Increasing Bradley's *emotional literacy* begins by helping him recognize when he is angry and, after that, by helping him better regulate his emotions when tricky social situations arise. A trusted adult would be well advised to introduce Bradley to his 'warning signs' to help him tune into his feelings and intuition. Feelings are our only evidence that an affect has been triggered. They are our first point of conscious awareness that something is right (enjoyable or interesting) or wrong (confusing, distressing, scary, disgusting) and in need of closer inspection.

If Bradley can be helped to pay close attention to the sensation he gets in his stomach, or the way he clenches his jaw or how his head feels heavy and hot when shame and anger are triggered, he will be afforded a few vital nanoseconds to think about what's happening inside him and say something kind to himself like 'I'm getting angry and I need to use a trick to keep myself safe.' Only then will he be able to call on a strategy he's been taught to short-circuit his normally volatile reactions.

Awareness of his feelings will be crucial in helping Bradley create more socially appropriate sets of instructions – *scripts* – for what to say and do when affects like shame, anger and fear are triggered. With support, Bradley will be more able to conduct himself in ways that won't cause those around him to also feel ashamed, fearful or distressed.

A long-term goal for Bradley will be for him to understand that anger is just what his brain does to help him feel big and strong when something happens that makes him feel weak and vulnerable (shameful). With guidance, Bradley will be able to learn what all our boys and men need to know: that angry feelings happen when we feel small and scared, and we all feel small and scared sometimes.

3. Explicit Teaching of Restorative Thinking and Behaviour to All Students

All of our Bradleys are completely reliant on emotionally aware adults who build and sustain relationships with them. These same adults need to build school cultures where understanding and compassion thrive, and teachers and students are expected to show empathy and care for one another. This doesn't happen by accident, and restorative schools don't happen by accident. Restorative thinking and behaviour can be explicitly taught to students and the adults who work with them. There are programmes[6] available for this.

An emotionally intelligent and skilled leadership team is needed. This team must do the necessary relational work with one another so they can share a clear vision of what an emotionally intelligent school looks like. Schools that achieve this either knowingly or unwittingly follow Tomkins's Central Blueprint by:

1. Deliberately creating opportunities for students and adults to engage together in mutually enjoyable and connecting activities.

   In other words: mutually maximize shared positive affect.

2. Minimize situations where negative affect will be triggered, even when addressing harm and conflict. (In Dana and Bradley's incident, Lydia's approach was focused on bringing emotional relief for Dana and Bradley so their distress could be minimized and connections restored – a central principle of restorative justice.)

   In other words: mutually minimize negative affect.

3. Allow for the expression of affect through restorative processes and, at the same time, explicitly teach children to express emotions in ways that are less likely to trigger negative affect in others.

   In other words: mutually minimize the inhibition of affect.

---

6   *The Grab and Go Circle Time Kit: 13 Sessions for Teaching Restorative Behaviour* (Hansberry and Langley) is a resource written for this purpose. It is available from www.hansberryec.com. au.

4. Create situations that maximize 1–3 such as:

- using restorative processes such as conferencing, problem-solving circles, caring circles; regular circle time in classrooms across the school as part of the curriculum

- explicitly teaching students how to think and behave restoratively in the early years

- planning circle time sessions across year levels (planned by students)

- planning whole-school fun events

- planning enjoyable peer-tutoring interactions across year levels.

These approaches build emotional vocabulary in all members of the school community. We already know that when we are taught to recognize and name the affects that run through us and others, negative affect isn't so negative and the good times can be made better.

4. A Behaviour Plan for Bradley

Despite the highly supportive interventions outlined so far, a management plan will need some rainy-day contingencies to support Bradley when he cannot muster the self-regulation to make safe decisions because he is emotionally overwhelmed and safety becomes an issue.

- A designated time-out place in the classroom or yard that Bradley can take himself to when he's feeling out of control.

- An identified member of staff that Bradley can seek out who will simply allow Bradley to be close when he's struggling – this will become 'time in' – a way Bradley can be away from the trouble but still feel connected to another person and not have to be alone with his vulnerable feelings.

- Designating particular members of staff who deal with Bradley when he is spinning out of control – Lydia would be one of these people.

- A plan for take-home that can be calmly and discreetly enacted when the school environment is completely overwhelming for Bradley. This is not to be confused with times when Bradley becomes non-compliant and gets caught in power-seeking behaviours with those trying to help him. These types of behaviours can be cleverly sidestepped by emotionally intelligent adults. We are referring to times when Bradley behaves in a physically or emotionally intimidating manner to staff or students and doesn't stop.

This plan needn't be complicated. In essence, it outlines who gets involved when Bradley unravels, where he can go within the school when he's overwhelmed and what happens when Bradley can no longer remain at school.

5. A Caring Circle

Bradley will benefit enormously from what we call a *caring circle*. This is a small group of peers and an adult facilitator who are willing to give up their time to sit in a circle once a week with Bradley to listen to him, share in his successes and empathize with what didn't go so well for him.

Facilitated by a skilled teacher or school counsellor, members of the group can gently share their own experiences and offer Bradley ideas for how the positive can be maximized and the negative minimized. Put simply, this caring circle is a space in Bradley's life where the Central Blueprint for emotion is strictly adhered to. Bradley's caring circle would become his lifeline to school – an engineered community of care. The students involved would take their understanding of Bradley back into the schoolyard and classrooms, gently advocating for him when life gets tough. Small acts like lightly touching his arm or saying his name when his tricky behaviours send him toward social disaster will make an enormous difference as the connections formed bolster Bradley's social functioning.

Caring circles are effective because they make it explicit for students like Bradley what they can do and say to be better accepted by their peers. This positive peer pressure and the need to belong become even more powerful with children from roughly eight years onwards, so Bradley is at a developmental stage where he is beginning to be able to take on board what his peers are saying and appreciate the help they are giving.

If you are thinking about a child in your school and thinking that none of his peers would willingly give up their time to help a student like Bradley, you are mistaken. They just haven't been asked yet. Young people have tremendous capacity for compassion. They also have unmatched power to rescue kids like Bradley. Adults just need to share their concern with them and then ask for their assistance.

What stops this happening as often as it should in schools is the mistaken assumption that asking young people to advocate for others in this way will put them in harm's way. Risk management (a common form of *avoidance* of shame affect) often prevents schools from responding to their Bradleys in such a way. The sad irony is that research from all over the world is now telling us that the risks of *not* asking young people to sometimes go out of their way to take care of one another are far greater. The social costs of prolonged disconnection and alienation are devastating. Incidents like the Columbine and Virginia Tech shootings are clear and confronting evidence of this.

Conclusion

Even with support, Bradley faces an ongoing struggle to make good choices in the heat of the moment because he lives with a point-of-performance deficit: ADHD. Bradley will continue to battle impulse control issues and unhelpful scripted responses to the affects of shame, anger and fear. He will still fall victim to his fast emotions and old scripts. The forming of new scripts (ways to behave) will take him time. Bradley is at the very least a ten-year project for his teachers while he attends school. Beyond this, Bradley will likely require ongoing and steady support into adulthood.

Adults in schools often become frustrated with children like Bradley because the investment in time is huge and the progress is slow and stilted. The unpredictability of functioning and behaviour in kids like Bradley offer us glimmers of hope, when we feel like we've had a breakthrough, only to trigger our collective shame when they make a spectacular mistake again. It's truly two steps forward and one and sometimes two steps backwards!

Teachers struggle to understand why children who are told over and over again to do the right thing still don't. The investment seems to outweigh the return, and adults, caught up in their own affects of shame, fear and anger, flick the 'justice switch' in their heads. When this anxiety-, shame-based switch is flicked, adults think and say things like 'What about the kids who are good all of the time? It's not fair that Bradley takes all our energy up and the good kids miss out.' For those of us who live with a brain with near-typical processing and normal executive functions, it's almost impossible to understand a mind that cannot dampen extreme emotions, cannot plan ahead, cannot sum up possible consequences of actions and cannot learn quickly from past events. Not understanding what drives Bradley's behaviours, it's easy to develop a misguided sense of social justice.

References

Baumeister, R.F., Twenge, J.M. and Nuss, C. (2002) 'Effects of social exclusion on cognitive processes: Anticipated aloneness reduces intelligent thought.' *Journal of Personality and Social Psychology 83*, 4, 817–827.

Gaffney, M. (2011) *Flourishing: How to Achieve a Deeper Sense of Well-Being, Meaning and Purpose – Even When Facing Adversity.* Dublin: Penguin Ireland.

Hansberry, B. (2009) *Working Restoratively in Schools: A Guidebook for Developing Safe and Connected Learning Communities.* Queenscliff, Australia: Inyahead.

Jaffe, E. (2011) 'The complicated psychology of revenge.' *Observer 24*, 8. Available at www.psychologicalscience.org/index.php/publications/observer/2011/october-11/the-complicated-psychology-of-revenge.html, accessed on 15 October 2011.

Kelly, V.C. (2012) *A Primer of Affect Psychology.* Available at www.tomkins.org/uploads/ASP_Primer_2012.pdf, accessed on 15 October 2012.

Lewis, T., Amini, F. and Lannon, R. (2000) *A General Theory of Love.* New York, NY: Random House.

Nathanson, D.L. (1992) *Shame and Pride: Affect, Sex, and the Birth of the Self.* New York, NY: W.W. Norton.

Nathanson, D.L. (2003) *The Role of Affect in Learning to Read: How Shame Exacerbates Reading Difficulties.* Available at www.childrenofthecode.org/interviews/nathanson.htm, accessed on 15 November 2011.

The Contributors

Lauren Abramson is Founding Director of the Community Conferencing Center in Baltimore, Maryland, and is Assistant Professor of Child Psychiatry at Johns Hopkins School of Medicine, USA. As a psychologist who has worked in communities for over 30 years, Lauren advances conferencing as an effective means of system reform, individual transformation and community building. She has written extensively on the role of emotion in conflict transformation, the theoretical underpinnings of conferencing and the implementation and practice of restorative justice.

Email: labramso@jhmi.edu
www.communityconferencing.org

Anne Burton assumed her current role as Coordinator of Goulburn Family Support Service (GFSS) in Goulburn, New South Wales, Australia, in 1999. After completing her degree in Sydney in 1990, she became determined to provide a more practical response for families affected by family violence. She played a pivotal role in the development of 'Explicit Affective Practice'. Anne has overseen the transformation of the service into a genuine learning organization at the leading edge of practice with families. It now consistently achieves improved outcomes for those with often chronically dysfunctional presentations around violence, abuse, relationship breakdown, child resident issues, parenting, mental health and life management.

Email: anne.burton@bigpond.com
http://gfss.ned.org.au

Matthew Casey is a counsellor and restorative practice consultant in Goulburn, New South Wales, Australia, who also serves a role in Professional Standards for the Catholic Archdiocese of Canberra and Goulburn. A former Head of the School of Investigation and Intelligence at the NSW Police Academy, he retired from policing and led a project for the Goulburn Family Support Service (GFSS) which developed, described and validated 'Explicit Affective Practice' as a successful mode of counselling based around the explicit application of affect script psychology. He has developed a range of vocational education-accredited training packages and seminars on the application of the practice model and the underpinning theory. These seminars include restorative practice, ministry and theology, and the management of stakeholder engagement, conflict and confrontation in the non-police law enforcement sector.

Email: matt.casey@catholiclife.org.au
http://gfss.ned.org.au

William Curry is a qualified counsellor and member of the Australian Counseling Association who lives in Goulburn, New South Wales, Australia. He moved from a career in the wool industry to disability services specifically in group homes with clients exhibiting challenging behaviours. Bill became interested in the unfolding practice at Goulburn Family Support Service (GFSS) and became a family worker in 2002. Since then he has further developed the practice model while completing a Diploma in Community Welfare and obtaining registration as a counsellor. He has wide experience successfully assisting clients with challenging and complex presentations around issues of relationship breakdown, domestic violence, sexual assault, abuse and neglect. Bill has also volunteered at the Goulburn Traffic Offender Program for the past five years, along with Matt Casey, presenting the service affect framework as a learning opportunity for traffic offenders.

Email: billcurry@optusnet.com.au
http://gfss.ned.org.au

Graeme George has taught science in an independent school in Brisbane for more than 30 years. For much of that time, he has held senior leadership positions within the school and across his schooling sector. An experienced trainer and facilitator of restorative practices, he has had a keen research interest in affect script psychology and its application to teachers' work in schools, both in restorative practices and in pedagogy. He maintains a website, RP for Schools, with an array of readily available resources including reading materials, videos, YouTube clips, links to RP topics and associations worldwide and PowerPoint presentations for schools engaging in restorative practice.

Email: gbgeorge@gmail.com
www.rpforschools.net

Katherine Gribben is a counsellor with more than 20 years' experience in the community sector working around domestic violence. She has been with Goulburn Family Support Service (GFSS) in Goulburn, New South Wales, Australia, for the past ten years. Kath had a range of jobs from family day care and teacher's aide in primary education in the UK and the Middle East before migrating in 1992 to Australia where she began working with families experiencing stress and crisis. When introduced to 'Explicit Affective Practice' she was attracted to what was, for her, a radicallu new concept, particularly as families reported how this new learning had improved their lives. Kath realized this was 'help' which did work. As an early intervention strategy, Kath works with playgroups using the developed model to assist families around relationship development and more effective parenting.

Email: kathgribben@optusnet.com
http://gfss.ned.org.au

Bill Hansberry works privately at Fullarton House in Adelaide, South Australia, as a teacher, counsellor and mentor to many amazing young people who live with a range of learning and emotional challenges that make school tough to navigate. This work naturally extends to supporting their incredibly brave parents and teachers who swim against the stream to support these young people who process the world differently. Most of this work places Bill in the lives of young people who live with dyslexia and autism spectrum disorder. Bill's background is in teaching, school counselling and behaviour management consultancy.

Bill works with schools and organizations that are looking for sustainable ways to implement a restorative ethos. Bill presents workshops across Australia on restorative practices, circle time, school climate and cultural renewal in educational settings. Bill's publications include *Working Restoratively in Schools: A Guidebook for Developing Safe and Connected Learning Communities* (Inyahead Press, 2009), *The Grab and Go Circle Time Kit for Teaching Restorative Behaviour*, co-authored with Jane Langley (Inyahead Press, 2013) and his most recent self-published book, *Raising Beaut Kids: Recipes for Parents in When to Say 'Yes' and How to Say 'No'*, written with Mark Le Messurier (2013).

Email: bill@hansberryec.com.au
www.hansberryec.com.au

Katy Hutchison is a native of British Columbia, Canada, who became a restorative justice advocate following the murder of her husband in 1997. Her work focuses on informing communities how alcohol and other drug use, bullying, peer pressure and misguided choices can cause irrevocable devastation. She strives to empower communities to make healthier choices so similar tragedies can be prevented. Most importantly, she explores the power of forgiveness and describes her own grassroots quest for restorative justice. Now a full-time professional speaker, Katy has spoken internationally to over 500,000 people. She addresses community groups, churches, schools, youth detention centres and prisons. Her keynotes have been shared with health and wellness, restorative practice, social responsibility, victim services, corrections, parole and law enforcement, and education conferences. Katy was nominated for the Courage to Come Back award in 2004 and the Women of Distinction award in 2005, and she received the Canadian 'Living From Me to We' award for social action in 2006. Katy courageously shares her story in depth in a book entitled *Walking After Midnight: One Woman's Journey Through Murder, Justice, and Forgiveness* (New Harbinger, 2006). Her story also inspired Lifetime Network's movie, *Bond of Silence*.

Email: katy@katyhutchisonpresents.com
www.katyhutchisonpresents.com

Vernon C. Kelly, Jr. is a psychiatrist based in Philadelphia, Pennsylvania, USA. He was a co-founder of The Silvan S. Tomkins Institute in 1991. As its first training director, he was involved in one of the initial presentations of restorative justice principles to an audience in the USA and the Mayor of Philadelphia in the mid-1990s. He is currently chair emeritus of the Board and was integral in the expansion of the organization as The Tomkins Institute: Applied Studies in Motivation, Emotion and Cognition.

His practice of psychiatry has included work with children, individuals, couples and families since 1969. His book, *The Art of Intimacy and the Hidden Challenge of Shame*, details insights gained from over 45 years working with troubled relationships. His expertise in the biology of emotion and affect script psychology has contributed to the understanding of the motivation for change during restorative interventions. He has lectured internationally about these principles in the USA, Canada, Norway, Australia and New Zealand.

Email: vickkellyrpi@verizon.net
www.shameandmarriage.com

John Lennox is currently in private practice as a partner in JLD Restorative Practices, Tasmania, Australia, and provides training and consultancy services to various government departments and non-government organizations. He served as a police officer for 30 years and became an early advocate of restorative conferencing in Tasmania Police and has been largely responsible for training of Authorized Police Officers (pursuant to the Youth Justice Act 1997) since 1997. He has also delivered training in restorative practices to all police cadets since 2004 and to staff at some 70 schools. He has contributed to the development of Tasmania Police youth policy and the development of a revised Authorized Officer training course.

Email: jolona@netspace.net.au
www.jldrestore.com.au

Margaret Thorsborne, managing director of Margaret Thorsborne and Associates and Thorsborne and Associates, UK, is a restorative consultant based in Queensland, Australia. She has a background in teaching and school counselling, and played a key role in the pioneering of restorative practices in schools and workplaces in the mid-1990s and continues to work across this field in Australia, New Zealand, the USA, Canada, the UK, Hong Kong and Singapore. She is a co-founder of Restorative Practices International, the world's first membership organization for restorative practitioners, and has authored and co-authored several training manuals for restorative practice in schools, classrooms, workplaces and restorative approaches to bullying. Her latest work, with Peta Blood, *Implementing Restorative Practices in Schools: A Practical Guide to Transforming School Communities*, concentrates on helping schools manage the complex process of culture change away from punitive to restorative approaches for managing disciplinary matters.

She continues to search for ways to adapt the restorative philosophy in varied settings, and is currently working on a manual for the application of the practice with young people in schools with special needs. All of her practice is now underpinned by a clear understanding of affect script psychology.

Email: marg@thorsborne.com.au
www.thorsborne.com.au

Siân Williams is an experienced educator, working independently as an adviser, facilitator and trainer in the field of restorative practice in the UK. She taught for ten years in inner-city London before joining a local authority for eight years. Here she led on many authority-wide initiatives including anti-bullying, restorative approaches, safer schools and social and emotional learning. Since 2010, she has worked independently as a restorative practitioner and trainer, and is currently principal consultant for Thorsborne and Associates, UK. She has worked as an education adviser for the Paul Hamlyn Foundation, as well as spending two years with the arts organization that is the subject of her chapter. She currently divides her time between the UK and Malawi, Africa.

Email: sian@thorsborne.co.uk

www.thorsborne.co.uk

Subject Index

Author Index

Made in the USA
Middletown, DE
24 November 2016